DAY HIKES ALONG THE

HIGHWAY 108 CORRIDOR

Photo: Cleo's Bath on the South Fork of the Stanislaus River above
Pinecrest Lake

DAY HIKES ALONG THE

HIGHWAY 108 CORRIDOR

OVER 70 HIKES
FROM KNIGHTS FERRY TO
LEAVITT MEADOW

Written by Katherine Joye

Published by
Sonora Press
www.sonorapress.biz
16964 Columbia River Drive
Sonora CA 95370
(209) 532 4202

Joye, Katherine, Betz, Sheri ed. *Day hikes along the Highway 108 corridor.*
Joye, Katherine, *Day hikes along the Highway 108 corridor.*
Joye, Katherine, Photos unless otherwise stated.
    Cover Photo: Middle Fork of the Stanislaus River below Relief Reservoir
    Page 3 Photo: Sword Lake in the Carson-Iceberg Wilderness
    Page 10 Map, Katherine Joye
    Back Photo: Author hiking on Sonora Pass Trail taken by Sheri Betz
Sonora: Sonora Press, 2014. Print.
Library of Congress Cataloging-in-Publication
Joye, Katherine
Day hikes along the Highway 108 corridor
ISBN 978-1-889409-92-4

First Edition
Printed in the United States of America

Dedication

To all my fellow hikers… may the trails always beckon, the body ever respond and the beauty never wane.

The mountains are calling and I must go.   John Muir

Photo: Herring Creek at the start of the Pinecrest Peak Trail in early spring

Acknowledgements

I would like to thank those of you who believed in this project. Numerous thanks to friends and family members for your companionship on various hikes: Sheri Betz, Wendy Hesse, Beth and Francesca DeLuca, Karen Spitze, Merv Cancio, Olivia LaPertche, Steve Joye (my husband), Keean Joye (my son) and my constant four-legged companions, Gloria and Stefano. Wendy also shared some of her photos of the McCormick Creek hike. I am grateful to Kaila Joye (my daughter) for teaching me how to edit photos and to Sheri, Kaila and Ashlin Joye (my son) for their help in selecting photos. I would like to thank Lowell Jones at Sonora Press for answering the many questions I had about preparing a book for print. And a huge 'thanks' goes out to Sheri for all the editing that she did but most of all, for introducing me to a number of places and helping me to live the dream.

Photo: Leichtlin's Mariposa Lilies

Table of Contents

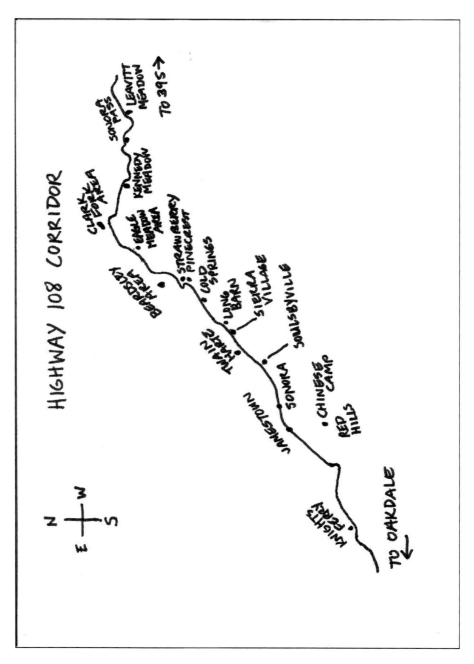

Map: The Highway 108 Corridor from Knights Ferry to Leavitt Meadow

Introduction

The Highway 108 corridor takes you through a variety of terrain, elevations and historical areas offering a plethora of opportunities for day hiking. After leaving the valley towns behind as you head eastward, low elevation hiking trails can be found amongst the rolling green hills near Knights Ferry, within the unique Red Hills outside of Chinese Camp, upon flat-topped Table Mountain out of Jamestown and around the foothills surrounding Sonora. As you climb further up, mid-elevation hikes abound along historic ditch systems and old railroad grades outside of Tuolumne City, Twain Harte, Sierra Village and Fraser Flat. There are also peaceful forest hikes through various areas of the Stanislaus National Forest at many elevations some of which take you to lakes, past historic dams on reservoirs or along streams. Others send you to tops of mountains for incredible views or through mountain meadows lush with wildflowers. Some are interpretive trails that have an informational focal point. High elevation hikes typically start from Carson-Iceberg, Emigrant or Humboldt-Toiyabe National Forest Trailheads and take you through some geologically and ecologically spectacular country.

Despite the richness of trails in the area, many people head up here to hike the same few 'most popular' trails. Although these 'most popular' trails are included (with suggested times to use them so that you are not inundated), this book includes many trails that are infrequently visited. This allows you to explore much more of the wonders found within 30 miles of the 108 corridor, in near solitude.

This book describes over 70 day hikes of varying distances and difficulties that start on actual trails and options for further exploration on the many other miles of trails and cross-country travels that beckon. This is more than a year's worth at a pace of one hike per week. There are nine different sections of hikes. A few hikes could be placed in more than one section but I have placed each in a 'best fit' section. There are also pages near the front that list hikes by area, difficulty, total hike distance, distance from 108 and starting elevation. So now it's time to lace up those shoes and hit the trails!

Explanations for Informational Sections

- **Highlights**: This section gives you a quick upfront blurb about what you can expect to see, hear or experience on the hike.

- **Distance**: Both one-way and round-trip mileage is provided as often there are options for loops or one-way shuttle trips. Mileage is always given as an approximation as its accuracy is only as good as the tool being used to measure it: a GARMIN Foretrex 401 GPS unit. Readings were similar to those obtained by other tools carried by friends.

- **Elevation Changes**: Although it is helpful to know the starting elevation and the destination elevation, the real question that we all have (though we might not admit it) is how much up and down we will be doing. Using the GARMIN Foretrex 401 GPS, I have provide approximations on how much total climbing you will have to do on the way out as well as on the return trip.

- **Difficulty**: Most of us are able to gauge how many miles we can hike comfortably and hikes longer than desired can be cut short. Typically what makes a hike difficult is the amount of climbing that is required. As a result, the difficulty ratings for each hike are based on cumulative roundtrip elevation gains. Typically, the easiest hikes are those along railroad grades and ditches whereas those taking you up and over high elevation passes are challenging or strenuous.
  - **Easy**: < 200 ft of roundtrip climbing
  - **Moderately easy**: 200-500 ft of roundtrip climbing
  - **Moderate**: 501-800 ft of roundtrip climbing
  - **Moderately difficult**: 801-1100 ft of roundtrip climbing
  - **Difficult**: 1101-1400 ft of roundtrip climbing
  - **Challenging (or Strenuous)**: >1400 ft of roundtrip climbing

- **Seasonality**: A 'best' season to go is listed for each hike along with an explanation for why that particular season is best. Obviously, hikes can still be enjoyed at other times but perhaps you might miss some of the great highlights. In general, low elevation hikes are best during the winter through mid-spring as conditions are too hot and dry during the rest of the year. Spring and fall are probably the best times to do mid-elevation hikes but early summer mornings and clear winter days could work as well. Higher elevation hikes are best to do during the summer and early fall as conditions can be treacherous and access restricted at other times of the year. Realize that hunting season starts towards the end of September and continues into November; if you are hiking at that time, you may be sharing the trails with people carrying guns. Cattle ranchers also begin to drive cattle from wilderness grazing areas down to trailheads to be rounded up into trailers around this same time period.

- **User Groups/ Permits**: It could be helpful to know who might be sharing the trail with you as this can also give you some idea of what the trail conditions might be like. Some of the trails described are used by horsemen (they have the right of way) and these trails tend to be thick with dust by the end of summer. Mountain bike riders enjoy some of these trails as well and they should be ceding the right of way to you; however, they might not see it that way and as my husband likes to say 'if they are bigger than you, then they have the right of way'. There are a few hikes where motorized vehicles have access to a section of the hike so proceed with caution. Permits are typically only required in wilderness areas if you are planning on staying overnight and these can be obtained at local ranger stations (Sonora, Mi-Wok or Summit).

- **Parking/ Facilities**: This section provides information about where you can park and whether or not there are any toilets located there or along the trail. If there is a fee for parking, that information is included.

- **Topographic Map**: The appropriate USGS 7.5 minute topographic map(s) is listed for each hike. It is highly recommended that you travel with a map of the area each time that you are out in wilderness or forested areas and that you have some skills in reading a map.

- **Hike Description**: This section is solely devoted to getting you from point A to point B without extraneous information that you have to skip over to find out whether or not you need to go right or left at a particular junction. Directions are provided by giving reference to notable benchmarks (signs, trail junctions, stream crossings etc.), approximate mileage between each benchmark and prompting when you need to head in a different direction after reaching a particular benchmark. This type of description can be particularly helpful along trails that are not well-marked with signs (such as in the Carson-Iceberg Wilderness or Peoria Wildlife Management Area). In addition, information is provided about trail conditions and when to look up to take in a particularly great view!

- **Trail Tidbits**: Knowing the history or some interesting relevant facts of an area often makes a hike more meaningful and allows the hiker to view the surroundings with a new perspective. Information has been gleaned from various resources to bring to light interesting tidbits for each hike so that you, the hiker, might give your surroundings additional scrutiny.

- **Need To Know**: Would you like to know when you will be traipsing through poison oak? Is the trail slippery with scree at any point? Are there any cross-country segments that require map reading? Perhaps you would like to be forewarned if you will be sharing the trail with large bovines and their soupy cow patties. This type of information is specifically provided for each hike. **NOTE: hiking, whether in the high elevation wilderness areas or low elevation foothills, has inherent risks that could threaten one's safety. Ultimately, each hiker needs to take responsibility for his or her own safety.** This section does not necessarily list every potential hazard and risk and certainly does not replace using good common sense but it does give you an idea of what you need to look out for when hiking the trail.

- **Want A Loop? or Want More?**: I like loops! I prefer to find alternative ways back to the start even if it means traveling cross-country. This section gives you loop options (if appropriate) and will let you know if cross-country travel (with map skills) is necessary. Sometimes loops are not an option. When this is true, ideas for further exploration of the area are presented.

- **Directions to Trailhead**: This section provides detailed directions (with mileage) to the start of each hike from highway 108. Total mileage from 108 is also listed.

List of Trails by Closest Area Along 108

List of Trails by Difficulty

Easy Trails (continued)

Moderately Easy Trails

Moderate Trails

Moderately Difficult Trails

Moderately Difficult Trails (continued)

Difficult Trails

Challenging or Strenuous Trails

List of Trails by Distance

Roundtrip distance of 2 miles or less

Roundtrip distance of 2 miles or less (continued)

Roundtrip distance between 2.1 and 4.0 miles

Roundtrip distance between 4.1 and 7.0 miles

Roundtrip distance between 4.1 and 7.0 miles (continued)

Roundtrip distance between 7.1 and 10.0 miles

Roundtrip distance more than 10 miles

List of Trails by Distance from 108

Trails 1 to 5 miles from 108 (continued)

Trails 5.1 to 10 miles from 108

Trails 10.1 to 20 miles from 108

List of Trails by Starting Elevation

Photo: Rivulet and tree roots along the Arnot Creek Trail

Low Elevation Trails

There are a number of low elevation hikes that are perfect for winter and early spring excursions when Sonora Pass is closed and access to higher elevation trails is limited. Most of these would be too hot to hike in the summer as they are at elevations below 2000 ft. They are found along the Highway 108 corridor from Knights Ferry up through Sonora. The majority of these low elevation trails are short and not too difficult making them a good choice for family outings.

The hikes in the Knights Ferry area are along the Stanislaus River. Not only does this offer recreational venues for hiking, swimming, wildlife viewing and picnicking, but it also provides historic and geologic educational opportunities with visits to the Knights Ferry Bridge and Information Center, the mill, the Iron Jail, California's oldest operating General Store and other historic structures. The hikes are all on land managed by the US Army Corps of Engineers with the book's lowest elevations of <400 ft.

The Red Hills, under the jurisdiction of the Bureau of Land Management, is a unique ecosystem. Although the area looks austere from the roadway, once you are on the trails, you encounter a variety of plants (and evidence of animals) that are successful in this environment. It has been designated as an area of critical environmental concern to protect the rare plants and other unique flora found there, and to preserve the habitat for the Red Hills roach (a rare minnow) and wintering sites of the bald eagle. The Red Hills are known as a premier place for wildflowers in spring; this is the best time to hike here as the streams typically are full of water. There are four hikes for this location, at elevations of ~1050-1550 ft, but there are also a number of other trails not included in this book.

There are three hikes that overlook New Melones Lake and offer excellent views of the lake, surrounding foothills and high elevation Yosemite peaks. Two are in the Peoria Wildlife Management Area which offers opportunities for wildlife viewing in a woodland setting dominated by oaks. The other is Table Mountain, a geologically unique feature. Wildflowers are rampant on Table Mountain in spring particularly around the vernal pools. The entire recreational area around New Melones Lake is operated by the Bureau of Reclamation. The elevations for these hikes range from 1000-1800 ft.

The Dragoon Gulch Trail is the only hike listed for the Sonora area. It is a pleasant walk through a lovely oak woodland along Woods Creek at the edge of the downtown area. Through a Roberti-Z'Berg-Harris Nonurbanized Area Grant (RZH), the City of Sonora was able to purchase the original 35 acres (at a reduced rate) and develop trails with the help of crews from the Stanislaus National Forest and Baseline Conservation Camp. There are plans to expand this area in the near future with additional trails through the aid of another RZH Grant. This trail has the highest elevation of the low elevation hikes (~1750-2000 ft) and is one of the few that could be comfortably walked on a summer morning or evening due to decent canopy cover.

Photo: View of New Melones Lake from top of Table Mountain

Dragoon Gulch Loop

Highlights: This trail is a woodland oasis in the middle of the city of Sonora. Although a section of it runs through a neighborhood, the majority of it is located in a secluded forest of oaks, manzanita and toyon with Woods Creek running through a portion of it.

Distance: 2.4 miles round trip (out on the longer trail and back on the shorter trail)

Elevation Changes: Cumulative ascent on loop is ~250 ft; elevation is ~1750-2000 ft

Difficulty: Moderately easy in terms of elevation change

Seasonality: This trail can be used all year. Although summers are hot in Sonora, this trail is sufficiently shaded so that morning or evening use is reasonable. There is little to no water running in Woods Creek late in the season. Wildflowers abound during the spring.

User Groups/Permits: The trail is used by hikers and dog walkers; part of the trail is ADA accessible. Permits are not needed to park or day hike; no camping is allowed.

Parking/Facilities: Parking is located just past Woods Creek Park. The ADA parking area is at the end of Alpine Lane. There are no facilities in the parking area or along the trail but there is a restroom at Woods Creek Park.

Topographic Map: USGS Sonora, CA Quadrangle (7.5 Minute Series)

Hike Description: From the trailhead parking area, look for the Dragoon Gulch sign. Cross the bridge and head right up South Forest Road through a neighborhood. This portion of the trail is marked with signs and a solid white line. At 0.2 miles into the hike, veer left onto North Forest Road. Travel another 0.1 miles then enter the park area on the right. Follow the trail up along Woods Creek. At 0.5 miles you can see the other trailhead parking area off to the right and the main trail turns to dirt. Soon after, you reach a junction. Continue straight along the North Creekside Trail (less steep trail); you will return on the trail that you see to the left. You bend to the left onto the Ridge Trail at 0.75 miles into the hike and bend to the right 0.4 miles later. At 1.4 miles, you reach another trail junction; stay straight to go to the end of the Ridge Trail and the overlook (~1.5 miles total). Spend a few minutes enjoying the view which stretches beyond the city of Sonora. Head back to the last junction (~1.6 miles total) and head downhill to the right. After traveling ~0.3 miles further (~1.9 miles total), you return to the main trail along Woods Creek; turn right to head back to the parking area the same way you came.

Trail Tidbits: Gold was discovered in 1849 in Woods Creek near the current site of Sonora High School. The Dragoon Gulch area was mined extensively after 1852 when water became more plentiful due to the construction of the ditch systems. This ravine was named Dragoon Gulch for the US Army cavalry soldiers or dragoons who stayed and mined in this area.

Need to Know: Beware of poison oak and rattlesnakes in this area. Check for ticks (particularly in the spring).

Want More? The trail is written as a loop. If you would like to hike more, you can explore the area along Woods Creek by the bridge near the parking area.

Directions to Trailhead: Go east on 108 past Jamestown. Exit on 49 North to Stockton Road. The 0.2 mile exit ramp takes you onto Stockton Road. Drive another 1.1 miles up Stockton Road then turn left onto Woods Creek Road (across from the Sonora Fairgrounds entrance). Go 0.3 miles to the parking area which is past Woods Creek Park. Distance from 108 is 1.6 miles.

For the ADA accessible parking area, follow the signs for Highway 49 North until you pass the Historic Red Church towards the end of downtown Sonora. Then turn left onto Snell Street. Snell Street becomes Bonanza Road after the first stop sign. Go one block and turn right onto Calaveras Street and then left onto Alpine Lane. Pass through the gate to the Alpine Lane parking area. The gate is locked at dark.

Knights Ferry North Canyon Trail

Highlights: The highlights of this trip include the historic sights of the old Knight's Mill and the longest covered bridge west of the Mississippi River, the spectacular views of the Stanislaus River and its canyon and the large beach area perfect for cooling off your feet. In addition, the Knights Ferry Information Center provides an opportunity to learn more about the area.

Distance: 0.8 miles to end of trail (1.6 miles roundtrip)

Elevation Changes: Cumulative ascent roundtrip is <200 ft; elevation is ~200-380 ft

Difficulty: Easy in terms of elevation change

Seasonality: This trail is best from late winter to mid-spring when water in the river is flowing and wildflowers are blooming. This area is hot and crowded in the summer so you should avoid it unless you are heading to the river to swim. It is cooler in the fall but dry; this is also the time of year that you can see the salmon run upstream.

User Groups/Permits: The trail is only open to foot traffic. The recreation area is used by picnickers, boaters and walkers. Permits are not needed to park or day hike.

Parking/Facilities: There is no fee for parking at this recreation area; there are numerous facilities at the parking area and another ~0.4 miles down the trail.

Topographic Map: USGS Knights Ferry, CA Quadrangle (7.5 Minute Series)

Hike Description: Start the hike at the Knights Ferry Information Center. Follow the trail to the right. Within 100 yards, you pass the old mill on the right. The trail heads up the stairs on the left and within 0.1 miles, you pass the entrance to the covered bridge (add 0.2 miles roundtrip if you walk across the bridge and back). To stay on the trail, head straight. From this point on, you should note numerous side trails that head off to the right to take you down to the water; for this hike, stay on the main trail which is fairly wide but rocky in some sections. At ~0.4 miles, you pass a bathroom and benches. Just past the benches, stay left to stay on the main trail. Note the sign on the right for North Canyon Loop Trail ~0.15 miles later (see Want a Loop?). At ~0.6 miles, you encounter a gate and fence; the trail narrows significantly and follows the fence line around to the right. At this point you are paralleling the San Joaquin Main Canal. The trail ends at the start of private property ~0.8 miles into the hike. This is the turnaround point unless you want to do a loop (see Want a Loop?).

Trail Tidbits: This area is part of the Stanislaus River Parks and is operated by the US Army Corps of Engineers. Dr. William Knight, with James Vantine, established a ferry boat crossing at a reasonable site along the Stanislaus River just after gold was discovered in the foothills in 1849. Although Knight was murdered later in 1849, his partner operated the ferry with new cohorts, the Dent brothers. A toll bridge replaced the ferry crossing in 1857. This bridge was destroyed in the Great Flood of 1862 when the bridge at Two-Mile Bar dislodged, floated downstream and rammed the Knights Ferry Bridge. A new covered bridge was built in 1863 at a higher elevation and it still stands today. Car traffic traveled over the bridge until 1985 but now its use is limited to pedestrians. It is the longest covered bridge west of the Mississippi River at a length of 330 ft.

Need to Know: Be aware that the river water can be moving faster than you think and can sweep you downstream if you are not careful (particularly at high flow levels). Some of the side trails are steep and can be slippery when wet; take extra caution on these trails.

Want A Loop? To do a loop, take the trail that heads downward just as the ridge trail ends. Veer right a short ways down. At ~0.1 miles from the start of the loop, you reach another trail junction; either one gets you where you need to go but the left one takes you down stairs, around and back up whereas the right one takes you over a rougher section. Less than 0.1 miles further, you encounter a sign that states 'Last Rapid Overlook'. Nearly 0.25 miles from the start of the loop (1.05 miles into the hike), you reach a junction with a number of trails. Take the middle trail that heads upward at a reasonable grade and this brings you back up to the main trail at the North Canyon Loop Trail sign. Continue back to the Knights Ferry Information Center the way you came for a 1.7 mile loop. If you want more, you could cross the covered bridge and take the walking paths along the opposite side of the river until you eventually reach Sonora Road. Walk on the sidewalk along the road until you cross the car bridge over the river then take the stairs down to the parking area. You could also explore the town of Knights Ferry and visit the Iron Jail and the General Store.

Directions to Trailhead: If you are approaching Knights Ferry from the west (just out of Oakdale), take the Kennedy Road exit to the left. Follow it 0.4 miles then turn left onto Sonora Road. If you are approaching Knights Ferry from the east, take the Sonora Road exit to the right. Follow this road 0.3 miles then bend to the right to stay on Sonora Road. From here (whether you came from the east or west), go 0.6 miles, crossing the river, to the junction with Covered Bridge Road. Turn right onto Covered Bridge Road and then an immediate right into the Knights Ferry Recreation Area. Distance from 108 is 0.9 or 1.0 miles depending on which 108 exit you used.

Photo: The historic mill at Knights Ferry

Knights Ferry Russian Rapid Trail

Highlights: This is a very short, easy hike to the section of the Stanislaus River that contains the Russian Rapid. The parking area contains a large beach area and picnic tables for some rest and relaxation afterwards and there is also the Knights Ferry Information Center which offers an opportunity to learn more about the area.

Distance: 0.5 miles to end of trail (1.0 miles roundtrip)

Elevation Changes: Cumulative ascent roundtrip is <35 ft; elevation is ~150-180 ft

Difficulty: Easy in terms of elevation change

Seasonality: This trail is best from late winter to mid-spring when water in the river is flowing and wildflowers are blooming. This area is hot and crowded in the summer so you should avoid it unless you are heading to the river to swim. It is cooler in the fall but dry; this is also the time of year that you can see the salmon run upstream.

User Groups/Permits: The trail is only open to foot traffic. The recreation area is used by picnickers, boaters and walkers. Permits are not needed to park or day hike.

Parking/Facilities: There is no fee for parking at this recreation area; there are numerous facilities at the parking area but none on the trail.

Topographic Map: USGS Knights Ferry, CA Quadrangle (7.5 Minute Series)

Hike Description: Start at the information placards below the stairs by the vehicular bridge that you just drove over. Head up the stairs and along the bridge. Cross the road at the end of the bridge to the start of the Russian Rapid Trail. Follow the trail down the wide but gravely path past blackberry bushes and bush lupine. At ~0.5 miles you reach the river.

Trail Tidbits: The Stanislaus River is popular with rafters and kayakers. The most used section of the river is from Knights Ferry to Orange Blossom Park, a section that is 8.5 miles long. The Russian Rapid, the first section of rapids that groups encounter from the Knights Ferry start, is a class II rapid. Knights Ferry receives ~1000 visitors a day on weekends during the summer months changing it from a small-time community to a hopping, bustling place reminiscent of its former days when it was the seat of Stanislaus County (1862- 1871). This area is part of the Stanislaus River Parks and is operated by the US Army Corps of Engineers.

Need to Know: Be aware that the river water can be moving faster than you think and can sweep you downstream if you are not careful (particularly at high flow levels).

Want More? It is not possible to do a loop on this trail. If you want more, you can go nearly 0.2 miles further (add 0.4 miles to the roundtrip total) on a much smaller trail that is somewhat difficult to walk on due to the large amounts of river rock. This smaller trail takes you to another section of the river. Otherwise, if you want more, head back to the Russian Rapid Trail sign and cross back over Sonora Road. Head up to the other parking area and follow the walking paths to the covered bridge. Cross over the bridge and then veer left to head back down to the information center. This can add another mile to your walk.

Directions to Trailhead: If you are approaching Knights Ferry from the west (just out of Oakdale), take the Kennedy Road exit to the left. Follow it 0.4 miles then turn left onto Sonora Road. If you are approaching Knights Ferry from the east, take the Sonora Road exit to the right. Follow this road 0.3 miles then bend to the right to stay on Sonora Road. From here (whether you came from the east or west), go 0.6 miles, crossing the river, to the junction with Covered Bridge Road. Turn right onto Covered Bridge Road and then an immediate right into the Knights Ferry Recreation Area. Distance from 108 is 0.9 or 1.0 miles depending on which 108 exit you used.

Peoria Mountain Trail Loop

Highlights: This trail climbs steeply right at the start but rewards you with great views of Table Mountain and the Stanislaus River (as it heads to Tulloch Reservoir) once you reach the summit. At the summit, you meander along the ridge looking down onto New Melones Lake before heading back down to the trailhead. A map of trails for this area can be downloaded from the internet or picked up at the New Melones Lake Visitor Center.

Distance: 2.7 miles roundtrip (4.0 miles roundtrip from equestrian staging area)

Elevation Changes: Cumulative ascent is ~850 ft; elevation is ~1000-1800 ft

Difficulty: Moderately difficult in terms of elevation change

Photo: Oak woodland in Peoria Wildlife Management Area

Seasonality: This hike is best during the spring when wildflowers are blooming. It is reasonable to do this hike in the late fall or winter. However, it is too hot to hike here in the summer and early fall.

User Groups/Permits: The trail is used by hikers, horsemen and mountain bike riders. Permits are not needed to park or day hike.

Parking/Facilities: Parking is located at the gated end of Old Melones Dam Road. Be sure not to block the gate. You could also park at the equestrian staging area just past Baseline Conservation Camp. There are no facilities if you park at the gate; there are portable potties at the equestrian staging area.

Topographic Map: USGS New Melones Dam, CA Quadrangle (7.5 Minute Series)

Hike Description: The trail begins behind the gate on the uphill side of Old Melones Dam Road (the trail on the other side of the road takes you down to the equestrian staging area). Once on the other side of the gate, find the trail that goes uphill directly to the left. The trail is steep and narrow for the first ~0.3 miles. It then levels out for a short bit before climbing again to the barbed wire fence beneath a tower just past 0.7 miles. There is a junction shortly after this; continue straight. You reach the top at ~0.85 miles. Be sure to take in the views of Table Mountain south and southeast and the Stanislaus River in the southwest. Once you reach the top, you travel on the northern edge of the ridge with views of New Melones Lake while heading mostly downhill. At ~1.8 miles you reach a junction; take the right trail downhill for nearly 0.7 miles. Turn right onto Green Springs Trail and head back 0.3 miles to the parking area.

Trail Tidbits: The Peoria Wildlife Management Area was established by the Bureau of Reclamation and covers 2500 acres. It was created to provide a habitat for native species in substitution for those lost when New Melones Lake was filled in 1983.

Need to Know: Beware of poison oak, ticks and rattlesnakes in this area. None of the trails in this area are marked. There are also extraneous trails heading off from the main trails. Typically, you can figure out which is the main trail based on its size and signs of travel but this is not always true. You should be comfortable reading maps and using a compass (or GPS device) to determine your general location. There is no water in this area.

Want More? The hike is written as a loop. If you want more, you can continue along the Peoria Ridge Trail. To do this, stay straight at the junction at ~1.8 miles. Peoria Ridge Trail eventually runs into Green Springs Trail in ~1.1 miles; take a right here and another right 0.2 miles further. This loop would be 4.9 miles.

Directions to Trailhead: Go east on 108 towards Jamestown. Turn left onto O'Byrne's Ferry Road. Go 0.2 miles then turn right onto Peoria Flat Road. Continue for 3 miles before turning right just before the Baseline Conservation Camp onto Old Melones Dam Road (note the signs for BOR Dam and TH Parking). The equestrian staging area is on the left ~0.1 miles down this road. To park closer to the trail, continue on Old Melones Dam Road for 0.9 miles until you see the gate. Park off the road on the right and don't block any gates. Distance from 108 is 4.1 miles.

Peoria Ridge and Green Springs Loop

Highlights: This is an enjoyable hike in an oak woodland community with views of Table Mountain and New Melones Lake once you have reached the ridge. There are a number of springs in the area off of Green Springs Trail. A map of trails for this area can be downloaded from the internet or picked up at the New Melones Lake Visitor Center.

Distance: 4.1 miles roundtrip (5.3 miles roundtrip from the equestrian staging area)

Elevation Changes: Cumulative ascent is ~730 ft; elevation is ~1000-1530 ft

Difficulty: Moderate in terms of elevation change (moderately difficult from equestrian staging area)

Seasonality: This hike is best during the spring when wildflowers are blooming. It is reasonable to do this hike in the late fall or winter. However, it is too hot in the summer and early fall and there is little water at this time.

User Groups/Permits: The trail is used by hikers, horsemen and mountain bike riders. Permits are not needed to park or day hike.

Parking/Facilities: Parking is located at the gated end of Old Melones Dam Road. Be sure not to block the gate. You could also park at the equestrian staging area just past Baseline Conservation Camp. There are no facilities if you park at the gate; there are portable potties at the equestrian staging area.

Topographic Map: USGS New Melones Dam, CA Quadrangle (7.5 Minute Series)

Hike Description: The trail begins behind the gate on the uphill side of Old Melones Dam Road (the trail on the other side of the road takes you down to the equestrian staging area). Once on the other side of the gate, continue straight up the main trail which is Green Springs Trail. Travel uphill ~0.3 miles where you should note the trail on the left; this is the trail you will come down to return to the parking area. At this point, stay on Green Springs Trail which starts wide but then narrows. Just past 0.6 miles into the hike, you reach a spring and a water tank. Veer right to stay on the Green Springs

Trail. From here, you hike up and down through beautiful oak woodlands and then begin to climb up to the ridge. Just before 1.8 miles, turn left to meet up with the Peoria Ridge Trail. Go up and over a small hump before reaching the junction with a large tract (just before 2 miles into the hike); turn left. This trail is mostly level as it travels along the ridge above New Melones Lake. At ~3.1 miles, you reach another junction; take the left trail downhill for nearly 0.7 miles. Turn right onto Green Springs Trail and head 0.3 miles back to the parking area.

Trail Tidbits: The Peoria Wildlife Management Area contains a variety of ecosystems including oak woodlands, conifer stands, vernal pools, riparian areas as well as the lake area itself. As a result, it supports a variety of native plant and animal species including American bald eagles, ospreys, mule deer, bats, hawks, California quail and grey foxes. In the scattered vernal pools, one can find tiger salamanders, fairy shrimp and toads.

Need to Know: Beware of poison oak, ticks and rattlesnakes in this area. None of the trails in this area are marked. There are extraneous trails heading off from the main trails. Typically you can figure out which is the main trail based on its size and signs of travel but this is not always true. You should be comfortable reading maps and using a compass (or GPS device) to determine your general location. There is little water in this area, particularly during the dry season.

Want More? The hike is written as a loop. If you want more, you can continue onto the Peoria Mountain Trail (go straight at the 3.1 miles junction) and follow this trail back down to the gate (this loop would be 4.9 miles). Another option would be to take Green Springs Trail further out towards Table Mountain before heading up to the Peoria Ridge Trail.

Directions to Trailhead: Go east on 108 towards Jamestown. Turn left onto O'Byrne's Ferry Road. Go 0.2 miles then turn right onto Peoria Flat Road. Continue for 3 miles before turning right just before the Baseline Conservation Camp onto Old Melones Dam Road (note the signs for BOR Dam and TH Parking). The equestrian staging area is on the left ~0.1 miles down this road. To park closer to the trail, continue on Old Melones Dam Road for 0.9 miles until you see the gate. Park off the road on the right and don't block any gates. Distance from 108 is 4.1 miles.

Red Hills Interpretive Nature Trail

Highlights: This is an easy hike that takes you out into the distinctive ecosystem that makes up the Red Hills. To help you understand the unique features that are a part of this environment, an interpretive trail has been developed along the south side of seasonal Horton Creek that runs parallel to North Serpentine Road. Brochures can be downloaded at the BLM webpage (http://www.blm.gov/pgdata/etc/medialib/blm/ca/pdf/folsom/brochures.Par.5 5238.File.dat/RedHills_nature_trail_brochure8x11.pdf).

Distance: 2.4 miles roundtrip

Elevation Changes: Cumulative ascent for loop is <200 ft; elevation is ~1050-1250 ft

Difficulty: Easy in terms of elevation change

Seasonality: This trail is best from late winter to mid-spring when water is flowing through the creek and wildflowers are blooming; it is too scorching hot to hike in this area in the summer particularly as there is no cover. It is cooler in the fall but dry.

User Groups/Permits: The trail is open only to foot traffic; the road is used by motorized vehicles, mountain bikes, horses and hikers. Permits are not needed to park or day hike.

Parking/Facilities: There is no fee for parking at the start of North Serpentine Road; there are no facilities here or on the trail but you do pass a vault toilet at the main trailhead parking area on Red Hills Road.

Topographic Map: USGS Chinese Camp, CA Quadrangle (7.5 Minute Series)

Hike Description: From the start of North Serpentine Loop, head up the road. [Note: this section could be driven but it requires a sturdy 4-wheel drive vehicle and it is more pleasant walking this as a longer loop.] The road is rocky and parallels Horton Creek which is a seasonal stream. Red Hills Trail heads off to the left ~0.2 miles into the hike. You cross the stream bed at ~0.8 miles. Just past 1 mile, the road opens up into a larger area; the interpretive trail starts just off to the left at the start of this opened area. You should see trail marker #1 at ~1.1 miles and markers #2 and 3 within another 0.1 miles. At this point the trail will follow the stream (or dry bed). Trail marker #4 appears just before a creek crossing and #5 occurs just after the crossing. There is a 'Y' in the trail at ~1.3 miles; the nature trail continues left following the stream. Over the next 0.3 miles, you will find markers #6-12. Another 'Y' is found at ~1.7 miles; stay left and cross the creek. The final marker, #13 is right there. Head up to the road and turn right to return back to the start of North Serpentine Loop for a roundtrip total of 2.4 miles. [If you drove to the start of the nature trail, you would turn left when the trail brings you back to the road and total mileage would be ~1.1 miles.]

Trail Tidbits: The interpretive trail was created by the high school students in the Ecology Club at Summerville High School (outside of Tuolumne City) in coordination with the California Native Plant Society and the Central Sierra Environmental Resource Center. The land is under the jurisdiction of the Bureau of Land Management, a federal government entity. The brochure primarily provides ecological information about the area.

Need to Know: This area is fairly exposed so it might be best to get an early start on warm days. If you are walking on the trail late in the season (like fall), be sure to pack enough water as there are no water sources at this time. The trail is rocky in most places so please watch your footing. Creek crossings can be slippery when water is present. Do not deface the stations at the interpretive trail; many volunteer hours went into creating this community asset. Do NOT leave VALUABLES in your car while out hiking; cars have been broken into in this area.

Want More? The trail is written as a loop. If you would like to hike more, you can explore the Red Hills Trail that heads off to the right on the return trip to the parking area.

Directions to Trailhead: Go east on 108 past Oakdale but before Jamestown. Turn right onto J-59. Travel down J-59 for ~2.1 miles then turn left onto Red Hills Road. You should see a sign for the Red Hills ~0.3 miles from J-59 but continue on this road for another 3.2 miles (past the large trailhead area on the right) until you come to North Serpentine Loop. Turn left and park at the start of this road. Distance from 108 is 5.6 miles.

Red Hills: Old Stage to Soaproot Ridge Long Loop

Highlights: This long loop hike takes you deep into the Red Hills Area of Critical Environmental Concern giving you ample opportunity to experience its unique ecology. As you head out on the trail, you travel up and over many low-lying hills dominated by low growing shrubs and plants and then further out on the loop, you climb up onto a high ridge with good views (including Don Pedro Reservoir) and stands of foothill pines and manzanita. A BLM trail map for this area can be downloaded from the internet.

Distance: 9.1 miles roundtrip

Elevation Changes: Cumulative ascent for loop is ~1200 ft; elevation is ~1190-1530 ft

Difficulty: Difficult in terms of elevation change

Seasonality: This trail is best from late winter to mid-spring when water is flowing through the creeks and wildflowers are blooming; it is too scorching hot to hike in this area in the summer particularly as there is little to no cover. Although cooler in the fall, it is still dry until the seasonal rains start.

User Groups/Permits: The trail is used by hikers, horseback riders and mountain bike riders. Permits are not needed to park or day hike.

Parking/Facilities: There is no fee for the large parking area at the trailhead. There is a vault toilet located in the parking area only.

Topographic Map: USGS Chinese Camp, CA Quadrangle (7.5 Minute Series)

Hike Description: From the trailhead parking area, look for the trailhead sign (off to the right with your back to Red Hills Road). Follow the trail that starts to the left of this sign; this is Old Stage Trail. It takes you around the side of a hill. At ~0.35 miles, the main trail goes right. At ~1.2 miles, you reach a trail junction near a stream bed. Cross the stream bed and continue up on the right-hand trail labeled Old Stage Trail. Continue uphill and at ~1.3 miles, you reach the first junction with Butterweed Trail; continue straight. Another 0.3 miles further, you enter into an area with more cover due to the greater number of pines and manzanita growing amongst the ceanothus plants. Cross a creek bed at ~1.8 miles and head uphill. At ~2.0 miles, you reach the second junction with the Butterweed Trail; stay on Old Stage Trail. Follow the fence line downhill and then veer left as you head uphill again. Soon you head right and pick up the fence line again. At ~2.5 miles, cross a streambed where you reach a junction. Old Stage Trail heads to the left but this section is difficult to follow and gets you to Don Pedro Overlook Road in ~2.7 miles. Instead, head right taking the trail to a parking area. Turn left onto Don Pedro Overlook Road (behind the locked gate) and up to the junction with Old Stage Trail in ~2 miles (4.5 miles into the hike). Once you reach the junction of Don Pedro Overlook Road with Old Stage Trail, turn right onto Old Stage Trail and head downhill. You pass a picnic table at ~4.7 miles; veer left. The trail climbs back up to the Don Pedro Overlook Road at ~5.0 miles. Cross the road to pick up the Soaproot Ridge Trail from which you can see a section of Don Pedro Reservoir. At ~5.7 miles, you reach the junction with Six Bit Trail; cross the trail to continue on the Soaproot Ridge Trail. There is another nice overlook area where the trail sharply juts to the north (at ~6.2 miles). Head along the ridge for the next ~1.3 miles (passing junctions for a trail that takes you back to the Old Stage Trail and another that takes you to the Butterweed Trail) before heading downhill on a steep and rocky section at ~7.5 miles. You reach the bottom at ~7.9 miles where you cross a creek bed and turn right. At ~8.1 you reach another trail junction with a trail that takes you to Old Stage Trail; continue right to stay on the Soaproot Ridge Trail. At ~8.3 miles, you reach an unmarked big 'Y' junction; go left. About 0.2 miles further, a trail off to the right takes you onto the Overlook Loop; stay on Soaproot Ridge unless you want to add this other loop onto your hiking distance. At ~8.8 miles, the trial on the right is the return trail for the Overlook Loop. You reach the outskirts of the parking area at 9.0 miles; circle to the left to return to the start of the trail.

Trail Tidbits: The Red Hills Area of Critical Environmental Concern was established in 1993 in an effort to protect the rare plant species that grow here and nowhere else. This land area consists of ~7,100 acres and has the largest exposure of serpentine rock in the Sierra Nevada foothills.

Need to Know: Due to the popularity of this area with horsemen and mountain bike riders, many extraneous trails have been created that are not marked. Most of the time you can discern which is the main trail and which is a side trail but this is not always true. This area is fairly exposed so it might be best to get an early start on warm days. If you are walking on the trail late in the season (like fall) be sure to pack enough water as there are no water sources at this time. The trail is rocky in most places so please watch your footing. Creek crossings can be slippery when water is present. Do NOT leave VALUABLES in your car while out hiking; cars have been broken into in this area.

Want More? The trail is written as a loop. If you would like to hike more, you can add the Overlook Loop as you head back on Soaproot Ridge Trail.

Directions to Trailhead: Go east on 108 past Oakdale but before Jamestown. Turn right onto J-59. Travel down J-59 for ~2.1 miles then turn left onto Red Hills Road. You should see a sign for the Red Hills ~0.3 miles from J-59 but go an additional 0.3 miles before turning right into the trailhead parking lot. Distance from 108 is 2.7 miles.

Photo: The austere look of the Red Hills

Red Hills: Old Stage to Soaproot Ridge Short Loop

Highlights: This is a short hike that still gives you a good perspective of the Red Hills Area of Critical Environmental Concern and its unique ecology. Only plants that are adapted to the inhospitable soils can grow here. When you begin to look around, you will notice quite a variety of species including some that are quite rare. A BLM trail map for this area can be downloaded from the internet.

Distance: 2.5 miles roundtrip

Elevation Changes: Cumulative ascent for loop is ~440 ft; elevation is ~1050-1350 ft

Difficulty: Moderately easy in terms of elevation change

Seasonality: This trail is best from late winter to mid-spring when water is flowing through the creeks and wildflowers are blooming; it is too scorching hot to hike in this area in the summer particularly as there is no cover. Although cooler in the fall, it is still dry until the seasonal rains start.

User Groups/Permits: The trail is used by hikers, horseback riders and mountain bike riders. Permits are not needed to park or day hike.

Parking/Facilities: There is no fee for the large parking area at the trailhead. There is a vault toilet located in the parking area only.

Topographic Map: USGS Chinese Camp, CA Quadrangle (7.5 Minute Series)

Hike Description: From the trailhead parking area, look for the trailhead sign (off to the right with your back to Red Hills Road). Follow the trail that starts to the left of this sign; this is Old Stage Trail. It takes you around the side of a hill where you can see the buildings for Diestel Turkey Ranch. At ~1.1 miles, you reach a trail junction near a stream bed. You want to turn left here and follow the stream before connecting to the Soaproot Ridge Trail. Just before 1.5 miles into the hike, there is another junction with the Soaproot Ridge Trail; head to the left. At ~1.7 miles, you reach a large unmarked 'Y' junction; take the left branch. About 0.2 miles further, the Overlook Loop trail heads off to the right; stay on Soaproot Ridge unless you want to add this other loop onto your hiking distance. At ~2.2 miles, the trail to the right is the return trail for the Overlook Loop; again, stay straight. You reach the outskirts of the parking area at 2.4 miles but you need to circle around the parking area to the left to return to the start.

Trail Tidbits: Look for the green rock that is found throughout this region. It is the serpentine rock which has been California's state rock since 1965. This rock, when it breaks down, contributes to the unique Red Hills soil composition which also contains dunite. Serpentine is high in magnesium and heavy metals. It is low in nitrogen, potassium and phosphorous which are elements that plants need to grow. The soils in this area are also high in oxidized iron which is what gives the hills their red color. All of these characteristics make it difficult for plants to grow and, as a result, only those specific plants adapted to these soil conditions thrive in the Red Hills.

Need to Know: This area is fairly exposed so it might be best to get an early start on warm days. If you are walking on the trail late in the season (like fall), be sure to pack enough water as there are no water sources at this time. The trail is rocky in most places so please watch your footing. Creek crossings can be slippery when water is present. This area is very popular with horseback riders; they have the right of way. Do NOT leave VALUABLES in your car while out hiking; cars have been broken into in this area.

Want More? The trail is written as a loop. If you would like to hike more, you can add the Overlook Loop as you head back on Soaproot Ridge. Another option is that you can make this loop longer by staying on the Old Stage Trail at the ~1.1 mile junction. From here head left at either the first or second Butterweed Trail junctions, then cross over to the Soaproot Ridge Trail (there are trails for this even though they are not on the map). Take the Soaproot Ridge Trail down to the Old Stage-Soaproot junction (see junction at ~1.5 miles on the short loop).

Directions to Trailhead: Go east on 108 past Oakdale but before Jamestown. Turn right onto J-59. Travel down J-59 for ~2.1 miles then turn left onto Red Hills Road. You should see a sign for the Red Hills ~0.3 miles from J-59 but go an additional 0.3 miles before turning right into the trailhead parking lot. Distance from 108 is 2.7 miles.

Red Hills Railroad Grade Trail

Highlights: This lesser traveled trail is predominantly level as it travels along the old Sierra Railroad grade. At its most southeast edge, there is a distinct demarcation between the unique ecosystem of the Red Hills and the surrounding oak woodlands. Another change in ecosystem zones occurs near the private property fence line further into the hike. Other highlights include the large quantities of exposed serpentine rock and the excellent views of the Red Hills area and beyond. A BLM trail map for this area can be downloaded from the internet.

Distance: 2.5 miles one way (5.0 miles roundtrip)

Elevation Changes: Cumulative ascent on the way out is 230 ft and 220 ft on the return trip; elevation is ~1160-1390 ft

Difficulty: Moderately easy in terms of elevation change

Seasonality: This trail is best from late winter to mid-spring when water is flowing through the creeks and wildflowers are blooming; it is too scorching hot to hike in this area in the summer particularly as there is no cover. Although cooler in the fall, it is still dry until the seasonal rains start.

User Groups/Permits: The trail is used by hikers, horseback riders and mountain bike riders. Permits are not needed to park or day hike.

Parking/Facilities: There is no fee for parking. There is a vault toilet located in the large trailhead parking area 0.25 miles further up Red Hills Road.

Topographic Map: USGS Chinese Camp, CA Quadrangle (7.5 Minute Series)

Hike Description: Cross the street from where you have parked the car to start the trail. Very quickly into the trail, you begin following a fence line (for a short while). At ~0.1 miles into the hike, take a look off to the left and note the demarcation between the oak woodlands typical of the foothills and the unique flora of the Red Hills. As you are heading down a hill at 0.4 miles, you encounter a junction with the Red Hills Trail (from Red Hills Road); veer left. The trail heads up and around a corner to the right at ~0.6 miles.

You now head along a ridge on a fairly level trail (there is some up and down near drainages and obstacles). Just before 1 mile, there is a split; the 2 trails meet up again later but stay left to stay on the main trail. The trail gets a bit rockier at ~1.2 miles and a short distance later, you climb and are treated to some excellent views of the Red Hills as well as some distant Yosemite Park peaks. The trail hits another fence line at ~1.6 miles as you skirt around a private residence. Go down and to the right at ~1.7 miles and at this point you should notice that you have entered a different ecological zone that contains toyon and a variety of oaks (including poison oak). At 2.0 and 2.1 miles, you cross some dirt tracks that lead to the private residence; stay straight at both locations to remain on the trail. You reach the junction with South Serpentine Loop at ~2.5 miles. This is the turnaround location.

Trail Tidbits: The railroad grade is part of the old Sierra Railroad system, constructed in the 1890's, which transported materials between the Central Valley and the southern mines. It has been out of service since 1979 but there are sections of rail still located in the Red Hills. The Red Hills, including scenes with or without railroad tracks, have been the site of many motion pictures and television series such as "Back to the Future III", "Unforgiven" and "Bonanza". A 1996 fire destroyed a number of structures used in the "Back to the Future III" set and burned many acres. Even today, you can still see black bark on some of the foothill pines scorched by the fire.

Need to Know: This area is fairly exposed so it might be best to get an early start on warm days. If you are walking on the trail late in the season (like fall), be sure to pack enough water as there are no water sources along this trail. The trail is rocky in most places so please watch your footing. There is one section of the trail where poison oak is evident; stay on the trail. Do NOT leave VALUABLES in your car while out hiking; cars have been broken into in this area.

Want A Loop? A reasonable but long loop would be to turn right onto the South Serpentine Loop and head back towards Red Hills Road. Near the junction of South Serpentine Loop and Red Hills Road, turn right onto Red Hills Trail. This trail parallels Red Hills Road for a short distance before bringing you back to Red Hills Road. Turn right onto the road and continue uphill until you reach the area where you parked.

Directions to Trailhead: Go east on 108 past Oakdale but before Jamestown. Turn right onto J-59. Travel down J-59 for ~2.1 miles then turn left onto Red Hills Road. You should see a sign for the Red Hills ~0.3 miles from J-59. Just past the Red Hills sign, you should see a different sign on the right that says "Vehicles restricted to designated routes" just before heading downhill (if you reach the large trailhead parking area down the hill and off to the right, you have gone too far). Park near this sign making sure your car is off the road. The trail starts across the street. [Note: there is another approach to this trail and that is to start on the Red Hills Trail on the left just down the hill past the large parking area. This trail will connect with the Railroad Grade Trail but entails a bit more climbing and distance.] Distance from 108 is 2.4 miles.

Photo: Red Hills vista along the Railroad Grade Trail

Table Mountain Trail

Highlights: Table Mountain, an iconic geologic feature, is in sections and visible throughout a portion of the Highway 108 corridor. This particular hike is on one section that is accessible to the public. Although the last 0.25 miles of the trail is steep and rocky, the climb to the flat top is well worth the views and is particularly rewarding in the spring when the entire top is covered with blooms of many different species of wildflowers (color photo page 167).

Distance: ~1.5 miles to the top (~3.0 miles roundtrip)

Elevation Changes: Cumulative ascent to the top is ~520 ft; elevation is ~1230- 1750 ft

Difficulty: Moderate in terms of elevation change

Seasonality: This hike is best during the spring when wildflowers are blooming. It is reasonable to do this hike in the late fall or winter but it is too hot to visit this area in the summer and early fall.

User Groups/Permits: The trail is used by hikers and rock climbers. Permits are not needed to park or day hike.

Parking/Facilities: Parking is located at the end of Shell Road. Be sure not to block any driveway entrances. There are no facilities in the parking area but there is a vault toilet ~0.9 miles up the trail.

Topographic Map: USGS Sonora, CA Quadrangle (7.5 Minute Series)

Hike Description: The trail begins off to the right just before the gate (note sign for trail). Pass through a small gate into an enclosed area (be sure to close the gate securely). The trail parallels the dirt road that continues beyond the gate. Nearly 0.2 miles into the hike, note a faint trail that heads off to the right. This trail is one that takes you down to New Melones Lake. Continue straight until you reach the vault toilet area at ~0.9 miles. Head up towards the road, go through (and secure) another gate, cross the road and continue up the trail on the other side. You should see a brown trail marker here and at other locations. Travel ~0.1 miles further and note a large mining shaft hole to the right. At ~1.2 miles, the trail bends to the left but you can see another mine shaft opening if you take a very short side trip to the right. Continue heading upwards and at ~1.3 miles, continue uphill to the right instead of veering left. The trail is quite rocky at this point and starts to become fairly steep; however, it is <0.2 miles further to the top. Once you reach the top, you have views in all directions: New Melones Reservoir to the northwest and Yosemite peaks to the southeast. Even though it is not included in the total trail mileage, you should continue hiking along the plateau to gain an appreciation for all that Table Mountain has to offer.

Trail Tidbits: A giant volcano near Sonora Pass erupted ~9 million years ago spilling lava into the giant, ancient Stanislaus River Canyon. The lava flowed downhill towards Knights Ferry, filling in all but the highest peaks within parts of Tuolumne and Calaveras Counties. The lava cooled and hardened blocking the original river channel. Water found new routes downhill eroding the softer material surrounding the lava and forming new stream beds and river channels. As the softer material was removed, the harder remains of the ancient lava flow became more evident and now are seen throughout both counties as unique geologic features (such as Table Mountain). Once gold miners in the area realized that a great river once flowed beneath the hardened lava bed of Table Mountain, they began to tunnel under it in search of gold.

Need to Know: Beware of poison oak, ticks and rattlesnakes in this area. The poison oak is particularly bad on the last section of the trail. There is no water available on this trail.

Want More? It would be difficult to turn this hike into a loop particularly with the steep sides of Table Mountain and the abundance of poison oak. If you would like to hike more, you can explore the flat ridge of Table Mountain by heading west. There is no official trail but you can follow paths already made that continue for quite a ways. In addition, on your return to the parking area, you can take the faint trail down to New Melones Lake.

Directions to Trailhead: Go east on 108 to Jamestown. Turn left onto Rawhide Road. Go 2 miles and when Rawhide Road takes a sharp right, turn left onto Shell Road. Drive 1.7 miles down Shell Road until you reach the closed gate. Park off the road and do not block driveways or other cars. Distance from 108 is 3.7 miles.

Two-Mile Bar Recreation Area

Highlights: This is a short and easy hike that takes you down to the Stanislaus River and provides views of the long flat bar on the opposite bank and cliff sides of a section of Table Mountain on both sides of the river. This is an excellent birding area.

Distance: 0.45 miles to water's edge past the bridge to nowhere (0.9 miles roundtrip)

Elevation Changes: Cumulative ascent roundtrip is <160 ft; elevation is ~250-400 ft

Difficulty: Easy in terms of elevation change

Photo: Section of Table Mountain at Two-Mile Bar

Seasonality: This trail is best from late winter to mid-spring when water in the river is flowing and wildflowers are blooming. This area can be quite hot in the summer; you might want to avoid it at this time unless you are heading to the river for a swim. It is cooler in the fall but dry.

User Groups/Permits: The trail is open only to foot traffic including those carrying boats to put into the river. Permits are not needed to park or day hike.

Parking/Facilities: There is no fee for parking at this recreation area; there is a portable potty in the parking area. There are also trashcans located in the parking area and down near the water.

Topographic Map: USGS Knights Ferry, CA Quadrangle (7.5 Minute Series)

Hike Description: Cross the bridge at the end of the parking area and follow the road downward. At ~0.15 miles, the road becomes more of a trail and veers to the right. At this and later points, there are trails to the left that take you down to the water's edge. To continue the hike, follow the trail through a section that is cut through the middle of blackberry bushes and poison oak. Stay on the trail! The trail becomes sandy at ~0.3 miles. At 0.4 miles, you cross the bridge to nowhere and over nothing. The trail becomes very narrow and takes you over a rocky section and through more blackberry bushes before bringing you to the water's edge at a good swimming hole.

Trail Tidbits: This area is part of the Stanislaus River Parks and is operated by the US Army Corps of Engineers. The canal that you cross at the start of the trail is part of the South Oakdale Main Canal that carries water to Cashman Reservoir outside of Oakdale. This canal has been the target of improvement project monies to stabilize the system and decrease water losses. The Two-Mile Bar Reach, 0.5 miles in length, is one of two flood plains located within the Goodwin Canyon of the Stanislaus River and is a critical spawning and rearing area for fish. The Goodwin Canyon is a 4 mile stretch of river from Goodwin Dam (below Tulloch Dam) to Knights Ferry.

Need to Know: There is poison oak in this area; try to avoid it. There is no camping allowed here. Be aware that the river water can be moving faster than you think and can sweep you downstream if you are not careful, particularly with high flow levels.

Want More? It is not possible to do a loop with this trail without going onto private property. If you want more, you can drive down to the Knights Ferry Recreation Area and do more hiking there. A trail from Two-Bar Recreation Area to Knights Ferry had been proposed in 2010 along a section of the canal; if the trail is now open for public use, you can try this as well.

Directions to Trailhead: The entrance to Two-Mile Bar Road can only be reached heading west on 108 as the turnoff for it occurs along the divided highway. If you are heading east from Oakdale, you will need to cross to westbound lanes of 108 at the Lake Tulloch South Shore exit. From this junction, travel ~0.9 miles (just before the divided highway ends) then turn right onto Two-Mile Bar Road. If you are paying attention to mile markers, this turnoff is just past the 0.5 mile marker for Tuolumne County. The recreation area is 0.9 miles down Two-Mile Bar Road. Distance from 108 is 0.9 miles.

Ditch Trails

Tuolumne County abounds with ditches which have trails paralleling them, offering fairly level and easy walking paths along a running stream of water. These trails typically can be accessed during most of the year. The ditches are valuable to most Tuolumne County residents as they serve as their water source; the trails provide access for ditch walkers who are employed to monitor the physical conditions of ditch structures and to ensure that water is flowing unimpeded. Since the ditch water is the source of drinking water for many communities, no human contact with the ditch water is allowed. Do NOT drink water directly from the ditch; it is not treated at this point.

Due to their historical role in the development of Tuolumne County, the various ditch systems had been submitted for consideration for the National Register of Historic Places. They were initially constructed to provide a year-round source of water to the mining communities in the 1850's both for mining purposes and for domestic use. Although no longer used for placer or quartz mining, the ditch systems still provide water for agricultural and household uses as well as for the generation of hydroelectric power.

The ditch systems consist of earthen areas, culverts, sections with piped water, narrow concrete & wooden channels, reservoirs and flumes. Flumes are half pipes that sit on top of wooden trestles; they are used to transport the water over steep areas in an effort to maintain the same percent grade. You can 'walk on water' or actually above it on single-wide or double-wide wooden planks that have been laid across the top of flumes from one end to the other to continue the path of the ditch trail. As flumes are not for everyone, the 'Need to Know' section of the hike will let you know if there are any flume crossings.

There are more ditch trails within the Highway 108 corridor that have not been included in this book for various reasons. For some, the trails are not very well established; for others, access is limited. Many of the ditch trails are easements on private property. Although these trails have been used by the public for decades, the easement is for employees that monitor the ditch systems. Please be respectful of property owners and their rights by staying on trails.

Main Tuolumne Ditch: 'C' Flume to 'I' Flume

Highlights: Once you reach this ditch trail after a gradual climb, it offers a fairly level path amidst mixed coniferous forests, oak woodlands and riparian habitats set to the gurgling and rushing movement of water. This ditch trail section is located just outside of downtown Twain Harte and involves some short flume crossings. Better yet, the trail is rarely used.

Distance: ~2.4 miles (4.8 miles roundtrip)

Elevation Changes: Cumulative ascent is ~265 ft on the way out and ~25 ft on the return trip; elevation ~3800-4050 ft

Difficulty: Moderately easy in terms of elevation change

Seasonality: This trail is suitable for all seasons but may be covered with snow at times in the winter. The trail can get muddy after heavy storms and snowmelt.

User Groups/Permits: The trail is used by walkers, runners and the occasional bike rider. No permits are needed to park or use the trail.

Parking/Facilities: Park off of South Fork Road and do not block the gate. You could park across South Fork Road at the entrance to Forest Service Road 3N99. There are no facilities here or along the trail.

Topographic Map: USGS Twain Harte, CA Quadrangle (7.5 minute series)

Hike Description: Head up the old logging road beyond the gate. Take in the view of the South Fork of Stanislaus River Canyon at ~0.3 miles. A short while later, the dirt road veers to the left and, at this point, you should hear rushing water. Continue a short distance until you note a flume structure and see a slight trail off to the right just past a corrugated pipe. Take this little side trail, at ~0.8 miles, up to the ditch trail at the junction with the 'C' Flume. Head right on the ditch trail and cross the very short 'D' Flume right away. At ~1.6 and 1.7 miles, you pass bridges that cross the ditch water. You cross 2 additional very short flumes at ~1.9 and 2.0 miles. The turnaround point is at the start of the longer 'I' Flume.

Trail Tidbits: The Main Tuolumne Ditch, also known as the Main Canal, was built in the early 1850's as a conduit to bring water from rivers that flowed year-round to the lower elevation mining camps for placer mining and then later on, hydraulic mining. Many miles of the various ditch systems in Tuolumne County have been abandoned but ~57 miles of ditches are currently used today for agriculture, hydroelectric power and domestic use for downstream communities. Numerous locks, flume structures and a concrete channel are seen on this particular section of the Main Canal, which is owned and operated by PG&E.

Need to Know: This hike involves some very short flume crossings on single-wide planks. The logging road that you take up to the ditch and the initial segment of the ditch trail could be overgrown since they receive minimal traffic.

Want A Loop? The loop actually shortens the roundtrip distance of the hike to 3.6 miles. On the trip back, look for a side trail off to the left after you pass both bridges that cross the ditch. The trail is at the end of the section that has a cement wall on the far side only (~3.3 miles into the hike). This trail takes you down a steep hill before bringing you to the logging road. If you want more, continue the hike over the 'I' flume or cross one of the bridges and explore areas on the other side of the ditch.

Directions to Trailhead: Go east on 108 and take the lower Twain Harte Drive exit into Twain Harte (1.8 miles). Go under the arch onto Joaquin Gully Road. Stay on this road until it puts you onto Middle Camp Road (another mile). Stay on Middle Camp until you reach a 'Y' (another 0.2 mile); take the left which becomes South Fork Road. Continue on South Fork Road for an additional 3.4 miles until you see a gate on the right side of the road. On the left side is the start of Forest Service Road 3N99. Total distance from 108 is 6.4 miles.

Main Tuolumne Ditch: Kewin Mill Road to Old Oak Ranch Road

Highlights: Although you pass through some Cedar Ridge neighborhoods at the start of this hike, you quickly feel as if you are out in the middle of nowhere when you leave the homes behind. This wide and level ditch trail meanders through mixed coniferous and oak forests with riparian habitats alongside the moving water.

Distance: ~5.3 miles (10.6 miles roundtrip)

Elevation Changes: Cumulative ascent of ~100 ft; elevation ~3850-3950 ft

Difficulty: Easy in terms of elevation change

Seasonality: This trail is suitable for all seasons but may be covered with snow at times in the winter. A variety of wildflowers can be seen from early spring through early fall. The trail can get quite muddy after heavy storms and snowmelt. Even on warm summer days, the trail is shaded offering a pleasant hiking temperature.

User Groups/Permits: The trail is used by walkers, runners and the occasional bike rider. No permits are needed to park or use the trail.

Parking/Facilities: There is a dirt area on the right side of Kewin Mill Road just before the junction with Mt. Elizabeth Drive where you can park. The start of the ditch trail is just past the junction with Mt. Elizabeth Drive on the left. There are no facilities here or on the trail.

Topographic Map: USGS Columbia SE, CA Quadrangle (7.5 minute series)

Hike Description: From the dirt parking area, head <0.1 miles up Kewin Mill Road until you reach the ditch trail located on the left just before the volunteer fire station. After 0.4 miles, you pass water storage tanks on the right. Cross North Oxbow at ~0.9 miles and Saddle Court at ~1.4 miles into the hike. At this point you leave behind Cedar Ridge and head into a forested area. You encounter bridges that span the ditch at 2.15 and 2.4 miles that, if crossed, would eventually lead you up to Old Oak Ranch Road. The water in the ditch drops 15 ft into a pool resulting in a waterfall at the 3 mile mark. Less than 0.2 miles further you pass a gravel road which connects to Old Oak Ranch Road. Nearly 3.6 miles into the hike, you reach a short double-planked flume crossing. You encounter another bridge at ~4.25 miles and then another 0.2 miles further, you reach a gravel road that ends at an overlook into the canyon. This gravel road also connects to Old Oak Ranch Road on Sierra Outdoor School property. Just beyond the junction with this gravel road, you reach a grated metal stairway that takes you up and then back down to the trail. The trail reaches Old Oak Ranch Road 0.8 miles past this stairway (at 5.3 miles).

Trail Tidbits: The water in this main canal began its journey at a small diversion dam below Lyons Dam. From here it traveled along the ridge at Middle Camp (bypassing the lock for the Section 4 Ditch) before reaching Cedar Ridge and then the Old Oak Ranch area. Just past the Old Oak Ranch area, a portion of the water travels through a penstock pipe to Phoenix Lake where it is stored behind an earthen dam that is 1150 ft long and 40 ft high. Phoenix Lake serves as a reservoir for the communities of Sonora and Jamestown and supplies water to the Algerine, Sonora and Shaw's Flat Ditches. Water not diverted through the Phoenix Lake penstock pipe continues onward in the Columbia Ditch which traverses Big Hill before dropping down into the Columbia area.

Need to Know: This section of the Main Tuolumne Ditch involves a short flume crossing on a double-wide plank. The ditch passes through some land that is privately owned; please stay on the trail.

Want A Loop? There are a number of loops that can be done from this trail. The longest would involve traveling the full 5.3 miles to Old Oak Ranch Road and then turning left onto it. Follow the road through the Sierra Outdoor School campus (be respectful if classes are in session). After traveling through the main part of campus, you reach a paved 'Y'; take the right. Less than 0.15 miles from the 'Y', the road is no longer paved. Continue on Old Oak Ranch Road for a total of 2.1 miles at which point it becomes a paved road named Pack Trail. Follow this road for just over 0.3 miles to turn right on Hitching Post. After 0.3 miles on this road, turn left onto Broken Pine. Follow Broken Pine just over 0.4 miles to Kewin Mill Road quite near the dirt parking area. Total mileage for this loop is just about 8.6 miles. Shorter loops can be done by crossing the ditch via one of the bridges or gravel roads mentioned and working your way up to Old Oak

Ranch Road. Once you reach the road, turn left and follow the directions above to return to the parking area.

Photo: A double-planked flume crossing

Directions to Trailhead: Go east on 108 and turn left at the Soulsbyville Drive exit (at the light). Head down this road until you reach a 4-way stop 0.2 miles from the light. Turn right onto Longeway Road. Veer left to stay on Longeway Road ~1.1 miles from 108. You reach a 'Y' 1.5 miles further; take the left branch to remain on Longeway Road. Turn left when you come to a 'T' 0.8 miles further or 3.4 miles from 108 (still on Longeway Road). Continue 0.4 miles to another 'T' (3.8 miles). Turn right onto Phoenix Lake Road and <0.1 miles further, veer right onto Kewin Mill Road (Big Hill Road veers off to the left). Drive nearly 2 miles up Kewin Mill Road before parking on the right in the dirt parking area where you can see the ditch. Total distance from 108 is ~5.8 miles.

Main Tuolumne Ditch: Mount Elizabeth Road to Kewin Mill Road

Highlights: This particular ditch trail is quite popular due to the fact that it is wide, level, shady and located just outside of downtown Twain Harte. At times the trail passes through stands of predominantly coniferous trees but at others, the landscape primarily consists of oaks. There are quite a few dogwood trees that grow along this trail that are gorgeous spring and fall.

Distance: ~2.5 miles (5.0 miles roundtrip)

Elevation Changes: Cumulative roundtrip ascent ~15 ft; elevation ~3960 ft

Difficulty: Easy in terms of elevation change

Seasonality: This trail is suitable for all seasons but may be covered with snow at times in the winter. A variety of wildflowers can be seen from early spring through early fall. The trail can get quite muddy after heavy storms and snowmelt. Even on warm summer days, the trail is shaded offering a pleasant temperature for hiking.

User Groups/Permits: The trail is used by walkers, runners and the occasional bike rider. No permits are needed to park or use the trail.

Parking/Facilities: There is a turnout on the left of Mt. Elizabeth Road immediately after the road crosses the ditch; parking is allowed here as this portion of the road is part of a subdivision. There are no facilities here but there is a portable potty just uphill from the water treatment plant at ~1.6 miles. This trail can also be accessed from Kewin Mill Road (for directions see Main Tuolumne Ditch Kewin Mill to Old Oak Ranch hike).

Topographic Map: USGS Twain Harte, CA and Columbia SE, CA Quadrangles (7.5 minute series)

Hike Description: Take the ditch trail that is on the same side of the road as the parking area. After 0.4 miles, cross a short double-plank flume; there is also a bridge and staircase that heads to Forest Service Road 2N26 (see Want A Loop?). At 0.8 miles you pass another bridge that also leads to 2N26. You reach a private property gate at 1.2 miles where the trail dips down and then back up again. The water treatment plant is located at ~1.6 miles. There are other bridges that you pass along the way but they are all privately owned and should not be used. As you continue on the trail, you pass an apple orchard on the left and more houses (Cedar Ridge) are evident. At ~2.4 miles, a fence line begins on the left. Continue walking until you reach the two big ponderosa trees forming a 'V' (2.5 miles) located at the edge of a dirt parking area. This is the turnaround point.

Trail Tidbits: The ditch systems were dug, either by hand or by scrapers drawn by horses or mules, during the 1850's (Gold Rush Era). Their purpose was to convey water from year-round flowing mountain rivers to mining towns. The water was used to wash gold from the gravels which exposed large swaths of limestone in the Columbia Basin. Once there were 250 miles of ditches, many of which have since been abandoned; currently, 57 miles of ditches are maintained either by PG&E or Tuolumne Utilities District (TUD). PG&E owns and operates the Main Canal also referred to as the Main Tuolumne Ditch and it continues to function as a source of water for downstream communities as well as a recreational spot for hikers and fishermen (Fish & Game stock the Main Canal with fish).

Need to Know: This trail involves a short flume crossing on a double-wide plank. The first half of the trail passes through Stanislaus National Forest land but the second half passes through private property. Please be courteous to property owners; respect their property by staying on the trail.

Want A Loop? There are 3 loops that can be done on this trail. The shortest loop (0.8 miles; ~45 ft elevation change) would entail that you cross the bridge just before the flume at ~0.4 miles and take the staircase up to the dirt road that is Forest Service Road 2N26. Turn right on this road and take it back to the parking area. The middle distance loop is 1.65 miles (elevation change of ~92 ft) and requires that you cross the bridge ~0.8 miles from the parking area. Head up to Forest Service Road 2N26 and then turn right traveling until you reach the parking area. The longest loop is still 5 miles but entails an elevation change of ~140 ft. Take the ditch trail to the dirt parking area past the 2 ponderosa trees then head up to Kewin Mill Road and turn right. Turn right onto Mount Elizabeth Drive. Travel through a neighborhood before the drive changes to a dirt road (at ~2.9 miles into the hike). Follow the dirt road past houses (and private property) before eventually reaching a locked gate (~4.1 miles). The road is now Forest Service Road 2N26. Follow it until you reach the parking area.

Directions to Trailhead: Go east on 108 and take the lower Twain Harte Drive exit into Twain Harte (1.8 miles). Go under the arch onto Joaquin Gully Road. Stay on this road until it puts you onto Middle Camp Road (another mile). At this intersection, make a very slight left onto Mt. Elizabeth Road. Drive up a fairly steep hill then down a smaller hill for 0.4 miles. At the bottom of this small hill (and before you begin to go up again), the road crosses the ditch. Park off on the left. Total distance from 108 is 3.2 miles.

Photo: A section of trail along the Main Tuolumne Ditch

Main Tuolumne Ditch: Mount Elizabeth Road to South Fork Road

Highlights: The start of this ditch trail section is located just outside of downtown Twain Harte, involves no flume walking and takes you through land that used to be part of an old golf course but is now reverting back to wild meadows fringed with trees.

Distance: ~0.6 miles (1.2 miles roundtrip) from Mount Elizabeth Road; ~0.5 miles (1.0 miles roundtrip) from Kit Carson Road.

Elevation Changes: Cumulative ascent is ~150 ft on the way out and ~50 ft on the return trip; elevation ~3980 ft.

Difficulty: Easy in terms of elevation change

Seasonality: This trail is suitable for all seasons but may be covered with snow at times in the winter. The trail can get quite muddy after heavy storms and snowmelt.

User Groups/Permits: The trail is used by walkers, runners, the occasional bike rider and disc golf players. No permits are needed to park or use the trail.

Parking/Facilities: There is a turnout on the left of Mt. Elizabeth Road immediately after the road crosses the ditch. There are no facilities here or on the trail. If you prefer to skip the short section between Mount Elizabeth Road and Kit Carson Road (which contains obstacles along a narrow, sometimes slippery trail), park at the end of Kit Carson Road.

Topographic Map: USGS Twain Harte, CA Quadrangle (7.5 minute series)

Hike Description: Take the ditch trail that is on the opposite side of the road from the parking area heading upstream. The first 0.1 miles is on a narrow path that takes you across wooden planks, over tree roots and a downed tree and through a marshy area. You then reach the cul-de-sac at the end of Kit Carson Road. Continue on the trail behind a few homes. Just past 0.2 miles, you come to a bridge crossing the ditch. Another bridge is located ~0.25

miles into the hike. At 0.35 miles, you reach a long, high flume that you may NOT walk on. Instead you parallel the flume on the trail that takes you down a hill and then up again until you reach the fishing access parking area off of South Fork Road.

Trail Tidbits: This part of the trail passes through what used to be the Sierra Pines Golf Course. Although the golf course has been closed for years, you can still see ponds and benches from the golf course's former days. Most of this land is now owned by Tuolumne Utilities District (TUD) but this ditch section is owned and operated by PG&E. Currently, parts of the golf course are being used for a disc golf course.

Need to Know: There are no flume crossings on this hike. The ditch passes through some land that is privately owned; please stay on the trail.

Want A Loop? You can turn this hike into a loop by heading cross-country for a short distance along the edge of the large meadow that parallels South Fork Road. At some point you need to dip down into the middle of the meadow and then head back up to the ditch trail. This is not recommended in the summer due to the copious amounts of brush with stickers. To do this hike in such a way that a part of it is a loop, follow the trail back to the section that has bridges that cross the ditch. Cross over on the first bridge and walk on the trail that takes you along the edges of the 'upper meadow' then back to the second bridge and the ditch trail. Otherwise, if you want more, continue hiking along either the Main Canal (see Main Tuolumne Ditch: South Fork to K Flume hike) or the Section 4 Ditch (see Section 4 Ditch: South Fork to Gurney Station Road hike).

Directions to Trailhead: Go east on 108 and take the lower Twain Harte Drive exit into Twain Harte (1.8 miles). Go under the arch onto Joaquin Gully Road. Stay on this road until its junction with Middle Camp Road (another mile). At this intersection, make a very slight left onto Mt. Elizabeth Road. Drive up a fairly steep hill then down a smaller hill for 0.4 miles. At the bottom of this small hill (and before you begin to go up again), the road crosses the ditch. Park off on the left. If you prefer to park at Kit Carson, then stay on Middle Camp Road for a short distance then turn left onto Kit Carson Road. Follow it to the end. Total distance from 108 is 3.2 miles.

Main Tuolumne Ditch: South Fork Road to 'K' Flume

Highlights: Ditch trails are known for their fairly level paths and the tranquility that comes from walking alongside water. The start of this ditch trail section is located just outside of downtown Twain Harte and involves some flume crossings. The latter portion of the trail is infrequently used.

Distance: ~1.75 miles (3.5 miles roundtrip)

Elevation Changes: Cumulative ascent is <15 ft on the way out and ~5 ft on the return trip; elevation ~4000 ft

Difficulty: Easy in terms of elevation changes

Seasonality: This trail is suitable for all seasons but may be covered with snow at times in the winter. The trail can get quite muddy after heavy storms and snowmelt.

User Groups/Permits: The trail is used by walkers, runners and the occasional bike rider. No permits are needed to park or use the trail.

Parking/Facilities: There is a parking area off of South Fork Road at its junction with Quaker Lane which is used as an access point for people fishing on the ditch. The gate to the parking area is open during fishing season during the day; it is still possible to park outside the parking area during non-fishing season. There are no facilities here or along the trail.

Topographic Map: USGS Twain Harte, CA Quadrangle (7.5 minute series)

Hike Description: From the parking area, cross the upstream grated metal bridge. Follow the trail 0.25 miles to the 'N' Flume. Go up the stairs and across the double-wide planks of the flume. At ~0.5 miles into the hike, cross Center Camp Road. At 0.7 miles, cross a private driveway and then the single-planked 'M' Flume (you can bypass this flume on a footbridge). You pass tennis courts on the other side of the ditch at ~0.8 miles and then cross South Fork Road at ~0.9 miles. At ~1.0 miles into the hike (just after crossing Manny Marshall Drive), you reach a very short section (<0.1 miles long) that is narrow and full of tree roots. From here you reach a less traveled section of the trail. At ~1.5 miles, there is a trail on the left that heads back down to South Fork Road; stay on the ditch trail where you soon reach the 'L' Flume and #3 Lock (at ~1.6 miles). A bit further up the trail, you reach the much longer 'K' Flume which is the turnaround point for this hike. [Note: if you wish to continue along the ditch trail, you can walk underneath the K Flume on a steep, rocky path.]

Trail Tidbits: The Tuolumne County Water Company (TCWC) began constructing the first ditch system in 1851 for the purpose of storing and conveying water from the Stanislaus River to the lower elevation mining towns in the Columbia Basin in an effort to provide a year-round water supply. Just one year later, 30 miles of ditches and 18 miles of flumes had been completed. It is said that 4/5 of the gold obtained in Tuolumne County was extracted with the direct or indirect assistance of ditch water. Over the next decades, TCWC constructed additional ditch systems, purchased others built by competing water companies and expanded their operation to provide water to the entire area between the Stanislaus and Tuolumne Rivers and not just the Columbia Basin.

Need to Know: There are three flume crossings: one on double-wide planks and two on single-wide planks. There is poison oak along the trail from the 'N' Flume to Center Camp Road. The ditch passes through some land that is privately owned; please stay on the trail.

Want A Loop? The loop includes more elevation gains and some walking on paved roads. Cross the footbridge just before the 'K' Flume and then turn left onto a dirt tract. Walk uphill ~0.4 miles to the Sugar Pine Railroad Grade. Turn right and walk 1 mile to Confidence South Fork Road. Turn right again and walk downhill ~0.5 miles until you reach the intersection with South Fork Road. Turn right and walk ~0.1 miles until you reach the ditch trail again and return the way you came (roundtrip total ~4.6 miles).

Directions to Trailhead: Go east on 108 and take the lower Twain Harte Drive exit into Twain Harte (1.8 miles). Go under the arch onto Joaquin Gully Road. Stay on this road until it puts you onto Middle Camp Road (another mile). Stay on Middle Camp until it you reach a 'Y' (another 0.2 mile); take the left which becomes South Fork Road. Head uphill an additional 0.4 miles and you will see the fishing access parking lot on the left opposite the entrance to Quaker Lane on the right. Total distance from 108 is 3.4 miles.

Philadelphia Ditch: Road 4N13 to Diversion Dam

Highlights: **Highlights**: This higher elevation ditch trail offers a level path amidst a coniferous forest with mountain misery, all set to the gurgling and rushing movement of water. You can also hear the rushing of the South Fork of the Stanislaus River and it will be visible through the trees for most of the hike. The trail begins at Forest Service Road 4N13 and is infrequently used.

Distance: ~1.5 miles (~3.0 miles roundtrip)

Elevation Changes: Cumulative ascent is <20 ft on the way out and <20 ft on the return trip; elevation ~4900 ft

Difficulty: Easy in terms of elevation change

Photo: The gaging station and flume

Seasonality: This trail is best used during late spring, summer and early fall. There is less cover on this ditch trail than other ditch trails; plan this hike for cooler times of the day. The roads to this area are closed during the winter.

User Groups/Permits: The trail is used by hikers. No permits are needed to park or use the trail.

Parking/Facilities: Park off the road either before or after Forest Service Road 4N13 crosses the ditch. There are no facilities here or along the trail.

Topographic Map: USGS Strawberry, CA Quadrangle (7.5 minute series)

Hike Description: Start the hike at the intersection of the ditch trail with Forest Service Road 4N13. Head upstream on the ditch trail (to the right). Less than 0.2 miles into the hike you cross the first single-plank flume which is <0.1 miles long. As you continue further, you should be able to see and hear the South Fork of the Stanislaus River through the trees (and Fraser Flat Road). You reach the second single-plank flume that is 0.1 miles long, ~0.8 miles into the hike. A very short flume appears ~0.2 miles from the end of the second flume (1.0 miles). The trail gets closer to the river just before the fourth and final flume (single-plank). This flume is just over 0.2 miles and ends at the Philadelphia Diversion Dam at ~1.5 miles. There is a trail that goes under the last flume near its beginning and then heads up to a dirt road that parallels the flume. Take this road to the diversion dam and gaging station if you don't feel comfortable walking on this flume.

Trail Tidbits: The Philadelphia Diversion Dam is located downstream of Pinecrest Lake. It was built in 1899 to supply water to mining camps in Jupiter. Today, the purpose of the dam is to divert water from the South Fork of the Stanislaus River into the flume and subsequent ditch to bring water to the Spring Gap forebay. The dam is 11 ft high and 56 ft long and can impound (or pool) ~0.25 acres of water. Located at the dam is a gaging station that monitors stream flow, a fish screen to keep fish out of the flume and a fish ladder to help spawning fish reach areas upstream from the dam.

Need to Know: There are a number of flume crossings on single-wide planks. The diversion dam and gaging station is located on private property owned by PG&E. Keep out of the enclosed area.

Want a Loop? One loop that you could do would be to take Forest Service Road 4N13 back to the start of the hike; however, it seems that it would be far less dusty, more scenic and far more tranquil to return on the ditch trail. To do this loop, follow the dirt road that parallels the last flume away from the dam. Continue on the road until it reaches the intersection with Forest Service Road 4N13; head left to return back to the start of this hike. Otherwise, if you want more, hike back to the start and then head on the ditch trail in the other direction. It is ~2.8 miles to the Spring Gap forebay (see Philadelphia Ditch Spring Gap to 4N13 hike).

Directions to Trailhead: Go east on 108 past Long Barn then turn left onto Forest Service Road 4N01 (or Fraser Flat Road) before Cold Springs (look for a brown forest service sign). Cross the bridge 2.5 miles down the road and continue another ~0.4 miles before turning right onto Forest Service Road 4N13. Drive up this road for ~0.2 miles until you reach the ditch. Find a place to park that is off the road either before or after it crosses the ditch. Total distance from 108 is 3.1 miles.

Philadelphia Ditch: Spring Gap to Road 4N13

Highlights: This higher elevation ditch trail offers solitude along a level walking path under a mixed coniferous forest with occasional views of the river canyon. It begins at the Spring Gap forebay for the hydroelectric plant.

Distance: ~2.8 miles (~5.6 miles roundtrip)

Elevation Changes: Cumulative ascent is <20 ft on the way out and <20 ft on the return trip (elevation changes mostly due to little dips in the trail when the water is channeled into concrete canals); elevation ~4900 ft

Difficulty: Easy in terms of elevation change

Seasonality: This trail is best used during late spring, summer and early fall. As there is less cover on this ditch trail than other ditch trails, plan to do this hike during cooler times. The roads to this area are closed during the winter.

User Groups/Permits: The trail is used by hikers. No permits are needed to park or use the trail.

Parking/Facilities: Park off the road at the Spring Gap forebay. Do not block the entrance to this area. There are no facilities here or on the trail.

Topographic Map: USGS Strawberry, CA Quadrangle (7.5 minute series)

Hike Description: Pick up the ditch trail from the road by heading upstream along the right side of the ditch. You parallel the forest service road that you arrived on for the majority of the time that you are on the ditch trail but you are above the road and eventually you move away from it. At 0.1 miles, you pass under power lines and, at ~1.3 miles, you pass a control gate. Spend some time at ~1.5 miles to take in the view across the river canyon. Another 0.1 miles further you encounter a rock wall and an intersection with a forest service road which parallels the trail for a short distance. At 2.6 miles, you pass a silo structure and < 0.1 miles further, you encounter a double-planked flume. You should be able to hear noise from the Fraser Flat Campground in the distance at this point (if not earlier). At ~2.8 miles into the hike, you reach Forest Service Road 4N13 to Strawberry (near Fraser Flat Campground). This is the turnaround point for this hike.

Trail Tidbits: This ditch is specifically used to deliver water from the South Fork of the Stanislaus River to the Spring Gap Hydroelectric Station located on the Middle Fork of the Stanislaus River. The ditch water arrives at the upper portion of Spring Gap into a forebay (used to pool sufficient amounts of water) and then is delivered to the hydroelectric plant at the lower portion of Spring Gap through a penstock pipe.

Need to Know: This hike involves one flume crossing on double-wide planks. This ditch trail is less established than other ditch trails so you need to watch your footing. The water smells like dead fish if there is little or no movement of water in the ditch.

Want a Loop? The only realistic loop would be for you to return on the forest service road back to the Spring Gap forebay; however, it seems that it would be more pleasant to return on the ditch trail. If you want more, you can continue on the ditch trail another ~1.5 miles to the diversion dam where water is channeled from the river into the ditch system (see Philadelphia Ditch Trail: 4N13 to Diversion Dam hike).

Directions to Trailhead: Go east on 108 past Long Barn then turn left onto Forest Service Road 4N01 (or Fraser Flat Road) before Cold Springs (look for a brown forest service sign). Cross the bridge 2.5 miles down the road and continue past the campground at ~3 miles. The road becomes a dirt road just past the campground. At 5.3 miles there is an OHV road that goes off to the left; stay to the right. Continue up to the Spring Gap forebay and find a place to park that is not blocking the road or the entrance to this upper portion of the hydroelectric station. Total distance from 108 is 5.6 miles.

Photo:
Water being channeled on the Philadelphia Ditch

Section 4 Ditch: Gurney Station Road Area to East Avenue

Highlights: The start of this ditch trail section is located just outside of downtown Twain Harte and takes you on the newly constructed section of the Sugar Pine Railroad Grade Trail. The trail is wide and fairly shaded.

Distance: ~0.75 miles (1.5 miles roundtrip)

Elevation Changes: Cumulative ascent is <10 ft on the way out and <150 ft on the return trip; elevation ~3880-3920 ft

Difficulty: Easy in terms of elevation change

Seasonality: This trail is suitable for all seasons but may be covered with snow at times in the winter. The trail can get quite muddy after heavy storms and snowmelt.

User Groups/Permits: The trail is used by walkers, runners and bike riders. No permits are needed to park or use the trail.

Parking/Facilities: Park on Korey Court at the start of the trail (minimal amount of parking available). Be sure to pull off the road so that local traffic can get by. There are no facilities at the parking area or along the trail.

Topographic Map: USGS Twain Harte, CA Quadrangle (7.5 minute series)

Hike Description: Although the trail can be accessed on Gurney Station Road (across the street from where the other Section 4 ditch trail ends), it would require some weed-whacking and then a walk across a single-plank flume to get to the trail. It is much easier to begin on the newly constructed Sugar Pine Railroad Grade (SPRG) Trail that begins up and around the corner on Korey Court. The trail begins with a downhill section on steps created from railroad ties. You reach the junction with the ditch trail at 0.1 miles. A left at this junction allows you to walk along the ditch for another 0.15 miles but then you need to take the trail off to the right just before the water disappears behind a metal grate (private property up ahead) to return to the SPRG Trail. A right at this junction keeps you on the SPRG Trail but you are no longer walking along the ditch. [Note: from the metal grate on, the ditch water is piped underground and does not return until the end of this hike.] Nearly 0.4 miles into the hike, you cross over Twain Harte Drive on a pedestrian overpass. Another 0.2 miles further, you pass the more recently built Black Oak Elementary School that no longer houses elementary students. The hike ends at East Avenue just at the point where the ditch water returns to the surface.

Trail Tidbits: The Section 4 ditch was constructed in 1887-1888 by the Tuolumne County Water Company to convey water for mining purposes from the Main Canal to the Soulsbyville and Eureka Ditches and then on to the communities of present-day Soulsbyville and Tuolumne. When the water goes underground mid-way through the hike, a portion of it is being diverted into the Eureka Ditch on the other side of Highway 108. The remainder returns as the Soulsbyville Ditch just before you reach East Avenue. This section of ditch is operated by Tuolumne Utilities District (TUD).

Need to Know: There are no flume crossings for this hike. The ditch passes through some land that is privately owned; please stay on the trail.

Want More? As most of the land on either side of the ditch is privately owned and passes through a number of Twain Harte neighborhoods, a loop would only put you on surface streets (some of them busy) and this seems less preferable to the quiet solitude of the trail. Instead, if you would like more, you can continue this hike by crossing East Avenue and veering to the right (slightly) on to the Soulsbyville Ditch (see Soulsbyville Ditch hike).

Directions to Trailhead: Go east on 108 and take the upper Twain Harte Drive exit towards Twain Harte. Go 0.2 miles and turn right on Tiffeni Drive. After another 0.2 miles, turn right on Gurney Station Road. Drive 0.1 miles up this road then turn right on Korey Court. The trail begins just past the 1st house on the right. Total distance from 108 is 0.5 miles.

Section 4 Ditch: South Fork Road to Gurney Station Road

Highlights: The Section 4 ditch is a much smaller ditch than the Main Canal; however, it is used by less people too. The start of this ditch trail section is located just outside of downtown Twain Harte. The trail is very shady and has a little more elevation change than most ditch trails.

Distance: ~2.1 miles (4.2 miles roundtrip)

Elevation Changes: Cumulative ascent is <40 ft on the way out and ~185 ft on the return trip; elevation ~3880-3980 ft

Difficulty: Moderately easy in terms of elevation change

Seasonality: This trail is suitable for all seasons but may be covered with snow at times in the winter. The trail can get quite muddy after heavy storms and snowmelt.

User Groups/Permits: The trail is used by walkers and runners. No permits are needed to park or use the trail.

Parking/Facilities: There is a parking area off of South Fork Road at its junction with Quaker Lane which is used as an access point for people fishing on the ditch. The gate to the parking area is open during fishing season during the day; it is still possible to park outside the parking area during non-fishing season. There are no facilities here or on the trail.

Topographic Map: USGS Twain Harte, CA Quadrangle (7.5 minute series)

Hike Description: Cross South Fork Road and walk up Quaker Lane. Turn right on the unmarked trail located about 15 yards past the line of mailboxes found on Quaker Lane. Follow this trail along the smaller Section 4 Ditch (paralleling Quaker Lane) until you can cross the ditch at the bridge (0.15 miles) and follow it to the other side. At ~0.5 miles you cross Middle Camp Road and veer just slightly to the right of the last house where there is open space. Pick up the trail again on a steep downhill section The ditch water is piped through this section and you can see the pipe in a number of areas over the next ~0.1 miles. Cross the bridge at the bottom of the hill then go up the hill on the other side to reach the open ditch water again (now at 0.65 miles). Head right and continue on the trail, crossing a bridge, bypassing a small flume and reaching another section where the water is again piped (~1.0 mile).The water appears in the ditch again a short ways later and the trail now parallels Joaquin Gully Road for a while. At ~1.2 miles, you cross over a large boulder and at ~1.25 miles you should note that the trail becomes rockier (watch your footing). You pass behind homes in a Twain Harte neighborhood from here to the end. At 1.6 miles, you reach water storage tanks and a water treatment plant. Just past the plant, the trail crosses a small access road and then a number of driveways. During the last section, you should note that the water is piped on and off again a number of times. Finally you reach a set of stairs that take you up to Gurney Station Road.

Trail Tidbits: Large portions of this ditch section are gunited. Gunite is a cement mixture that is sprayed onto rebar framework using compressed air. The final product is a dense, strong layer that is impermeable to water. On this section, you pass a number of water treatment areas and storage tanks. The small one that you pass near the bridge on Quaker Lane belongs to Twain Harte Valley Mutual Water Company. The larger ones belong to Tuolumne Utilities District (TUD) which supplies water to most homes in Twain Harte.

Need to Know: The one flume on this hike can easily be bypassed by walking on the trail beside it. The ditch passes through some land that is privately owned; please stay on the trail.

Want More? As most of the land on either side of the ditch is private property, a loop would only put you on busy surface streets and this seems less preferable to the quiet solitude of the trail. If you want more, continue the hike along the ditch trail (see Section 4 Ditch: Gurney Station Road to East Avenue hike).

Directions to Trailhead: Go east on 108 and take the lower Twain Harte Drive exit into Twain Harte (1.8 miles). Go under the arch onto Joaquin Gully Road. Stay on this road until it puts you onto Middle Camp Road (another mile). Stay on Middle Camp until it you reach a 'Y' (~0.2 miles); take the left which becomes South Fork Road. Head uphill and you will see the fishing access parking lot on the left opposite the entrance to Quaker Lane on the right (another 0.4 miles). Total distance from 108 is 3.4 miles.

Soulsbyville Ditch: East Avenue to Highway 108

Highlights: As is true of most ditch trails, this trail is shady and involves easy walking along a pleasantly gurgling stream. The Soulsbyville Ditch is a small, shallow ditch found on the outskirts of Twain Harte that passes behind neighborhoods and is popular with walkers with and without dogs.

Distance: ~1.1 miles (2.2 miles roundtrip)

Elevation Changes: Cumulative ascent is <5 ft on the way out and <50 ft on the return trip; elevation ~3800-3880 ft

Difficulty: Easy in terms of elevation change

Seasonality: This trail is suitable for all seasons but may be covered with snow at times in the winter. The trail can get quite muddy after heavy storms and snowmelt.

User Groups/Permits: The trail is used by walkers and runners. No permits are needed to park or use the trail.

Parking/Facilities: Park off the road on East Avenue across from where the trail starts or around the corner on Cedar Pines Avenue. There are no facilities here or along the trail.

Topographic Map: USGS Twain Harte, CA Quadrangle (7.5 minute series)

Hike Description: The trail starts off East Avenue just to the right of a post that is a trail marker. Less than 0.1 miles into the hike, the trail dips next to a small flume; it is fairly narrow at this point. At 0.75 miles, the ditch water is piped underground for <0.1 miles. Near where it reappears, you need to cross over a tree. Someone has kindly cut a notch through the tree trunk that you can use as a step. You reach the end of the trail and the turnaround point when you note the ditch veering to the left through a control gate before passing under Highway 108.

Trail Tidbits: The Soulsbyville Ditch was built to provide water for mining soon after gold and quartz were discovered in 1857. In 1878, the ditch was reconstructed at a higher elevation to avoid flooding issues in the Twain

Harte Meadow. At the time that the Tuolumne County Water Company purchased the old Soulsby Ditch (its original name) in the late 1800's, the Section 4 Ditch was built to connect the Soulsby Ditch to the Main Tuolumne Ditch off of Middle Camp Road in an effort to bring additional water to the Soulsby Mine and to serve areas further away. This section of the ditch is maintained and operated by Tuolumne Utilities District (TUD).

Need to Know: This hike does not involve any flume crossings. Poison oak is rampant along the latter half of the trail. It is far enough off the trail that you will not inadvertently brush up against it but you should be sure to stay on the trail and keep any dogs that you have with you on the trail too. The ditch passes through some land that is privately owned; please stay on the trail.

Want A Loop? The loop option is simply to take the dirt road on the opposite side of the ditch back towards East Avenue. Although it parallels the ditch trail most of the way, this side trail includes a few brief hills. Once you reach the gate that crosses the dirt road, you can return to East Avenue by walking down Cedar Pines Avenue or you can cross back onto the ditch trail using one of the occasional footbridges that have been set up for ditch crossings.

Directions to Trailhead: Go east on 108 and take the upper Twain Harte Drive exit towards Twain Harte. Go ~0.6 miles and then turn left on East Avenue. Another 0.2 miles brings you to the section of the road where the ditch crosses (just before the highway overpass). Park on the left-hand side of the road or find a spot along Cedar Pines Avenue. Total distance from 108 is 0.8 miles.

Interpretive Trails

There are a number of interpretive or self-guided trails throughout the Stanislaus National Forest (SNF) and outlying areas that have been put in place to educate the public about unique geologic, cultural, historical and/or ecologic features of the area. The geologic self-guided trails include: Column of the Giants, Trail of the Gargoyles and Donnell Vista & Interpretive Trail. The Shadow of the Miwok Trail provides cultural information about the Native Americans that inhabited this area long before the discovery of gold. There are two railroad grades that serve as historic interpretive trails: Westside Railroad Grade & Interpretive Trail and Fraser Flat South Side Railroad Grade & Interpretive Trail; the latter trail is found in the section entitled South Fork of the Stanislaus River Canyon along with the other railroad grade hikes on the South Fork. The Trail of the Ancient Dwarfs (SNF spelling) and the Trail of the Survivors primarily provide an ecological perspective of the area although this perspective is intertwined with geologic, cultural and/or historical details. The Red Hills Interpretive Trail (found in the Red Hills section with the other Red Hills trails) also focuses on its unique geology and the impact the geology has on the ecology of the area.

The interpretive trails either have informative signs posted along the way or marked posts that correspond to numbers in a brochure. Those with permanent placards include Column of the Giants, Donnell Vista & Interpretive Trail, Westside Railroad Grade & Interpretive Trail and Trail of the Survivors (although a number of these are missing). The rest require a brochure to provide information about the numbered posts. Brochures for Trail of the Gargoyles, Shadow of the Miwok, Fraser Flat South Side Railroad Grade (Sugar Pine Railway, the Strawberry Branch) and Trail of the Ancient Dwarfs can be obtained at the Summit or Mi-Wok Ranger Stations. The Red Hills Interpretive Trail brochure can be downloaded from the BLM website for this area (see Red Hills Interpretive Trail hike for website). Some of the numbered posts appear to be missing along the Trail of the Ancient Dwarfs; consider the hike to include a scavenger hunt as you try to find as many of the numbered posts as you can.

In addition to being informative and interesting, these trails are great for entire families to visit. Most are short and fairly easy to walk. You can usually find a great picnic spot nearby as well.

Column of the Giants

Highlights: This hike is an easy walk on a paved trail across the scenic Middle Fork of the Stanislaus River and through a geologically unique area. There are informative placards along the trail that explain how the basalt columns were formed. This is a great area for a picnic as well!

Distance: Nearly 0.4 miles one-way (0.75 miles roundtrip)

Elevation Changes: Cumulative ascent roundtrip is ~40 ft.; elevation ~5960-6000 ft

Difficulty: Easy in terms of elevation change

Seasonality: This trail is best during summer months to fall. The road to this area is closed during winter months.

User Groups/Permits: The trail is used by walkers and is also wheelchair accessible. Motorized vehicles are prohibited. Permits are not needed to park or day hike.

Parking/Facilities: There is a parking area at the Columns of the Giants. There is a vault toilet located near the parking area.

Topographic Map: USGS Dardanelle, CA Quadrangle (7.5 Minute Series)

Hike Description: The trail begins across from the vault toilet on blacktop. In less than 0.1 miles, you cross the Middle Fork of the Stanislaus River. Continue following the blacktop trail reading the informational signs along the way. There are a total of five signs with the last two being at the end of the trail.

Trail Tidbits: Basalt columns are found in other areas of the world, including the nearby locations of Devils Postpile National Monument located east of Mammoth Mountain and Little Devils Postpile in Yosemite National Park west of Tuolumne Meadows. They are all formed when pooled molten lava cools evenly causing fracturing along angles that create hexagonally-shaped rods; the rods or columns are then exposed by glacial activity. The longer it takes for the lava to cool, the longer the columns are. Basalt is a black, fine-grained and dense, volcanic rock. It makes up most of the earth's surface found under the oceans but can also be found on land through lava flows.

Need to Know: The water in the river can be quite cold and flowing very quickly. If you take a side trip down to the river's edge, be sure to watch small children and pets carefully.

Want More? A loop is not possible with this hike. You could explore the area upstream.

Directions to Trailhead: Go east on 108 past Strawberry. The parking area is ~1.9 miles past the Brightman Forest Service Station and ~1.6 miles past the Dardanelles Resort. Look for the USFS sign indicating 'Column of the Giants'. Total distance from 108 is 0 miles.

Photo: Basalt columns found at Column of the Giants

Donnell Vista and Interpretive Trail

Highlights: This hike offers an easy jaunt with great views of the Dardanelles, Donnell Reservoir and its dam as well as the Middle Fork of the Stanislaus River Canyon. There are informational placards along the beginning of the trail (steeper northeast section) down to the overlook explaining the geology of the area and the necessity of the reservoir below. This is a superb location to have a picnic.

Distance: The loop is just under 0.5 miles roundtrip.

Elevation Changes: Cumulative ascent on the loop is <100 ft.; elevation ~6200-6300 ft

Difficulty: Easy in terms of elevation change

Seasonality: This trail is best at any time that there is access to the vista point. The road to this area is closed during winter months.

User Groups/Permits: The trail is used by visitors and walkers interested in the views; climbers also like to top-rope in the area. One direction of the trail to the overlook is wheelchair accessible (requires an out and back trip rather than a loop). Motorized vehicles are prohibited on the trail. Permits are not needed to park or day hike.

Parking/Facilities: There is a decent number of parking areas in a loop around the vault toilets.

Topographic Map: USGS Donnell Lake, CA Quadrangle (7.5 Minute Series)

Hike Description: The trail begins just past the restrooms on the one-way parking loop. You should note a number of informational placards explaining the geology of the area as you pass large granite boulders. At just before 0.2 miles, you reach a trail junction. The right takes you to the overlook, great views and more informational placards; the left takes you back to the parking area on long, easy switchbacks (this portion of the trail is wheelchair accessible). Head to the overlook and spend some time drinking in the views of Donnell Reservoir, the Dardanelles and the Middle Fork of the Stanislaus

River Canyon (0.2 miles). Then head back to the trail junction and go right to take the easier route to the parking lot to complete the loop. The trail ends at just under 0.5 miles in the parking lot.

Trail Tidbits: You can see two different types of igneous rock from this trail (igneous rocks are those formed by cooled magma). Igneous rock can be intrusive or extrusive. Intrusive rock forms when molten magma cools slowly within the earth crust. Due to the slow cooling, the resulting rock is course-grained. Although it was formed beneath the surface, uplifting, erosion and/or glacial activity often exposes the rock beneath. Granite is the predominant intrusive rock found in the Sierra Nevada Mountains and you can see the light-colored granite all along the trail. Across the river canyon, you can see that the Dardanelles are much darker in color. They are composed of extrusive igneous rock meaning that molten magma forced its way towards the earth's surface as lava and flowed across the landscape, cooling quickly. As a result of the rapid cooling, the rock is typically fine-grained. Basalt, andesite and rhyolite are types of extrusive igneous rock found in the Sierra Nevada Mountains.

Need to Know: It is not advised for wheelchairs to travel on the steeper section of the trail. Those with difficulties walking should take the long, easy switchbacks down to the overlook and return the same way.

Photo: Donnell Reservoir

Want A Loop? The hike is written as a loop.

Directions to Trailhead: Go east on 108 past Strawberry. After seeing the Eagle Meadow turnoff on the right, begin looking for the 'Donnell Vista' sign. The vista area is on the left ~0.25 miles past this sign. Turn into the area and head one-way around the small loop to find parking. Total distance from 108 is 0 miles.

Shadow of the Miwok

Highlights: This is a trail that provides cultural information about the Native Americans that lived in this area called the Sierra Miwok. This is an interpretive trail; pamphlets can be picked up at the Summit Ranger Station across the street. There are 14 posts marking the key displays that show how the Miwok lived and their relationship with the natural environment. To make this a longer hike, you can combine it with the 'Trail of the Survivors' that is located within walking distance (see Want More?).

Distance: ~0.3 mile loop

Elevation Changes: Cumulative ascent ~30 ft; elevation ~5600 ft

Difficulty: Easy in terms of elevation changes

Seasonality: The trail is accessible year round but it is difficult to follow if there is snow on the ground.

User Groups/Permits: The trail is used by those interested in learning about the Miwok Indians. The trail is off limits to motorized vehicles. No permits are needed to park or use the trail.

Parking/Facilities: There is a parking area at the Summit Ranger Station across the street. There are restrooms at the ranger station as well as vault toilets in the campground on the far side of the trail.

Topographic Map: USGS Strawberry Quadrangle (7.5 Minute Series)

Hike Description: The trail starts across the street from the Summit Ranger Station. The posts are numbered and fairly easy to follow. After meandering through the village, you head down a small hill and along a swampy meadow which has a bridge across it. You then head back up the hill to the start of the trail until you have visited all 14 posts.

Trail Tidbits: Today, the Miwok are an integral part of Tuolumne County communities. A portion of them live on the Tuolumne Rancheria outside of Tuolumne City where the Acorn Festival is held each year. Some Miwok devote time to share the ways of their ancestors with others in an effort to preserve what we know about them. As the Miwok did not have a written language, the name 'Miwok' has many correct phonetic spellings including Me-Wuk, Mi-Wok, and Mi-Wuk.

Need to Know: To understand what each post is referring to, pick up the informational pamphlet from the Summit Ranger Station across the street. Please observe the structures within the exhibit but do not remove or alter them.

Photo: Miwok Indian 'oomacha'

Want More? This hike is written as a loop. If you would like more, walk to the 'Trail of the Survivors' which is on the other side of the campground (across the bridge) and do its loop before heading back to your car. Cross the bridge and go up the path until you reach the campground road (100's loop). Turn left and follow the road towards the campground entrance. At the entrance, head right on the paved bike path until it reaches Pinecrest School Road. Turn right, and about ~0.1 miles further, you will see the sign for 'Trail of the Survivors' on the left. Roundtrip distance for combining both trails is ~2 miles.

Directions to Trailhead: Go east on 108 past Cold Springs. Turn right at the Pinecrest turnoff onto Pinecrest Lake Drive. Turn left into the Summit Ranger Station less than 0.1 miles down this road. Total distance from 108 is <0.1 miles.

Trail of the Ancient Dwarfs

Highlights: This is a fairly easy hike through a forest of ancient dwarf trees on the remnants of the Old Mono Wagon Road to Sonora. There are occasional glimpses of the Middle Fork of the Stanislaus River Canyon as well as the current Highway 108. A trail brochure can be obtained at the Summit or Mi-Wok Ranger Stations that provides an ecologic, geologic and historical perspective of the area.

Distance: ~1.1 miles to end of paved road (~2.2 miles roundtrip)

Elevation Changes: Cumulative ascent on the way out is ~90 ft and ~130 ft on the return trip; elevation ~6500-6650 ft

Difficulty: Moderately easy in terms of elevation change

Seasonality: This trail is best during summer to fall months. The roads to this area are closed during winter months.

User Groups/Permits: The trail is used by hikers. Motorized vehicles can travel on the road from access points on Highway 108 but only up to a point where boulders block the path. Permits are not needed to park or day hike. Fees are charged at the campgrounds along Eagle Meadow Road for overnight stays.

Parking/Facilities: There is a dirt parking area to the right of the road block at Niagra Creek. There are no facilities located here or on the trail.

Topographic Map: USGS Donnell Lake, CA Quadrangle (7.5 Minute Series)

Hike Description: From the dirt area, cross the creek either directly or, if the water is running too high, on the bridge. Stay on the road and follow it up into the mixed conifer forest. The road bends to the left at ~0.2 miles and just past ~0.3 miles, you can see posts and a damaged metal container that mark the start of the 'Trail of the Ancient Dwarfs'. You begin to see numbered posts ~0.4 miles into the hike that are placed to point out unique features. At nearly 0.6 miles into the hike, there are a cluster of posts off the road to the left. One points out a tree growing out of the side of a boulder. At ~0.7 miles, a 'granite table' appears on the left side of the road. Continue heading down the road for a serene walk on what used to be the old wagon road. At times, Highway 108 is visible below and the river canyon of the Middle Fork of the Stanislaus River can be seen in the distance. At ~1.1 miles, the paved road ends near some boulders. This is a good turnaround point as the dirt road drops down to OHV trails and an area that is used for target practice.

Trail Tidbits: The original toll road that passed through this area was built in the 1860's in an effort to connect Sonora with the mining communities on the eastside of the Sierra Nevada Mountains. When the silver deposits diminished, the eastside mining towns became ghost towns. As a result, the toll road was infrequently used and fell into disrepair. Eventually, the state took over its maintenance (early 1900's) turning it into a usable road for travel over Sonora Pass until the construction of the current highway.

Need to Know: The interpretive portion of the trail has not been maintained. Some of the numbered posts appear to be missing or hidden. Thus, the hike also becomes a scavenger hunt as you try to find as many of the numbered posts as you can. Although repairs for this trail are not slated for any time soon, the trail still makes for a nice hike. A trail brochure can be obtained at the Mi-Wok or Summit Ranger Stations.

Want More? There is not a reasonable loop to do for this hike. If you want more, you can explore the area along the creek heading upstream.

Directions to Trailhead: Go east on 108 past Strawberry ~13 miles. Turn right onto Eagle Meadow Road which is Forest Service Road 5N01. At ~0.3 miles from 108, turn left onto Forest Service Road 6N24 and drive past the Niagra Creek Campground. You will note that the road is blocked at Niagra Creek 0.7 miles from 108. Turn right and park in the dirt area. Total distance from 108 is 0.7 miles.

Photo: One of the 'Ancient Dwarfs'

Trail of the Gargoyles

Highlights: Does the name of the hike invoke sufficient intrigue? There are a number of interesting geologic features such as 'Death Slide', 'Wall of Noses' and 'Gargoyle Ridge' found at the top of a steep U-shaped ridge overlooking Cow Creek. It is well worth the stop at either the Summit or Mi-Wok Ranger Stations to pick up the interpretive trail brochure so that you can learn about the geology that shaped these unique features (color photo on page 163).

Distance: North Rim Trail roundtrip to parking area is ~0.75 miles; South Rim Trail roundtrip is ~1 mile (total is ~1.75 miles)

Elevation Changes: Cumulative ascent roundtrip on North Rim 180 ft; cumulative ascent on the South Rim is 140 ft; elevation ~7350-7450 ft

Difficulty: Moderately easy in terms of total elevation changes

Seasonality: This trail is best during late spring to early fall. The roads to this area are closed during the winter. The wildflowers are rampant during late spring to early summer.

User Groups/Permits: The trail is used by hikers. No motorized vehicles are allowed. No permits are needed to park or use the trail for day hikes.

Parking/Facilities: There is a parking area at the end of Forest Service Road 4N12F. There are no facilities here or along the trails.

Topographic Map: USGS Pinecrest & Donnell Lake, CA Quadrangles (7.5 minute series)

Hike Description: To visit the North Rim, follow the trail behind the sign. Within 0.1 miles, you reach the signposts for interpretive markers #1 and 2. The signposts for #3-6 occur within the next 0.1 miles of meandering up, down and around. At this point you begin to climb quickly reaching signpost #7. At 0.3 miles into the hike, you reach signpost #8 and shortly after, #9. To get to #10 and 11, you need to climb on a steeper, rocky section. At this vantage point, you have an excellent view of 'Gargoyle Ridge' as well as the grand perspective view of the South Rim. Return as you came. To visit the

South Rim, follow the trail in the other direction. Within 0.1 miles, you should note signposts #1-3. Work your way up a gradual slope to visit #4-6. You pass through a space in a fence 0.3 miles on the trail and within another 0.1 miles you should see signposts #7 and 8. To visit signpost #9, you need to drop down behind the 'Wall of Noses' and out onto the lower part of the ridge. Return as you came.

Trail Tidbits: The area of the Trail of the Gargoyles is the result of several geologic forces acting over time. Millions of years ago, the blocks of granite that are the foundation of the Sierras, were uplifted from the east side then altered by additional geologic events. The volcanic rock found throughout the area, provide evidence of former lava flows; the granitic erratics that are scattered about were left by glaciers that have scraped the area. You can also see in the layers of the rock evidence of flows that are a mix of lava and mud (called lahars) that form a type of concrete ash-like mud. Erosion by water and snow has also helped to create the unique features that make up this ridge of gargoyles.

Need to Know: Both trails are set along very steep ridges with unstable edges. Be sure to stay on the trail away from the edges and keep small children and pets close. Despite the easy distance and moderate elevation gains, the trail can be challenging in a few areas due to loose rock on somewhat steep terrain particularly on descents. Be sure that you have established good footholds before placing weight on each foot when stepping down. This area is very exposed and once the small creek on the North Rim dries up, there is no water. Come early in the day or earlier in the season to avoid being baked on the volcanic rock.

Want More? There is not an easy loop to do with this hike as you are on a U-shaped ridge which limits where you can hike. However, if you want more, continue taking the trail past interpretive marker #9 on the South Rim section down to the end of the ridge. You descend an additional 250 ft over the extra 0.75 miles. This gives you additional views of the Middle Fork of the Stanislaus River Canyon, the Punch Bowl off to the left of the ridge and Herring Creek Dome (visible on the return trip).

Directions to Trailhead: Go east on 108 past Strawberry and take Herring Creek Road. Continue on this road for ~6.7 miles (it becomes Forest Service Road 4N12 at ~4.5 miles and is no longer paved at ~5.5 miles). Turn left onto Forest Service Road 4N12F with several visible signs marking it as the turnoff for the Trail of the Gargoyles. Continue 0.2 miles to the parking area. Total distance from 108 is ~6.9 miles.

Photo: 'The Wall of Noses' found at the Trail of the Gargoyles

Trail of the Survivors

Highlights: This is a short informational hike about some of the struggles that trees must endure to survive. To make this a longer hike, you can combine it with the interpretive trail 'Shadow of the Miwok' that is located within walking distance (see Want More?).

Distance: ~0.4 mile loop

Elevation Changes: Cumulative ascent ~10 ft; elevation ~5600 ft

Difficulty: Easy in terms of elevation changes

Seasonality: The trail is accessible year round but it is difficult to follow if there is snow on the ground.

User Groups/Permits: The trail is used by walkers. The trail is off-limits to motorized vehicles. No permits are needed to park or use the trail.

Parking/Facilities: There is a parking area at the start of the trail. There are no facilities here but there are vault toilets in the campground across the street.

Topographic Map: USGS Strawberry Quadrangle (7.5 Minute Series)

Hike Description: The trail begins to the left of the sign and continues to circle in a counterclockwise direction. Some informational placards are posted at sights of interest.

Trail Tidbits: Within an ecosystem, trees face many challenges to their survival. These include natural forces such as competition for light or water, heavy winds or snows, insect invasions, herbivore munching and lightning strikes that often cause forest fires. In addition, trees must survive the challenges that humans impose upon them. Humans cause damage to the growing layers of wood by tying rope or wire around them or by nailing or carving their sides. This makes the trees more vulnerable to insect infestations. Man-made fires and air pollution can also hinder tree survival.

Need to Know: It appears that some of the informational placards are missing. It is the intent of the US Forest Service to work on restoring the placards in the next few years as part of a joint project with the campgrounds. If you are doing this hike in conjunction with the 'Shadow of the Miwok' hike, be sure to pick up the interpretive trail pamphlet for that hike at the Summit Ranger Station.

Want More? This hike is written as a loop. If you would like more, walk to the interpretive trail 'Shadow of the Miwok' and do its loop before hiking back to your car. The 'Shadow of the Miwok' loop is on the other side of the campground. Walk towards the junction of Pinecrest School Road and Dodge Ridge Road until you see the paved path to the left. Stay on this path until you come to the campground entrance where there is a large stop sign. Go onto the campground road and walk down the 100's loop. Just between campsite spots 113 and 116, turn right onto the path and across the bridge.

You pick up the 'Shadow of the Miwok' trail at its #10 post. Turn left (clockwise direction) to reach posts #11-14 before heading up the short hill to the start of the trail. Complete the loop then head back to your parked car. Total roundtrip distance is 1.8 miles.

Directions to Trailhead: Go east on 108 past Cold Springs. Turn right at the Pinecrest turnoff onto Pinecrest Lake Drive. Continue down this road for ~0.3 miles before turning right onto Dodge Ridge Road. Continue another 0.3 miles before turning right onto Pinecrest School Road. The trail begins on the left ~0.1 miles down this road. Total distance from 108 is 0.7 miles.

Photo: Trees along the Trail of the Survivors

West Side Railroad Grade and Interpretive Trail

Highlights: The trail is an easy jaunt on the old West Side Railroad Grade which was cut into the ridge overlooking the North Fork of the Tuolumne River. Railroad artifacts abound including ~3 miles of rails and ties. Interpretive trail signs have recently been erected along the path to provide information about the area's railway history and picnic tables have been placed beneath shade trees for resting and eating. If you are willing to travel the entire railroad grade plus an extra 0.3 miles, you can have the added bonus of lounging in the shade and dipping your feet into the cool waters of the North Fork Tuolumne River (see Want More?).

Distance: 3.0 miles to the end of the interpretive trail (6.0 miles roundtrip); 5.0 miles to the end of the developed railroad grade (10.0 miles round trip)

Elevation Changes: Cumulative ascent is <150 ft roundtrip on the railroad grade; elevation ~2630-2750 ft

Difficulty: Easy in terms of elevation changes

Seasonality: This trail is best during the spring when the wildflowers are in bloom. It can be done in the fall and winter but it is too hot to travel in the summer particularly as there are many sections that are fully exposed to the sun. The trail can be pretty muddy in sections after a series of rainstorms.

User Groups/Permits: The trail is popular with hikers, runners, cyclists and horseback riders. It is off-limits to motorized vehicles. No permits are needed to park or use the trail.

Parking/Facilities: Parking is at the start of the trail just off Buchanan Road (note West Side sign). There are no facilities here or on the trail. There are vault toilets at the River Ranch Campground if you choose to continue on to the river (see Want More?).

Topographic Map: USGS Tuolumne, CA Quadrangle (7.5 minute series)

Hike Description: The trail starts on the uphill end of the parking area where there is a staircase that takes you down to the trail and the first of 7 informational signs; go to the right. The second informational sign gives the history of the West Side Railroad and is 0.1 miles from the start. The third sign and views of the river canyon become apparent after 0.3 miles. Shortly after this, you cross a seepage area (muddy trail). At ~0.7 miles, you can see the North Fork Tuolumne River at the base of the canyon and just past this great view, you come to the fourth sign. Rails parallel the trail from ~1.2 miles onward. The fifth sign is just before 1.4 miles and less than 0.1 miles later the trail crosses a dirt road (left takes you into Ponderosa Hills; right takes you down to Cottonwood Road). At 2 miles, you pass a spring on the left and at 2.3 miles you reach Torment Gulch and the sixth sign. This section of track and trail were nearly washed out by the heavy storms in the winter of 2011; the trail has been rerouted into the ravine and back out again as the old section has been significantly eroded. You arrive at the seventh and final sign just before the 3 mile mark. This is the turnaround point if you are just interested in the interpretive portion of the trail. Otherwise, continue on the trail which is more overgrown from this point. You enter an open 'rock tunnel' (no ceiling) at ~3.5 miles that had to be blasted into the hillside for the tracks to be laid down. You cross a seasonal stream at ~3.8 miles. The trail 'ends' at 5.0 miles as it is not maintained beyond that. There is a trail that heads downhill off to the right. This trail takes you down to Cottonwood Road at the River Ranch Campground that straddles the North Fork Tuolumne River (See Want More?).

Trail Tidbits: This trail was part of the West Side Railroad that brought logs from the forests between Cherry Valley and the North Fork of the Tuolumne River to the West Side Lumber Mill in Tuolumne starting in 1889. The mill was located on the land just off Tuolumne Road below the current location of Summerville High School. Although this section of the trail is only 5 miles long, the actual railroad lines reached over 70 miles.

Need to Know: There is privately owned land on both sides of the trail (particularly at the start); please respect the owners' rights to privacy by staying on the trail. During most months, there is little running water so be sure to carry enough. The trail receives high use in the spring particularly on the weekends; please be respectful of the horseback riders and cyclists as they move past you at a faster pace. There is poison oak along the trail; try to avoid it. Also check for ticks when you return from your hike.

Want More? A loop is possible but not recommended as you would be returning on Cottonwood Road which can be busy. If you want more, hike the entire grade and then take the trail down to Cottonwood Road. Cross the road into the River Ranch Campground and spend some time exploring the North Fork Tuolumne River. This extension adds 0.6 miles roundtrip to the railroad grade total.

Directions to Trailhead: Go east on 108 to Soulsbyville. Turn right onto Soulsbyville Road and go 2.6 miles (veer left at 2.0 miles). Turn left onto Tuolumne Road and travel 2.1 miles past the high school on the right and through the stop light until you reach a stop sign. Turn left onto Carter and drive another 0.3 miles. Turn right onto Buchanan and travel 0.5 miles before reaching the parking area on the left with the West Side sign visible just before the parking area (Mira Monte Road turns left just before the parking area). Total distance from 108 is 5.5 miles.

Photo: Historic railroad rails on the West Side Railroad Grade

South Fork of the Stanislaus River Canyon Trails

The South Fork is a smaller fork of the Stanislaus River. Its origin is in the high country above Pinecrest Lake. The South Fork of the Stanislaus River is joined by Herring Creek outside of Strawberry, Lyons Creek at Lyons Reservoir, Deer Creek below Lyons Reservoir and Five Mile Creek northeast of Columbia. The South Fork joins with the North and Middle Forks after their confluence and then flows into the northern end of New Melones Lake just northwest of Columbia as the Stanislaus River.

Water was essential to the development of Tuolumne County for use in mining practices as well as to supply households, especially during the California dry seasons. As a result, the South Fork of the Stanislaus was dammed in a number of places to provide water storage and control over its release. At the same time, extensive ditch systems were built to transport the water to the mining communities. The 5 original storage reservoirs were Lyons, Herrin, Lower Strawberry, Middle Strawberry and Upper or Big Strawberry. Today, the dams still serve as a way to store water for use by downstream communities but the 3 Strawberry Reservoirs have been replaced by Pinecrest Lake after the construction of Strawberry Dam. There is also the Philadelphia Diversion Dam between Pinecrest Lake and Lyons Reservoir that is used to funnel water to the Spring Gap Hydroelectric Plant.

The river canyon of the South Fork is quite steep. However, many of the trails in the lower forested portions of the canyon are easy (in terms of elevation change) as they travel along old railroad grades. Miles of track connected mills outside of Sonora to the forested areas along the South Fork Stanislaus River; five hikes in this section of the book are along various parts of the Sugar Pine Railroad Grade and include those leaving from Fraser Flat, Lyons Reservoir and Twain Harte. Hikes further up the South Fork Canyon (closer to the headwaters of the river) can be more challenging as they do involve moderate to serious amounts of elevation change (see Pinecrest Peak hike in this book section and the Waterhouse hike in the Emigrant Wilderness section). However, the climbs on these trails are well worth the price paid in sweat as the views are always spectacular due to the fact that the upper portion of this river canyon is primarily granitic rock with little to impede the far-reaching panoramic sights.

Catfish Lake from Strawberry Trailhead

Highlights: This hike has it all. A stream crossing, a walk along a scenic river, a climb up to Strawberry Dam, panoramic views of Pinecrest Lake, a jaunt through pine forests and a visit to an 'off the beaten path' lake well above Pinecrest Lake. If you take the loop, the last section takes you along the crest above Herring Creek through quiet pine forests before returning back to the trail along the river.

Distance: ~2.4 miles to Catfish Lake (4.8 miles roundtrip); loop is ~3.9 miles

Elevation Changes: Cumulative ascent to Catfish Lake is ~800 ft and ~160 ft on the return trip; elevation ~5300-6050 ft

Difficulty: Moderately difficult in terms of elevation changes

Seasonality: This trail is suitable for most seasons but preferable in the off-season. During summer months, people (boaters, hikers, swimmers) swarm Pinecrest Lake. It would be a good idea to avoid this trek after a recent snowstorm but it is passable in the winter.

User Groups/Permits: The trail is popular with hikers and Pinecrest Lake is popular with everyone (it seems). The section described in the loop is popular with mountain bike riders. It is off-limits to unauthorized motorized vehicles. No permits are needed to park or use the trail.

Parking/Facilities: Parking is limited to a few spaces at the start of the trail in the area before the gate. There are no facilities here or on the trail.

Topographic Map: USGS Pinecrest Quadrangle (7.5 Minute Series)

Hike Description: The trail starts at the end of Herring Creek Lane in Strawberry at the gated dirt road. Nearly 500 ft up the trail, you reach a 'Y'. Take the right hand branch which takes you down to Herring Creek (just upstream from its junction with the South Fork of the Stanislaus River); when you see the old cement bridge foundation, you know you are in the right place. You need to cross the stream either by walking across the available log or hopping from rock to rock (or wading). At ~0.3 miles, you can see another trail coming down on the left to meet the trail you are on; this is the trail you will return on if you take the loop. Just past this junction you come within sight of the South Fork of the Stanislaus River. Another 0.3 miles upstream, the trail begins climbing towards the dam which you can see in the distance. You reach the top of the dam 0.75 miles into the hike. Spend a few minutes gazing at the unobstructed view of the lake then head up the trail on the left and continue above the edge of the lake. As soon as you reach a section with houses (1.2 miles into the hike), begin looking for the metal trail marker that indicates the offshoot for Catfish Lake. Turn left onto this trail (ignoring an intersecting path a few yards later that connects houses) and meander through a pine forest for a short ways before climbing a rocky section. 0.3 miles (1.5 miles total) on the Catfish Trail, you see Pinecrest Lake again and get a reprieve from climbing. If it is late spring or early summer, enjoy the incredible wildflower display along this section. At 1.7 miles you reach a shady shelf and another 0.1 miles up the trail you should note some stagnant ponds on the right. Just after this point, you begin climbing again (over 200 ft) until you reach a trail marker and small pond (~2.2 miles into hike). Turning right takes you on a trail to Pinecrest Peak but a left takes you to Catfish Lake. [Note: you might want to take a few minutes to visit this small pond and the Me-Wuk structure made from cedar bark that is known as an 'oomacha'.] Nearly another 0.2 miles up the trail you reach a larger body of water (but still quite shallow) and this is Catfish Lake. Most likely, there will be no one else visiting the lake as the majority of Pinecrest visitors tend to stick to the trail around Pinecrest Lake. This is your turnaround point unless you are doing the loop.

Trail Tidbits: Strawberry Dam was originally built in 1856 by the Tuolumne County Water Company to provide a water storage area (initially called Strawberry Lake) to ensure a more constant supply of water to the ditch systems that supplied water for mining operations throughout the county. The more modern dam replaced the original one in 1916; it is said that you can see parts of the original dam when lake levels are at their lowest during the fall and winter. Strawberry Dam is 133 ft high and 720 ft long and continues to function as a water storage reservoir for the ditch systems which provide domestic water for county communities. In addition, the water that leaves Pinecrest is used for hydroelectric power at the Spring Gap station.

Need to Know: The trail around the lake can be quite busy during the summer months. There may be groups of people passing you or coming at you from the opposite direction which can be disconcerting, particularly on narrow sections of the trail. Continue to take your time and watch your footing while on this section of the trail. Also be aware that the river levels can change quite dramatically depending on how much water is being let out of the dam. A siren should go off if more water is to be let out; head for higher ground if you hear this.

Photo: Catfish Lake

Want A Loop? You can turn this hike into a loop by continuing on the trail that takes you past Catfish Lake. From the lake, you drop down for a short while and then meander above the drainage for Herring Creek. Nearly 3.2 miles into the hike, you begin a more serious descent and the trail becomes rockier. Soon you should hear the roar of the South Fork of the Stanislaus River. Just past 3.6 miles into the hike, you return to the river trail; head right to return back towards the parking area. You need to cross Herring Creek again 0.2 miles down the trail; the parking area is <0.1 miles from the creek.

Directions to Trailhead: Go east on 108 past the Pinecrest turnoff until you reach the store at Strawberry on the right (just past the bridge). Turn into the store parking lot and continue down the road on the store's right side; this is Herring Creek Lane. The trailhead parking area is at the end of Herring Creek Lane (0.3 miles). Total distance from 108 is 0.3 miles.

Fraser Flat North Side Railroad Grade Trail

Highlights: The trail starts as an easy, wide tract that parallels the South Fork of the Stanislaus River. It narrows as it continues to head upstream before climbing up and under a flume for the Philadelphia Ditch to a dirt road. This trail is much like the trail on the south side except that it is closer to the river with easier access to sandy beaches.

Distance: 0.9 miles (1.8 miles roundtrip) to flume for Philadelphia Ditch; 1.9 miles (3.6 miles roundtrip) to Forest Service Road 4N13

Elevation Changes: Cumulative ascent is ~350 ft on the way out and ~40 ft on the return trip; elevation ~4850-5200 ft

Difficulty: Moderately easy in terms of elevation changes

Seasonality: This trail is suitable for most seasons. Although mostly forested, this side of the river gets more sun so it can get warm in the exposed areas, particularly in the summer. The road to Fraser Flat is closed for the winter season.

User Groups/Permits: The trail is used by hikers, fishermen and mountain bikers. It is off-limits to motorized vehicles. No permits are needed to park or use the trail.

Parking/Facilities: Parking is just after the bridge. Please be sure that your car is off the road. There are no facilities here or on the trail.

Topographic Map: USGS Strawberry, CA Quadrangle (7.5 minute series)

Hike Description: The trail starts on the right just after you cross the bridge. It begins as a gravel road up to the gate then becomes a wide, forested tract. You cross a small stream and what looks like railroad ties at ~0.2 miles. At 0.4 miles, there is a faint trail off to the left; stay on the river trail. You begin climbing just after 0.8 miles until you pass under the flume for the Philadelphia Ditch and onto a dirt road (now just past 0.9 miles). This could be your turnaround point. Otherwise, you can head right on the road and parallel the flume until it reaches the gaging station and diversion dam. At the end of the road, a trail starts. Follow this trail along the ridge that overlooks the river. Towards the end of the trail, you cross a number of planks placed over wet areas. You ascend to Forest Service Road 4N13 <0.1 miles past the last plank.

Trail Tidbits: A branch of the Sugar Pine Railroad (SPR) traveled along this north bank of the South Fork of the Stanislaus River for a distance of less than one mile starting at Camp Fraser (now Fraser Flat Campground) and ending at Camp Lowell. As was true of most base camps, Camp Lowell operated for only a few seasons (1918-1919) and was already in disuse by the time the Strawberry Branch of the SPR was built on the south bank of the river. If you look closely, it is possible to see stumps with wire ropes around them. These were used as anchor points for the steam donkeys as they dragged large logs over the ground.

Need to Know: Cattle graze this area during summer months. If you encounter a mountain biker on the narrow part of the trail, please step off to the side and let them pass. There has been construction on the dirt road past the diversion dam recently; do not attempt to travel on the road if heavy equipment is being operated in the area.

Want A Loop? A loop is possible but it means traveling on forest service roads. To do this, take the option to 4N13 and then turn left. Continue until you reach Fraser Flat Road then turn left and walk along the road until you reach the bridge (total of ~5 miles). If this loop does not sound appealing but you want more, you could take a right onto 4N13 instead and, < 0.1 miles later, pick up the trail on the other side of the road. Continue on this trail until it reaches Forest Service Road 4N67A in just over 0.3 miles. A long loop option would be to turn right onto 4N13 and take it until it reaches Old Strawberry Road. Follow Old Strawberry Road past the bridge over the river then uphill until you reach the south side trail on the right. This trail will take you back to 4N01 along the river (see Fraser Flat South Side hike).

Directions to Trailhead: Go east on 108 from the Long Barn exits then turn left onto Forest Service Road 4N01 (or Fraser Flat Road) before Cold Springs (look for a brown Forest Service sign). Travel 2.5 miles down the road and park just after crossing the bridge on the right-hand side of the road. Total distance from 108 is 2.5 miles.

Fraser Flat South Side Railroad Grade & Interpretive Trail

Highlights: The trail is an easy, wide tract that gradually narrows as it ascends gently towards Old Strawberry Road while paralleling the South Fork of the Stanislaus River (most of the way). Interpretive trail markers have been placed along the path to provide information about the area's railway history; pick up the interpretive trail guide for the Sugar Pine Railroad Grade, Strawberry Branch at either the Summit or Mi-Wok Ranger Stations.

Distance: 2.9 miles (5.8 miles roundtrip)

Elevation Changes: Cumulative ascent is <150 ft on the way out and <10 ft on the return trip; elevation ~4850-5000 ft

Photo: Fivespot flowers along the trail

Difficulty: Easy in terms of elevation changes

Seasonality: This trail is suitable for most seasons. Wildflowers are more abundant in late spring or early summer. The trail is still sufficiently shady in the summer. In the winter, the trail is only accessible from Old Strawberry Road as the road to Fraser Flat closes for the winter season. If there is snow, it is possible to snowshoe the trail.

User Groups/Permits: The trail is popular with hikers, runners, cyclists and even the occasional kayaker carrying a kayak back up to Old Strawberry

Road after coming down the river. It is off-limits to motorized vehicles. No permits are needed to park or use the trail.

Parking/Facilities: Parking is at the start of the trail just before the bridge. Please be sure that your car is off the road. There are no facilities here or on the trail.

Topographic Map: USGS Strawberry, CA Quadrangle (7.5 minute series)

Hike Description: The trail starts at the side of the river just before the bridge. The first interpretive trail marker is just past the start of the trail. The second marker is 0.2 miles up the trail with the third following at ~0.3 miles. At 0.35 miles, you cross a small stream (seasonal) and just before the first mile, you arrive at interpretive trail marker #4. Shortly after, you should note the flume on the opposite side of the river. At ~1.1 miles into the hike, you cross another small creek and should see the diversion dam on the other side of the river. The dam pools river water where some is channeled into the flume and the rest is returned back to the river bed. You reach a gate (and possible cattle guard) at ~1.4 miles. Interpretive trail marker #5 appears at ~1.6 miles and #s 6 and 7 are near the 2.0 and 2.1 mile marks, respectively. If you are interested in taking a water or lunch break down near the water, there is a side trail off to the left at ~2.2 miles into the hike. You head up a small hill and begin to head away from the river <0.1 miles later. Interpretive trail marker #8 is at 2.5 miles and #9 appears a bit more than 0.1 miles further. Nearly 2.75 miles into the hike you reach a 'Y' in the trail. The left branch takes you through private property; a sign directs you to take the right branch towards the road. You reach the road in just over 0.1 miles from this point.

Trail Tidbits: This trail was part of the Strawberry Spur of the Sugar Pine Railway (SPR) where steam engines carried logs down to Standard Lumber Company (SLC) mills from higher elevations starting in 1927 (for this spur). Fraser Flat Campground was originally called Camp Fraser and is the location where the Strawberry Spur split off from the main line of the SPR. The Strawberry Spur split into other spurs to allow logging in deeper parts of the forest. The Stanislaus National Forest has placed interpretive trail markers along the way to provide information about the history of the Strawberry Branch of the SPR.

Need to Know: The trail receives high use in the summer particularly on the weekends; please be respectful of the horseback riders, runners and cyclists as they move past you at a faster pace. Cattle graze this area in the summer.

Want A Loop? A loop is possible but it takes you on some paved and forest service roads and increases the roundtrip distance considerably to 8.5 miles (the loop is popular with bike riders and runners). Once you reach Old Strawberry Road, turn left and follow this road down into the town of Strawberry. You cross the bridge over the South Fork of the Stanislaus River 0.7 miles from where the trail met the road. You reach a junction 0.4 miles further; take the left to stay on Old Strawberry Road. Turn left on 4N13 another 0.4 miles further. Follow this road 3.6 miles until it ends at 4N01 or Fraser Flat Road. Turn left and continue another 0.4 miles to the bridge near where you parked. There is more elevation change with the loop so it would be considered a moderate hike in terms of difficulty.

Directions to Trailhead: Go east on 108 from the Long Barn exits then turn left onto Forest Service Road 4N01 (or Fraser Flat Road) before Cold Springs (look for a brown Forest Service sign). Travel 2.5 miles down the road and park just before crossing the bridge on the right-hand side of the road. Total distance from 108 is 2.5 miles.

Photo: South Fork of the Stanislaus River near Fraser Flat

Lyons Reservoir North Side Trail

Highlights: This hike is a tranquil jaunt that takes you first across the dam, then along a narrow trail before reaching a pine needle-carpeted dirt road, keeping the reservoir or inlet (South Fork Stanislaus River) in sight most of the way. As no boats are allowed on the lake and no motorized vehicles are allowed on the dirt roads, it is a quiet haven.

Distance: 2.8 miles to the inlet at Rushing Meadow (5.6 miles roundtrip)

Elevation Changes: Cumulative ascent is ~150 ft from parking area to Rushing Meadow and <50 ft on the return trip; elevation ~4200-4300 ft

Difficulty: Easy in terms of elevation changes

Seasonality: Lyons Reservoir is officially open for day use from May 1 through November 1 but these dates could be extended depending on conditions. The road is gated during the off-season.

User Groups/Permits: Lyons Reservoir is a day use area popular with fishermen, hikers, runners, cyclists and horseback riders who tend to populate the south side more than the north side of the lake. It is off-limits to unauthorized motorized vehicles. No permits are needed to park or hike.

Parking/Facilities: There is a medium-sized parking area located at the end of Lyons Dam Road. It contains a pit toilet but no drinking water is available.

Topographic Map: USGS Twain Harte, CA Quadrangle (7.5 minute series)

Hike Description: To head to the north side of the reservoir, walk to the gate at the left side of the parking area (when facing the lake). A dirt road continues beyond the gate for ~0.25 miles before reaching the dam staircase. Go down the stairs, turn right and head across the dam stopping to enjoy both the lake and downstream views. As you exit the dam, you find yourself on a helicopter pad (0.3 miles). Take the narrow dirt trail to the right that parallels the shore of the lake. At ~0.5 miles you come to a faint 'Y'. The right branch takes you to the lake but you want the left branch that eventually brings you to a dirt road. Nearly 0.1 miles further, you reach a more distinct 'Y'. Either branch brings you to Forest Service Road 4N02 but the left branch entails more climbing to reach it; turn right onto the road. At ~1.1 miles you head away from the lake for a short while and eventually start walking uphill on a short grade. You crest the hill at ~1.4 miles and begin heading downhill where the arm of the reservoir is again visible. At this point you enter a wildlife and research area on land that is owned by Sierra Pacific Industries (SPI); please be respectful of the area. As you continue along the road, you should notice that the reservoir arm is gradually narrowing until it is better described as the South Fork of the Stanislaus River. At ~2.5 miles you reach another 'Y'. The left branch heads away from the water whereas the right branch leads you out on a grassy and rocky area next to the water. Head along the right branch and when there is no longer a distinct tract, stay close to the river so that you can avoid the boggy area off to the left. The suggested turnaround location is by the field with the barbed wire fence located across from a good-sized, treed island in the middle of the river. This area is Rushing Meadow.

Trail Tidbits: The Tuolumne County Water Company erected a dam on Lyons Flat in 1857 creating Lyons Reservoir. This was done in an effort to create a water storage area that was capable of providing year-round water to downstream mining communities. This dam was rebuilt in 1897-1898 at a height of 55 ft and length of 210 ft. It withstood one of the greatest floods on the South Fork of the Stanislaus during the spring of 1907. The modern single arch dam was built in 1930 by PGE and is 132 ft high and 535 ft long with four flood gates. It continues to act as a water storage area today to provide water to downstream communities via the Main Tuolumne Ditch system.

Need to Know: Lyons Reservoir supplies drinking water to downstream communities. No swimming or other human contact with the water is allowed. No boats are allowed on the reservoir. In addition, camping is strictly prohibited as it is a day use area.

Want A Loop? You can turn this hike into a loop if you can find a way to cross the South Fork of the Stanislaus River. If it late in the season, you might be able to rock hop your way across but if there is a significant amount of water coming down the river, you might be getting your shoes wet while crossing it. Once across the river, turn right on the trail. Shortly after the dam comes into view in the distance (~4.4 miles into the hike), head uphill on the trail to the left (the trail that continues straight dead-ends at the water). As you crest the hill, continue straight ignoring the lesser trails off to the left.

You cross Lyons Creek at 4.7 miles and head to the right until you reach a cattle guard and gate (4.9 miles). Continue on the trail past the gate until you reach the parking area. The loop is 5.1 miles total with the uphill stretches amounting to <250 ft in ascent.

Directions to Trailhead: Go east on 108 past Sierra Village. Shortly after leaving Sierra Village, turn left onto Lyons Dam Road. Drive ~2 miles down a narrow road to the parking area. Be ready to pull to the side of the road to allow oncoming cars to squeeze past. Total distance from 108 is 2.1 miles.

Photo: Lyons Reservoir Dam early in the season

Lyons Reservoir South Side Railroad Grade Trail

Highlights: This hike is a pleasant walk that circles around a small inlet where you cross Lyons Creek and then heads along the shore of the reservoir until reaching its major inlet, the South Fork of the Stanislaus River. As no boats are allowed on the lake and no motorized vehicles are allowed on the dirt roads, it makes for a peaceful hike.

Distance: 2.25 miles to Rushing Meadow (4.5 miles roundtrip).

Elevation Changes: Cumulative ascent is ~150 ft from parking area to Rushing Meadow and <50 ft on the return trip; elevation ~4200-4300 ft

Difficulty: Easy in terms of elevation changes

Photo: Lyons Reservoir

Seasonality: Lyons Reservoir is officially open for day use from May 1 through November 1 but these dates could be extended depending on conditions. The road is gated during the off-season.

User Groups/Permits: Lyons Reservoir is a day use area popular with fishermen, hikers, runners, cyclists and horseback riders who tend to populate the south side more than the north side of the lake. It is off-limits to unauthorized motorized vehicles. No permits are needed to park or hike.

Parking/Facilities: There is a medium-sized parking area located at the end of Lyons Dam Road. It contains a pit toilet but no drinking water is available.

Topographic Map: USGS Twain Harte, CA Quadrangle (7.5 minute series)

Hike Description: To walk along the south side of the reservoir, hike to the gate that is on the right side of the parking area (when facing the lake). A dirt road continues beyond the gate for ~0.2 miles before reaching a cattle guard and gate. Pass through the gate and head downhill where you cross Lyons Creek at ~0.4 miles. Head uphill while ignoring the faint trail off to the left and those off to the right at the crest of the hill. From here, go downhill until you reach the reservoir again (~0.7 miles); turn right and follow its shore. As you continue along the road, which becomes rocky in places, you should notice that the reservoir arm is gradually narrowing until it is better described as the South Fork of the Stanislaus River. The suggested turnaround location is by the field with the barbed wire fence located across from a good-sized, treed island in the middle of the river. This is area is Rushing Meadow.

Trail Tidbits: Lyons Reservoir was created in 1857 as a water storage area for the ditch systems that provided water for mining during the Gold Rush era; it was one of 5 storage areas at the time. The reservoir has a maximum capacity of 6400 acre feet. The primary inlet is the South Fork of the Stanislaus River which comes from Pinecrest Lake. Cattle graze in the meadow along the inlet called Rushing Meadow. Most of the land along around Lyons Reservoir is owned by PG&E, Sierra Pacific Industries or the Stanislaus National Forest.

Need to Know: Lyons Reservoir supplies drinking water to downstream communities. No swimming or other human contact with the water is allowed. No boats are allowed on the reservoir. No camping is allowed.

Want A Loop? You can turn this hike into a loop if you can find a way to cross the South Fork of the Stanislaus River. If it late in the season, you might be able to rock hop your way across but if there is a significant amount of water coming down the river, you might be getting your shoes wet while crossing it. Once across the river, head to the left along the shore until you reach a grassy area. You can see the forest service road through the trees just off the bank to the right. Head left on the road and follow it for ~2.2 miles (4.5 miles into the hike) until you reach a gate. Take the narrow trail that drops off to the left at the gate; the trail takes you to the dam (ignore the few trails off to the left that take you to the shore of the reservoir). At the dam, cross its top, climb up the stairs and head left on the dirt road until you reach the parking lot. The loop is 5.1 miles total with <250 ft in ascent.

Directions to Trailhead: Go east on 108 past Sierra Village. Shortly after leaving Sierra Village, turn left onto Lyons Dam Road. Drive ~2 miles down a narrow road to the parking area. Be ready to pull to the side of the road to allow oncoming cars to squeeze past. Total distance from 108 is ~2 miles.

Pinecrest Lake Loop: National Recreation Trail

Highlights: For the majority of this hike, you have scenic views of beautiful Pinecrest Lake and the granitic majesty of the South Fork of the Stanislaus River Canyon. This trail and lake draw people from all around for hiking, swimming, boating and camping.

Distance: ~4.1 miles around the lake

Elevation Changes: Cumulative ascent for loop ~500 ft; elevation ~5600-5750 ft

Difficulty: Moderate in terms of elevation changes

Seasonality: The lake area can be quite crowded during the summer months (May 15 – September 15). Less people visit during the off-season but lake levels tend to be much lower during this period. The lake often freezes over in the winter. The trail is open year-round and is usually quite accessible unless there has been recent heavy snow.

User Groups/Permits: The trail is popular with hikers and fishermen. The lake is popular with everyone: swimmers, picnickers, boaters, etc. The trail is off-limits to motorized vehicles. No permits are needed to park or hike.

Parking/Facilities: Once you have passed the main campground, there are numerous parking areas on both sides of the road located at the southwest end of the lake. There are flush toilets near the parking and swimming areas; there is also a vault toilet on the other side of the lake near Sunset Point.

Topographic Map: USGS Pinecrest Quadrangle (7.5 Minute Series)

Hike Description: The trail starts wherever you have found a parking spot. You can choose to go in either direction but this guide is written such that you are going counterclockwise. Follow the path around the swimming and picnicking area. At the end of this area, you should note a concrete fishing dock; this dock is used as a mileage reference point. The trail continues from here as an old concrete walk. 0.4 miles from the fishing dock, you climb a staircase. From here until the far side of the lake, the trail is a mixture of sand, granite and concrete remnants. You encounter some wet, seep areas

~0.9 miles into the hike, and then 0.25 miles later, you begin to head away from the lake. You should see a sign pointing to the left for Sunrise Point (and the vault toilet) at 1.3 miles from the fishing 'dock'; head right. Just ahead you come to another trail junction that is more like a 'Y' and is easy to miss. The right branch takes you uphill quickly and continues on to Cleo's Bath (see Want More?); to continue around the lake, take the left branch. This section of the trail involves some up and down hiking on granitic slabs and rocky areas until you reach the dam. However, before you reach the dam, you pass the inlet to Pinecrest Lake (the South Fork of the Stanislaus River) on a bridge. At ~2.4 miles from the fishing 'dock', you pass the trail junction to Catfish Lake; stay on the main trail here and ~0.45 miles further, you reach the dam. This is always a great place to look around: take in views of the lake as well as the canyon where water is being released. Continue the hike by walking across the dam and then up the staircase on the far side. Pay close attention to where you are heading in this section as there are side trails that have been made both to the lake by swimmers as well as up to the water storage tanks above; stay on the main trail which climbs upwards to a saddle. As you head down from this saddle, you can see the boat ramp and docks in the distance. Continue past them and onto the walkway to the parking areas.

Trail Tidbits: Pinecrest Lake has been a water storage area (originally called Strawberry Reservoir) since 1856 and was created to ensure a more constant supply of water to the ditch systems that supplied water for mining operations throughout the county. Prior to Strawberry Reservoir, there were 3 storage reservoirs: Lower, Middle and Upper (also called Big) Lakes. The lake sits at an elevation just above 5600 ft during the summer season and is 300 acres in size. Although Pinecrest Lake is within the boundaries of the Stanislaus National Forest, the dam and lake levels are operated by PG&E.

Need to Know: The trail around the lake can be quite busy during the summer months. There may be groups of people passing you or coming at you from the opposite direction which can be disconcerting particularly on narrow sections of the trail. Continue to take your time and watch your footing while on the trail. Most of the trail is exposed; even on a late fall day, you can get warm if it is bright and sunny.

Want More? This hike is written as a loop. If you would like more, you can take a side excursion to Cleo's Bath (described in this section) or to Catfish Lake (see Catfish Lake hike). The hike to Cleo's Bath is not well marked and involves an additional ~650 ft of climbing, with some of it requiring both hands and feet on steep rock. As this section makes the hike 'difficult', it is only recommended for those fit enough and sure-footed enough to make the climb successfully. To do this additional section, turn right at the sign indicating the direction of Cleo's Bath. Follow the 'primitive' trail carefully. Shortly into the hike, you pass an old steam donkey and some historical information. Continue on the trail as it takes you up the South Fork of the Stanislaus River towards a waterfall (if enough water is flowing).The trail crosses a streamlet just before the waterfall; this area can be very wet and slippery in the spring when large amounts of water are flowing. Once past the streamlet, you need to climb up the rocks to the right of the waterfall. Look for trail signs such as 'ducks' or painted arrows. After climbing to the top, you reach some campsites off to the left; pass through these and head down to the water. There are numerous pools that are wonderful to swim in both upstream and downstream but the official 'Cleo's Bath' is to the left and above the waterfall. The Cleo's Bath excursion adds another 3.1 miles to your roundtrip total around the lake.

Directions to Trailhead: Go east on 108 past Cold Springs. Turn right at the Pinecrest turnoff onto Pinecrest Lake Drive. Continue down this road for ~0.8 miles before reaching the main parking lot for the lake on your left. There are other parking lots on the right and further down the road on your left. Total distance from 108 is 0.8 mile to the beginning of the parking areas.

Photo: Pinecrest Lake (and some smoke from the Rim Fire)

Pinecrest Peak Trail

Highlights: This hike involves lots of climbing but the views are well worth the sweat factor. Initially you are treated to sights of Pinecrest Lake, Dodge Ridge and the South Fork of the Stanislaus River Canyon but as you work your way up to the top past layered granite rocks, you can then relish the views of the Middle Fork of the Stanislaus River Canyon and Herring Dome. Although you can drive to the top of Pinecrest Peak on an ATV road from the other direction, you miss out on some of the views and you lose the sense of satisfaction from a climb well-done!

Distance: ~3.0 miles to the top (6.0 miles roundtrip)

Elevation Changes: Cumulative ascent is ~1620 ft on the way there and ~70 ft on the return; elevation ~6450-8025 ft

Difficulty: Strenuous in terms of elevation changes

Photo: Layered granitic rock on Pinecrest Peak

Seasonality: This trail is best done during the early summer or early fall. There are areas that are exposed so the trail can be hot in the late summer. The roads to this area are closed during the winter.

User Groups/Permits: The trail is used by hikers and mountain bike riders. No motorized vehicles are allowed on the trail. No permits are needed to park or use the trail for day hikes.

Parking/Facilities: There is a parking area at the trailhead. There are no facilities here or on the trail.

Topographic Map: USGS Pinecrest Quadrangle (7.5 Minute Series)

Hike Description: Start the hike at the bridge that crosses over Herring Creek. The beginning part of the trail is an old forest service road; initially, there are some plastic trail signs along the way. You climb briefly before walking down a short ways to a 'Y'; veer left and go up the road. At nearly 0.8 miles, you turn left onto a trail where a rock wall has been built. There is also a trail that heads off to the right of the road that goes to Catfish Lake (see Want A Loop?). Just over a mile into the hike, you reach a small seasonal pond. Take a side trip to the right of the pond to reach an overlook of the South Fork of the Stanislaus River Canyon. To continue the hike, go around the pond and begin another ascent (steeply at this point) with other opportunities for great views of the canyon. You reach a brief plateau at ~1.7 miles and ~0.2 miles further, there is a faint split in the trail; go to the left of the large boulder. You begin climbing some more from here. At ~2.3 miles, the dirt trail changes over to granitic rock and you begin to see large layered granite boulders. The trail becomes more difficult to delineate but keep following the 'ducks' or cairns. Head to a different overlook at ~2.8 miles (left off the trail) where you have views of Herring Dome and the Trail of the Gargoyles area. Continue climbing until you reach the peak and the end of the dirt ATV road.

Trail Tidbits: There used to be an observation tower at this location for spotting forest fires. It was built during WWII and destroyed by fire in 1973. The remainder of the tower was dismantled in the 1970's but you can still see evidence of it if you look carefully.

Need to Know: There are portions of the trail that are exposed. At times the trail surface becomes more challenging as you have to step over granite boulders or on loose granitic rubble on top of granite which is slippery.

Want A Loop? If you arrange a shuttle ahead of time, you could do a shuttle loop. Descend the way you came back to the old forest service road with the rock wall marking the trail. Cross the road and head down the trail 1.4 miles to Catfish Lake. From Catfish Lake, head to the Strawberry Trailhead (see Catfish Lake hike) for a total of 8.1 miles.

Directions to Trailhead: Go east on 108 past Strawberry. Turn right on Herring Creek Road. Continue on this road for ~2.8 miles. Turn right onto 4N27 where you can see a sign that says 'Message Board'. Follow this road 1.3 miles to the end then park in the dirt area near the bridge. Total distance from 108 is 4.1 miles.

Twain Harte to Lyons Dam Railroad Grade

Highlights: The trail is an easy, wide tract with great views of the South Fork of the Stanislaus River Canyon and the Dardanelles in the east. The roar of the river as it cascades downstream becomes audible as you near the dam.

Distance: 4.6 miles to the dam (9.2 miles roundtrip)

Elevation Changes: Cumulative ascent is <25 ft from road to dam and <5 ft on the return trip; elevation ~4220-4240 ft

Difficulty: Easy in terms of elevation changes

Seasonality: This trail is suitable for all seasons. The dogwoods and wildflowers are spectacular in the spring. The trail goes in and out of tree cover, so you might get warm and dusty walking on summer afternoons. The tract can be muddy following rain or snow storms.

User Groups/Permits: The trail is popular with hikers, runners, cyclists and horseback riders. It is off-limits to unauthorized motorized vehicles. No permits are needed to park or use the trail.

Parking/Facilities: Parking is limited to a few spaces at the start of the trail and a few more on Confidence South Fork Road heading towards Middle Camp Road. Please be sure that your car is off the road. There are no facilities here or on the trail. If you hike this trail in reverse, there is a pit toilet in the Lyons Reservoir parking area (add 0.5 miles round trip).

Topographic Map: USGS Twain Harte, CA Quadrangle (7.5 minute series)

Hike Description: The trail starts off on the uphill side of Confidence South Fork Road on a dirt tract. You encounter a gate with a sign that indicates that the land is private property <0.1 miles into the hike. Go around the gate and continue down the tract. Take time to enjoy the panoramic view of the river canyon at 0.5 miles into the hike. There are logging roads that branch off the tract in various locations; most of the ones that head downhill bring you to the Main Tuolumne Ditch (see section Want A Loop?). To reach the dam, stay on the main tract. At 4 miles, you round a corner and the dam becomes visible in the distance. Continue until you reach the staircase at the dam.

Trail Tidbits: This tract was part of the Sugar Pine Railway (SPR) where steam engines carried logs down to Standard Lumber Company (SLC) mills from higher elevations starting in 1903. SPR owned 9 miles of the track from Lyons but the remainder of the track to the Sonora area was leased from Sierra Railway Company. A second track was created by the Empire City Railway (ECR) and serviced the 12 mile area from Lyons Dam to the Empire Mill in Cold Springs. Pickering Lumber Company (PLC) purchased the SPR and SLC in 1921 and operated the more than 400 miles of track until 1965. The land is currently owned by Sierra Pacific Industries (SPI) and has been logged in various locations. SPI allows non-motorized use of the trail.

Need to Know: Much of the land on both sides of the initial segment of tract is privately owned; please respect the owners' rights by staying on the trail. During most months, there is little running water; be sure to carry enough. The trail receives high use in the summer particularly on the weekends; be respectful of others as they move past you at a faster pace.

Want A Loop? To turn this hike into a loop, take one of the downhill branches that lead to the Main Tuolumne Ditch. Most of these require that you can **walk on single-wide board planks on flumes**. For the longest loop, go down the staircase at the dam, turn left at the path and left again at the bottom. You cross a helicopter pad before starting off on a board plank on the 'A' flume which is >1 mile long. The 'B', 'C' and 'D' flumes follow shortly after but then you spend more time walking on a dirt path along the ditch. For the shortest loop and the only one that skips all but a very short flume, take the first trail off to the left about 1 mile from Confidence South Fork Road. Regardless of which loop you do, to return to the parking area, you need to walk the ditch until it crosses South Fork. Turn left onto South Fork Road (leaving the ditch trail) and go ~0.1 miles. Turn left onto Confidence South Fork Road and head uphill for ~0.5 miles to the trailhead. The shortest loop would be 1.7 miles; the longest is closer to 10 miles.

Directions to Trailhead: Go east on 108 past Twain Harte, turn left onto Confidence South Fork Road and drive 1.2 miles. Turn left on Middle Camp Sugar Pine Road and go <0.1 miles before turning right back onto Confidence South Fork Road. The trail begins on the right on a dirt tract. Total distance from 108 is 1.3 miles.

Middle Fork of the Stanislaus River Canyon Trails

The Middle Fork of the Stanislaus River is the largest of the 3 forks that eventually become the Stanislaus River. In the 1800's, this fork was referred to as the Main Fork of the Stanislaus River. Its origin is in the high country above Relief Reservoir. The Middle Fork of the Stanislaus River is joined by Kennedy Creek above Kennedy Meadow, Deadman Creek at Kennedy Meadows, Eagle Creek near the Dardanelles Resort area and Clark Fork River just above Donnell Reservoir. From Donnell, the river flows down to Beardsley Reservoir and Sand Bar Flat before joining with the North Fork and finally, the South Fork just above New Melones Lake.

A year-round water supply was essential for mining and household use in the early years of Tuolumne County. As a result, the Middle Fork of the Stanislaus was dammed in a number of places to provide water storage and control over its release. Ditches and flumes were built to transport the water to the mining communities. Today, the dams are primarily used to deliver irrigation water to the valley and generate hydroelectric power. Powerhouses are located downstream from Donnell Reservoir, below Beardsley Dam, at Spring Gap, upstream from Sand Bar Flat and below the confluence of the North and Middle Forks (Stanislaus Powerhouse).

Although the Middle Fork of the Stanislaus River Canyon is steep, many of the trails in the area are not. Railroad spurs were built in this canyon in an effort to pull out timber for the construction of flumes as well as homes for the growing communities downstream. Trails along these old railroad grades maintain ~3.5% grade and, therefore, have minimal elevation gains. They are also high above the river but give a better perspective of the grandeur of this river canyon. The trails that follow alongside the river have more changes in elevation due to the terrain of the canyon walls but they allow you to keep pace with the river current and its sounds and provide you with closer views of the powerhouses.

Photo: Powerhouse above Sand Bar Flat

Beardsley Dam to Spring Gap Railroad Grade

Highlights: This trail is an easy walk along an old railroad grade high above the river canyon of the Middle Fork of the Stanislaus River. Beardsley Powerhouse is visible below at the start. Near the end, in the Spring Gap area, you can see the old tramway and the penstock pipe that travels between the forebay at upper Spring Gap and the hydroelectric plant at lower Spring Gap. If you are so inclined, you can take the steep spur to the power plant and to the water's edge.

Distance: ~2.8 miles (5.6 miles roundtrip) to bridge above power station; ~3.6 (7.2 miles roundtrip) to actual power station

Elevation Changes: Cumulative ascent is ~300 ft on the way to the bridge above the power station and ~20 ft on the return with elevations of ~3400-3700 ft.; cumulative ascent is ~300 ft on the way to the actual power station and ~720 ft on the return with elevations of ~3000-3700 ft

Difficulty: Moderately easy in terms of elevation changes to the bridge above the power station; moderately difficult if you go to the power station

Seasonality: This trail is really best during the fall, winter and spring. The road to Beardsley Reservoir closes temporarily when there is snow on it. The streams (with waterfalls) should be running in the spring. The grade is gorgeous in the fall when the deciduous trees change color. Although there is shade for a good portion of the trail, this area can get hot in the summer.

User Groups/Permits: The trail is used by hikers, fishermen and mountain bikers. No unauthorized motorized vehicles are allowed; at times, a PG&E vehicle might be on the road to access the power plant. No permits are needed to park or day hike.

Parking/Facilities: Park off the road just before crossing the dam. Do not block the gate when you park. There are no facilities here or along the trail; however, there are restrooms at Beardsley Day Use Area, Beardsley Campground and China Flat Day Use Area.

Topographic Map: USGS Strawberry Quadrangle (7.5 Minute Series)

Hike Description: The hike is on a wide forest service road that is packed gravel and dirt that starts just beyond a typically locked gate. It parallels the river canyon of the Middle Fork of the Stanislaus. Nearly 0.2 miles into the hike, you see an old water pipe off to the right and just around the corner you should note the water tank hidden on the hill. You cross a cattle guard with a gate just a short bit later. At ~0.4–0.8 miles, you start to have unobstructed views of Beardsley Dam including its spillway and power station. You can see and hear the churning of water as it leaves the powerhouse and enters the afterbay reservoir. The China Flat Day Use Area, gaging station and afterbay dam are also visible from this vantage. After ~0.8 miles, the views of the river are occasional (or through trees). You pass a solar panel at ~1.5 miles and ~0.2 miles farther, you catch a glimpse of the Spring Gap Power Station further downstream. There is a spring off to the left at ~2 miles that runs even in the fall. An ancient artifact (an old steam engine) is visible off to the left at ~2.2 miles. You cross the first bridge at ~2.5 miles; a nice waterfall should be visible in the spring when water levels are high. You reach the bridge in the Spring Gap area ~0.3 miles from the first bridge (~2.8 miles total). Take a look at the old tramway line and the steep hill that it used to travel. Feel how cold the penstock pipe is as it carries water down to the powerhouse. You can see the river downhill in the distance. This can be your turnaround point or you can take the spur road off to the right down to the power station.

Photo: Historic Artifact

Trail Tidbits: This trail was once a segment of the Sugar Pine Railroad, operated first by Standard Lumber Company and then Pickering Lumber Company from the early 1900's to 1965. There is a section of the grade that was named and is still referred to as the 'Peeled Onion'; it is the section where the railroad tracks were cut into the side of the steep granite wall (~0.5-1 mile from the start of the hike). The Sugar Pine Railroad traveled along the 'Peeled Onion' and then crossed the Middle Fork of the Stanislaus River on a trestle (Pickering Bridge) to logging areas on the north side of the canyon and beyond. When Beardsley Dam was built in the 1950's, the trestle was submerged. Beardsley Dam is 284 ft high and 1000 ft long and is part of the Stanislaus River Tri-Dam Project that brings irrigation water to the San Joaquin Valley.

Need to Know: The Stanislaus National Forest has closed off certain areas on the sides of the road where ancient artifacts have been found; please stay on the road. It is against the law to remove, alter or destroy any of these artifacts. There is no accessible water during the hike (unless you drop down to the water's edge at Spring Gap); be sure to pack enough water.

Want A Loop? A loop is possible. Walk down to the power station, cross the bridge to the other side of the river and pick up the trail that heads upstream along the river to the China Flat Day Use Area. From here, walk up the dam road back to your car. The roundtrip mileage for this hike would be closer to 7 miles and would involve more climbing. If you want more but don't want to do additional climbing, continue along the railroad grade. It goes for ~4 miles before reaching the forest service road that leads to Sand Bar Flat Campground.

Photo:
Beardsley
Reservoir,
Dam
Powerhouse
and Spillway

**Directions
to Trailhead**: Go east on 108 past Strawberry. Turn left on Beardsley Road (5N02). Take the paved road all the way down to the dam (veer left at the junction with the day use area at 7.7 miles). Park off the road just before it crosses the dam. Total distance from 108 is 8.1 miles.

China Flat River Trail

Highlights: This trail is a varied river trail that takes you past dams, power stations, a tramway, gaging stations and granite walls and across bridges while following the numerous river pools and cascades of the Middle Fork of the Stanislaus River (color photo page 170). You start along the drier north edge of the river canyon from China Flat Day Use Area before crossing over at the Spring Gap Hydroelectric Plant to the cooler south edge on your way to Sand Bar Flat Campground. A particularly appealing aspect of this trail is that very few people use it. This hike is the longer version of the Sand Bar Flat River hike.

Distance: ~5 miles one-way (10 miles roundtrip)

Elevation Changes: Cumulative ascent is ~350 ft on the way there and ~660 ft on the return; elevation ~2750-3200 ft

Difficulty: Moderately difficult in terms of elevation changes

Seasonality: This trail is really best during the fall, winter and early spring. The road to Beardsley Reservoir can close temporarily if there is snow on the ground. The north side of the trail can be very hot during the summer. The trail is gorgeous in the fall when all the deciduous trees change color.

User Groups/Permits: The trail is used by hikers and fly fishermen. No motorized vehicles are allowed. No permits are needed to park or day hike.

Parking/Facilities: There is a parking area at the China Flat Trailhead. There is a vault toilet at the trailhead as well as at Sand Bar Flat campground but no facilities along the trail.

Topographic Map: USGS Crandall Peak and Strawberry Quadrangles (7.5 Minute Series)

Hike Description: The hike begins on the gravel road that starts at the parking area and continues past a locked gate heading downstream. This road parallels the afterbay below Beardsley Dam Powerhouse and at ~0.6 miles, brings you to the afterbay dam (you can walk out onto it). To continue on the hike, take the narrow dirt trail that continues heading in the downstream direction just as the road ends at the afterbay dam. This section of the hike has quite a bit of up and down on the hotter, drier north side of the canyon. Nearly 1 mile into the hike, you cross a small footbridge and then~0.2 miles later you pass a gaging station (measures water flow from the river). You encounter a PG&E residence at ~2.2 and this is where you cross a bridge over the river to the lower portion of Spring Gap where a power station is located. You might want to take a few minutes to explore the old tramway and the penstock pipe that carries water down from the Philadelphia Ditch to the power station. Now that you are on the south side of the canyon, the trail is cooler with the cover of more deciduous trees. As you continue down the trail, you cross a few footbridges and some small streams (or dry beds depending on the season) and pass huge granite walls and an open-top granite tunnel while following the meanderings of the river. At ~4.7 miles, you see the Sand Bar Powerhouse on the other side of the river. You reach Sand Bar Flat Campground just to the left of a floating bridge that crosses the river at ~5 miles.

Trail Tidbits: Water that flows through the Beardsley powerhouse (at the bottom of the dam) is returned to the river in the afterbay, which is an impoundment or collection of water created by a downstream dam (in this case, the afterbay dam). At the afterbay dam, some of the water is diverted from the river into a tunnel to the Sand Bar Powerhouse, located 4 miles downstream, where it is eventually returned to the river just upstream from the Sand Bar Diversion Dam. However, only 2 miles from the afterbay dam, water from the South Fork of the Stanislaus River joins the Middle Fork after traveling through a penstock pipe and the Spring Gap Powerhouse. Even further downstream, the Sand Bar Diversion Dam allows water to be sent through an 11.4 mile tunnel (originally a flume was used) to the Stanislaus forebay, the Stanislaus Powerhouse and then, finally, New Melones Lake.

Need to Know: The area is grazed by cattle during the summer to early fall. The trail is rocky at times; watch your footing. There is poison oak along various sections of the trail. Water might be discharged from the Beardsley Dam Powerhouse at any moment so keep away from the water in the afterbay area. The Sand Bar Flat Campground area is closed from June 2013 through December 2014 as new fish ladders are being constructed.

Want A Loop? You could do a loop by walking along the old Sugar Pine Railroad Grade (4N88) but it would involve hiking ~18 miles. To do this, head up 4N85 from the campground, turn left onto 4N88, cross the top of

Beardsley Dam and then hike down to China Flat Day Use area. If you want more, explore the Sand Bar Flat area including the dam with its fish ladders.

Photo: The Middle Fork of the Stanislaus River

Directions to Trailhead: Go east on 108 past Strawberry. Turn left on Beardsley Road (5N02). Take the paved road all the way down to the dam (veer left at the junction with the day use area at 7.7 miles). Cross the dam (8.1 miles) and when you reach the end of the dam, turn left onto the steep road that takes you down to the power station. At 8.7 miles, the road turns to dirt and 0.2 miles later you cross a washboard bridge. Continue another 0.1 miles to the parking area of China Flat Day Use Area (picnic area and vault toilet are on the right). Total distance from 108 is 9.0 miles.

Donnell Reservoir Forest Road

Highlights: This trail is an easy trek high above the river canyon of the Middle Fork of the Stanislaus River to an 'overlook' area with nice views. Along the way, you pass a penstock pipe that carries water via a tunnel from Donnell Reservoir down to the Donnell Powerhouse and an old adit (underground entrance) to a former waterway. The road passes numerous streams, granite rock walls and cross-canyon waterfalls along the way to the overlook or, if you are interested in going further, Donnell Reservoir.

Distance: ~2.75 miles (5.5 miles roundtrip) to river overlook

Elevation Changes: Cumulative ascent is ~60 ft on the way out and ~120 ft on the return with elevations of ~4570-4750 ft

Difficulty: Easy in terms of elevation changes

Seasonality: This trail can be done in any season although it can be warm in the summer (go early). The road to Beardsley Reservoir closes temporarily when there is snow on it and Forest Service Road 5N95 is closed the entire winter season except for power station traffic. If you do this hike in the winter when this road is closed, add 4.2 miles to the roundtrip total. The streams (with waterfalls) will be more spectacular in the spring.

User Groups/Permits: The trail is used by motorized vehicles (not many) as well as hikers, rock climbers and mountain bike riders. No permits are needed to park or day hike.

Parking/Facilities: Park off the road just at the junction of 5N09X and 5N95. Do not block the gate or roadways when you park. There are no facilities here or along the trail.

Topographic Map: USGS Strawberry and Liberty Hill Quadrangles (7.5 Minute Series); Donnell Lake too if plan to go the distance to the reservoir

Hike Description: The hike is on a wide forest service road (5N09X) that is packed gravel and dirt that starts at the junction with 5N95. Shortly after starting down the road, you pass a gate. Keep your eye out for waterfalls on the opposite side of the canyon (at ~0.35 and 0.9 miles). About 0.5 miles down the road, you cross over the penstock pipe that carries water from Donnell Reservoir via an underground tunnel to the Donnell Powerhouse which you can see down below in the river canyon. There is an old rock quarry ~0.1 miles further along the road. You begin to travel through a burned area ~1 mile into the hike; this is from the 2013 Power Fire. You cross an unnamed creek ~1.25 miles into the hike and continue through more burned forest. At ~2.1 miles, you can see an old concrete foundation and tucked back behind trees into the rock wall, the opening (adit) for an old water transport system. Just past this area, you cross Lily Creek and another rock quarry. Note the open overlook of the river ~0.6 miles past this second rock quarry. This is the turnaround point for this hike. Take some time to view the river canyon including Dome Rock to the northeast.

Trail Tidbits: Donnell Reservoir was named for the man who owned and operated the Donnell and Parsons Sawmill which was once located on a flat near the Middle Fork of the Stanislaus River but is now underwater. The sawmill cut timbers that were used by the Columbia Stanislaus Water Company to build the flumes used to transport water to mining towns. The dam was built to create a storage reservoir and limit the amount of water spilling downstream. Today, most of the water flowing from Donnell Dam is diverted into an 8 mile tunnel and penstock pipe to the Donnell Powerhouse located upstream from Beardsley Reservoir.

Need to Know: As motorized vehicles are allowed on this road when the gates are open, please step to the side of the road when you hear one coming. Be careful to stay on the road through the burned area as many of the trees have been weakened as a result of the fire.

Want More? A loop is not possible with the steep canyon walls above and below you. However, if you want more, continue further down the road until you reach Cascade Creek, Mill Creek or even Donnell Dam and Reservoir.

Directions to Trailhead: Go east on 108 past Strawberry. Turn left on Beardsley Road (5N02) following the paved road down ~1 mile. Turn right onto Forest Service Road 5N95. Continue down this road for 2.1 miles until you see the junction with 5N09X which heads off to the right (if you stay on 5N95, it takes you down to Donnell Powerhouse and Hell's Half Acre Campground & Beach Area). Be sure to park off the road and out of the way of any gates. Total distance from 108 is 3.1 miles.

Sand Bar Flat River Trail

Highlights: This trail offers a gorgeous meander along the Middle Fork of the Stanislaus River up to the hydroelectric plant at Spring Gap. Along the way, you cross a few footbridges and some small streambeds and pass huge granite walls and an open-top granite tunnel while heading upstream past deep pools and cascades. This hike is the shorter, easier version of the China Flat River hike.

Distance: ~2.8 miles (5.6 miles roundtrip)

Elevation Changes: Cumulative ascent is ~320 ft on the way there and ~110 ft on the return; elevation ~2750- 3000 ft

Difficulty: Moderately easy in terms of elevation changes

Seasonality: This trail is really best during the spring and fall. Although it is shaded, it could be quite warm in the summer particularly in the middle of the day. It is gorgeous in the fall when all the deciduous trees change color. The roads to Sand Bar Flat are closed during the winter.

User Groups/Permits: The trail is used by hikers and fly fishermen. No motorized vehicles are allowed on the trail. No permits are needed to park or day hike; fees are charged for overnight camping in the campground.

Parking/Facilities: There is a parking area at the campground. There are vault toilets located in the campground but there are no facilities on the trail.

Topographic Map: USGS Crandall Peak and Strawberry Quadrangles (7.5 Minute Series)

Hike Description: The hike begins at the back of the campground; look for the trail off to the right just past a vault toilet but before the floating bridge that crosses the river. Hike upstream. About 0.25 miles into the hike, you cross a footbridge (over a small creek) and shortly after, you should see the Sand Bar Flat Power Station on the other side of the river. There is a bit of a bog area ~ 0.5 miles into the hike. You walk through the open-topped granite 'tunnel' ~0.5 miles later (~1 mile into the hike). After passing by granitic walls, you spend the remainder of the hike walking under a thick forest canopy, crossing bridges over small streambeds before reaching the powerhouse at the lower portion of Spring Gap.

Trail Tidbits: The Sand Bar Diversion Dam was first constructed in 1909 by the Stanislaus Electric Company. PG&E reconstructed it in 1939 as part of the Spring Gap-Stanislaus System. The dam is known as a timber crib hydroelectric dam and is so unique that it may be the only one of its kind in California. It consists of a timber crib that is filled with rock and decked with timber and then plywood. The Sand Bar Dam is 24 ft high and 174 ft long; its purpose is to create a pool of water (impoundment) so that the water can be diverted through an 11.4 mile long tunnel to the Stanislaus powerhouse.

Need to Know: The area is grazed by cattle during the summer to early fall. The trail is rocky at times; watch your footing. There is poison oak along various sections of the trail. Sand Bar Flat Campground is closed from June 2013 through December 2014 for construction of new fish ladders at the Sand Bar Flat Dam.

Want A Loop? You could do a loop by heading up the dirt road at the Spring Gap Powerhouse to Forest Service Road 4N88. Turn right on 4N88 and then right on Forest Service Road 4N85 to reach the campground again. If you just want more, take some time to explore the fish ladders at Sand Bar Flat Dam or the old tramway and penstock pipe in the area around the Spring Gap Powerhouse. To add more mileage, cross the river at Spring Gap on the bridge and head upstream towards Beardsley Dam; it is 2.2 miles more to the dam.

Directions to Trailhead: Go east on 108 past Long Barn but before Cold Springs. Turn left on Fraser Flat Road (4N01). You will be on 4N01 for 6.9 miles. As you travel that distance, you cross a bridge at 2.5 miles, pass the campground at 3.0 miles, begin traveling on dirt at 3.2 miles, veer left at 5.2 miles (right goes to upper portion of Spring Gap) and veer left again at 6.4 miles. After 6.9 miles, turn right onto Forest Service Road 4N88. After traveling 2.2 miles (9.1 from 108) on this road, you reach a junction; stay straight to remain on 4N88 (right is 4N86). Continue another 2.1 miles further (11.2 from 108) on 4N88 before turning left onto 4N85. Go 2.9 miles on this road to Sand Bar Flat Campground. Total distance from 108 is 14.1 miles.

Other Stanislaus National Forest Trails

Located just north of Yosemite on the western slopes of the Sierra Nevada Mountains, the Stanislaus National Forest consists of 898,099 acres which includes Emigrant Wilderness and large portions of Carson-Iceberg Wilderness. The forest is divided into 4 Ranger Districts: Groveland (along Highway 120), Calaveras (along Highway 4), Mi-Wok (along lower elevations of 108) and Summit (along upper elevations of 108).

The Stanislaus National Forest is named for the Stanislaus River which has its headwaters within the Stanislaus National Forest boundaries. The original name for the Stanislaus River was 'Our Lady of Guadalupe' given in 1806 by a Spanish explorer. It was renamed 'Rio Estanislao' for Estanislao, a Me-Wuk tribal leader who fought the Mexican government. Fremont anglicized the name to 'Stanislaus' in 1844.

In 1891, Congress authorized the establishment of forest reserves in an effort to diminish the rampant cutting of trees and reduce the destruction of forests due to fire. The Stanislaus National Forest Reserve was created in February of 1897. Soon after, a federal law was passed to protect National Forests and the Stanislaus National Forest (SNF) came into being. Originally, the SNF consisted of 995,000 acres and was used for ranching, mining, logging, railroad construction, agriculture, hunting and more.

Known as the 'Land of Many Uses', the Stanislaus National Forest is a popular destination today for many outdoor enthusiasts. There are over 800 miles of rivers and streams which attract fishermen, boaters, campers, picnickers and hikers and are also used to generate electricity. The area is infused with a large number of OHV trails that are used by all-terrain vehicles most months and snowmobiles in the winter. The granitic peaks and walls are popular with rock climbers. In the fall, hunters flock to the forest. The many miles of trails used by mountain bike riders, horsemen and hikers most months are available for use by cross-country skiers and those on snowshoes during the winter. Ranching and logging still continue today in the forest. Despite these many uses, you can still find places to hike in near solitude.

Although many of the trails found in this book are located in the Stanislaus National Forest, most of them have been listed in more specific book sections due to the unique settings of these areas (Emigrant Wilderness, Carson- Iceberg Wilderness, Middle Fork of the Stanislaus River Canyon, South Fork of the Stanislaus River Canyon, many of the Interpretive Trails, and certain Ditch Trails). The hikes that are listed here in this section are those without a home in other sections; however, it does not make them any less special.

Photo: Waterfall along Herring Creek

Eagle Meadow from Dardanelles Resort Trailhead

Highlights: This hike is a strenuous climb up through the shady, heavily forested Eagle Creek drainage to the easy grade through Lower Eagle Meadow, then across numerous creeks before the final ascent to Eagle Meadow. It offers great views of the Dardanelles, Bald Peak and Eagle Peak. A popular way to do this hike is using a shuttle and just hiking in the direction from Eagle Meadow to Dardanelles skipping most of the uphill.

Distance: 4.4 miles one-way (8.8 miles roundtrip)

Elevation Changes: Cumulative ascent to Eagle Meadow is ~1680 ft and ~190 ft on the return trip; elevation ~5900-7550 ft

Difficulty: Strenuous in terms of elevation change for the roundtrip hike; easy for the return direction

Seasonality: This trail is best during summer months to fall. There are wildflowers and more water in the creeks earlier in the season. The roads to this area are closed during winter months.

User Groups/Permits: The trail is used by hikers, horseback riders and mountain bike riders. Motorized vehicles are prohibited. Permits are not needed to park or day hike.

Parking/Facilities: There is limited parking at the start of the hike. There are no facilities at the trailhead but there are vault toilets in the Eagle Meadow Horse Camp across from the turnaround point in the hike.

Topographic Map: USGS Dardanelle, CA Quadrangle (7.5 Minute Series)

Hike Description: The trail begins at the Eagle Meadow Trailhead sign. Follow the dirt track up the hill past cabins following the signs. Turn left (uphill) onto an actual trail at the last cabin (Cabin 4 Fallen Fir). You then cross numerous streams (or dry creek beds depending on the season) with the largest one being at ~0.2 miles. You pass a water tank off to the right at 0.3 miles and begin to hear Eagle Creek down below you to the right for a short bit. At ~0.5 miles, there is a good spot to stop and view the Dardanelles to the northwest and Eagle Creek down below. The Dardanelles continue to be in view on and off (when you turn around) as you head up the steep section of the trail. Bald Peak also comes into view in the northwest once you get higher. At ~1.4 miles, you reach a plateau where you can catch your breath for a short while. Soon after you cross a small stream and near ~1.5 miles you begin to climb again but less steeply. You begin a short downhill at ~1.9 miles to some creek crossings just over 2 miles into the hike. At this point you walk along a flat shelf. At nearly 2.3 miles, you cross a large drainage then begin to climb to a knob, steeply at first then more gradually as you continue to ~2.6 miles. At the top of the knob you descend and on your descent, you should note a sign that tells you the trail goes left at the 'Y'. Once you are nearly to the bottom, there is another sign for travelers going in the other direction (at ~2.8 miles). You have now reached another flat section. Prepare for numerous stream crossings: the first is at ~2.9 miles, then Eagle Creek at ~3.1 miles (before heading through Lower Eagle Meadow at the edge of the forest), Eagle Creek again at ~3.5 miles and finally, a significant feeder creek into Eagle Creek at just past 3.6 miles. After crossing the 'feeder creek', you begin a significant climb up to Eagle Meadow. At nearly 3.8 miles, follow the directional sign for horses (and people!). The original trail past this section was damaged by the fall of a large tree but the 'horse' trail is fairly obvious. At ~4.1 miles, you start to see glimpses of Eagle Peak in the distance and just past 4.2 miles you reach a 'Y'. The sign indicates that you should go right as the left branch takes you onto private property (the direction of the original trail). Take the right, cross the creek but then leave the trail and follow the creek upstream for ~0.1 miles until you reach Eagle Meadow Road; there is a cow camp across the road to the left and the Eagle Meadow Horse Camp to the right. This is the turnaround point. [Note: the trail that heads off to the right after crossing the creek goes into the woods for a long ways and away from Eagle Meadow Road which is not what you want.]

Trail Tidbits: The Dardanelles Resort was established in 1923 and offers a multitude of services including a general store, restaurant and bar, cabins, motel and RV park. It is located near the confluence of Eagle Creek with the Middle Fork of the Stanislaus River. The resort most likely was named for the Dardanelles structures visible in the northwest. Near the resort is the historic Dardanelles Bridge built in 1933 which once carried Highway 108 traffic over the Middle Fork.

Need to Know: The water in the creeks can be flowing heavily in the early part of the summer making crossings more difficult. There is little access to water from the beginning of the trail until you begin to cross creeks at ~2 miles; be sure to pack enough water. Cattle graze in this area during the summer months. Sections of the trail consist of loose rock on top of larger rocks making the trail slippery; watch your footing going downhill.

Want More? A loop is not possible with this hike. If you want more, you can continue onward from here and do the loop through Eagle Meadow (see Eagle Meadow Loop hike).

Directions to Trailhead: Go east on 108 past Strawberry. Turn right on the dirt road just past the Eagle Creek Bridge (0.2 miles past the first Dardanelles Resort entrance). Stay left for 0.2 miles until you cross a creek bed. The next few right turns after the creek bed are driveways but ~0.3 miles from 108 there is a right turn into a dirt parking area. Turn right here and note the sign that says Eagle Meadow Trailhead. Total distance from 108 is 0.3 miles.

Photo: Eagle Peak as viewed from Eagle Meadow

Herring Creek Trail

Highlights: This trail offers views of Herring Creek Reservoir nestled amongst Stanislaus National Forest mountain peaks and then showcases one beautiful wilderness meadow after another as you head up to the confluence of Herring Creek and Willow Creek and then follow Herring Creek upstream along a trail that gently ascends to level plateaus.

Distance: ~3.5 miles (7.0 miles roundtrip) to sign that says 'Main Trail'

Elevation Changes: Cumulative ascent is <200 ft on the way out and <20 ft on the return trip; elevation ~7580-7780 ft

Difficulty: Moderately easy in terms of elevation changes

Seasonality: This trail is best during early to mid-summer; the wildflowers are rampant during late spring to early summer. The amount of water decreases in the creeks and the reservoir by late summer. The roads to this area are closed during the winter.

User Groups/Permits: The trail is used by hikers, fishermen and horseback riders. No motorized vehicles are allowed. No permits are needed to park or day hike. No fees are charged for overnight stays in the campground.

Parking/Facilities: There is a parking area at the end of the road at the back of the campground. There is a vault toilet located in the campground.

Topographic Map: USGS Donnell Lake, CA Quadrangle (7.5 minute series)

Hike Description: Follow the trail that starts on the other side of the gate. Stay to the left when there appears to be a split in the trail (the right takes you to an old campground area). At ~0.3 miles from the parking area, you should note another campground area to the right. This area is designated for walk-in campers only and is also where you pick up the trail to the reservoir's dam. To continue the hike, stay on the main trail. At ~0.5 miles into the hike, you get your first views of Herring Creek Reservoir. The trail continues along the edge of the reservoir and at ~0.8 miles, you reach the confluence of Herring Creek (the stream closest to you) and Willow Creek in the middle of a gorgeous meadow. The trail continues alongside Herring Creek and ~1 mile into the hike, you should hear a waterfall on the creek. Veer off-trail to get a peek at it. The trail continues meandering alongside the creek up through Hammill Canyon, occasionally climbing gently and passing through somewhat dense stands of trees and then open pockets of meadows. At ~3.5 miles you reach a sign that says 'Main Trail'. This sign is the turnaround point for this hike as the hike difficulty changes considerably (the trail begins climbing uphill until it reaches 4N12).

Trail Tidbits: Herring Creek Reservoir, originally named Herrin Reservoir, was created in 1857 (during the Gold Rush era) as a water storage area for mining operations downstream. It was one of 5 water storage areas in the county at the time; the others were Lyons, Lower Strawberry, Middle Strawberry and Big or Upper Strawberry. Herring Creek Reservoir was the only one of the 5 reservoirs created by damming a feeder creek (Herring Creek) rather than the South Fork of the Stanislaus River. Herring Creek merges with the South Fork of the Stanislaus just downstream of Pinecrest Lake.

Need to Know: The meadow areas can be boggy during late spring and early summer which attracts droves of mosquitoes. Be prepared for this, particularly if you are out in the early morning or early evening. Cattle graze throughout the area.

Want More? There is not an easy loop to do with this hike. However, if you want more, take the trail indicated by the 'Main Trail' sign and climb ~600 ft over the next 1.7 miles to 4N12. Once you reach the road, turn right and go <0.1 miles. Turn left into a dirt area and take the trail that heads off to the left of the dirt area and parallels the creek. It brings you to grassy Bloomer Lake within 0.2 miles. The total additional distance one-way is now 1.9 miles.

Directions to Trailhead: Go east on 108 past Strawberry and take Herring Creek Road. Continue on this road for ~6.8 miles until you reach a 'T' (it becomes Forest Service Road 4N12 at ~4.5 miles and is no longer paved at ~5.5 miles). At the 'T', turn right onto the 4N12 loop. When the road reaches a 'Y', take the left branch for 0.1 miles (Forest Service Road 5N50Y). After another 0.1 miles, turn left and cross the creek into Herring Reservoir Campground. Follow the campground road to the end (another 0.1 miles) and park when you see the gate. Total distance from 108 is ~7.1 miles.

Mt. Elizabeth Peak and Fire Lookout Tower

Highlights: This is a pleasant mountain hike on a dirt road that climbs through a mixed forest of sugar pine, ponderosa pine, cedar, fir, dogwood and oak that has spectacular panoramic views particularly from the top of the forest service fire lookout tower. The road is located just outside of downtown Twain Harte.

Distance: ~1.5 miles (3.0 miles roundtrip) from suggested parking area

Elevation Changes: Cumulative ascent is ~650 ft ascent from suggested parking area to fire lookout tower; elevation ~4300-4950 ft

Difficulty: Moderate in terms of elevation change

Seasonality: This trail is suitable for all seasons but may be covered with snow at times in the winter. The dogwoods are spectacular in the spring. The trail gets dusty in spots in the summer and the 'eye flies' appear when conditions are dry. During the fire season, the forest service fire tower is open to the public during daytime hours. Fire season varies from year to year but typically is summer to early fall.

User Groups/Permits: The road is used by mountain bikers, walkers, horseback riders and some motorized vehicles. No permits are needed to park or use the trail.

Parking/Facilities: The road is accessible to motorized vehicles meaning you can drive to the top in vehicles with good traction; however, if you wish to make it a reasonably distanced hike, park somewhere along Mt. Elizabeth Road. I suggest that you park at the pull-out area off to the right just past where the paved road ends. If you park further up Mt. Elizabeth, the distance hiked will be shorter. There are no facilities here or along the road.

Topographic Map: USGS Twain Harte, CA Quadrangle (7.5 minute series)

Hike Description: Start up the road from the gravel pull-out area. In 0.1 miles, the road will make a sharp left hook. Continue up the road until you come to a 'Y' about 0.4 miles into the hike. The left branch is a private drive; take the right branch to continue up the mountain. You are now on Forest

Service Road 2N03Y. There is a somewhat cleared area ('landing') off to the right shortly after you turn onto 2N03Y; stay on the main track veering left. At 0.65 miles, you encounter the first of 2 green gates on the left that block access to private property; stay on the main dirt road. At nearly 1 mile, you reach a forest service gate that seems to stay open all the time. Continue up the mountain getting glimpses of great views to the east through the trees. At 1.2 miles you reach another 'Y'. The left branch takes you up to the fire lookout tower and the peak of Mt. Elizabeth and the right branch heads to a plateau and then to a trail that leads to lower Cedar Ridge; stay left. There is another forest service gate at 1.35 miles and at this point you can see the forest service fire lookout tower rising above the trees. It is ~1.5 miles to the enclosure around the tower.

Trail Tidbits: In days past, Mt. Elizabeth was known for its gold mines. Today, there are remnants of mining activity in various areas of the mountain. Mt. Elizabeth also boasts one of the last manned fire lookout towers. If it is fire season and the enclosure around the fire tower is open, head on up the stairs to the top of the tower to take in the 360 degree views. These days it is only manned during daytime hours. The people who man the tower are friendly and give lots of topographic information about the peaks and lakes that you can see. Be sure to sign in as a guest in the log book.

Need to Know: There is no running or standing water along this road and only non-potable water at the tower. The 2N03Y portion of the road is in the Stanislaus National Forest where all forest rules apply. The Mt. Elizabeth portion of the road travels through land that is privately owned; please stay on the road. If there is an active forest fire, the tower is off limits to the public so that personnel can focus on their job.

Want A Loop? If you are adventurous, you can turn this hike into a moderately difficult loop (after taking in the view). Head around the back of the lookout enclosure and turn left towards another fenced area with cell towers. Head right at this fenced area and follow the power lines down the mountain. This is a **VERY STEEP, RUGGED** trail that drops nearly 900 ft in just over 0.5 miles with lots of loose rock. This rutty, narrow trail takes you down onto Forest Service Road 2N26 (also called Mt. Elizabeth Drive). Cross it and head down a small dirt path that leads you to stairs on the right; take these down to the ditch trail. Turn left and walk the ditch trail until you reach Mt. Elizabeth Road. Head left at the road and walk back to where you parked. This loop is ~4.3 miles with a total elevation gain of ~865 ft.

Directions to Trailhead: Go east on 108 and take the lower Twain Harte Drive exit into Twain Harte (1.8 miles). Go under the arch onto Joaquin Gully Road. Stay on this road until the junction with Middle Camp and Mt. Elizabeth Road (another mile). At this intersection, you want to make a very slight left onto Mt. Elizabeth Road. Drive for another 1.1 miles until you reach the end of the pavement. Total distance from 108 is 3.9 miles.

Photo: Mt. Elizabeth Fire Lookout Tower

Carson-Iceberg Wilderness Trails

The Carson-Iceberg Wilderness was designated as a federal wilderness area in 1984. It encompasses just over 161,000 acres that spread east and west from the Sierra Nevada crest and north and south between Highways 108 and 4. Nearly half of the wilderness area is found in the Humboldt-Toiyabe National Forest and the other half is part of the Stanislaus National Forest. The Pacific Crest Trail travels 26 miles along its crest from Sonora Pass on Highway 108 to Ebbetts Pass on Highway 4.

The Carson-Iceberg Wilderness has a distinctive name. The 'Carson' portion is named for its main watershed, the Carson River. Fremont named the river after Kit Carson, who was a scout for one of Fremont's expeditions in the area. They crossed the Sierra Nevada Mountains from the east, near current day Carson Pass. The 'Iceberg' attachment is derived from the granitic iceberg-like structure found across Iceberg Meadow and along Disaster Creek in the southern region of the wilderness area.

This high elevation region has a rugged beauty. It is known for its deep river canyons, small waterfalls, year-round creeks fed by numerous springs, meadow-filled valleys and few lakes. There are over 12 peaks that top out above 10,000 ft. The lowest elevation of the area is 5,000 ft around Donnell Reservoir and the highest is over 11,400 ft at the top of Sonora Peak. Although mostly granitic, there are volcanic peaks and ridges throughout the wilderness area, including the Dardanelles, which are structures recognized from far distances.

There a number of trailheads for Carson-Iceberg Wilderness along the 108 corridor. They include St. Mary's Pass, Seven Pines, Clark Fork, Disaster Creek, Arnot Creek, Wheats Meadow and County Line. There is at least 1 hike leaving from each of these trailheads in this book, with the exception of Seven Pines. When you are out on these trails, you will encounter an abundance of water in creeks and streams yet you will see few people (with the exception of trails leaving from the County Line Trailhead). This wilderness area, in comparison to others, is one less traveled, most likely due to the scarcity of lakes, the steepness of some of its trails and the minimal amounts of signage found along the trails.

Arnot Creek Trail

Highlights: This hike offers a wide and shady, forested trail along the rushing, cool waters of Arnot Creek with minimal elevation gain. Along the way, you are treated to some lush meadows and deep pools as well as views of Lightning Mountain, Iceberg Peak and Airola Peak.

Distance: ~2.0 miles to the junction for Woods Gulch and Upper Gardner Meadow (~4.0 miles roundtrip)

Elevation Changes: Cumulative ascent to the junction is ~220 ft and ~150 ft on the return trip; elevation ~6100-6400 ft

Difficulty: Moderately easy in terms of elevation change

Seasonality: This trail is best during summer or fall months and can be attempted on warmer days as there is a reasonable amount of cover. The roads to this area are closed during winter months.

User Groups/Permits: The trail is used by hikers, backpackers and horseback riders. Motorized vehicles are prohibited. Permits are not needed to park or day hike but wilderness permits are required for any overnight stays. Fees are charged at the campgrounds along the Clark Fork River.

Parking/Facilities: There is limited parking near the trailhead sign. There are no facilities here or on the trail; however, there are facilities found at the picnic and camping areas along Clark Fork Road.

Topographic Map: USGS Dardanelles Cone, CA Quadrangle (7.5 Minute Series)

Hike Description: The trailhead sign marks the start of the trail. Initially, you travel through a thinned forested area until you reach the Carson-Iceberg Wilderness boundary sign with the creek becoming audible off to the right at ~0.3 miles. Now that you are in the wilderness area, the forest becomes thicker but the tract still remains wide, cushiony and predominantly level with a few gentle hills. You cross a decent-sized stream at ~0.9 miles and some smaller streams nearly 0.5 and 0.7 miles further. You cross a substantial feeder stream near its junction with Arnot Creek at ~1.9 miles.

The trail junction for Woods Gulch and Upper Gardner Meadow (and the turnaround point) is <0.1 miles further at nearly 2.0 miles into the hike. There is a nice meadow just north of the creek junction (but before the trail junction) that looks inviting for picnicking and resting.

Trail Tidbits: Arnot Peak and Creek were named for an Alpine County Superior Court Judge (1879-1904) named Nathaniel Arnot. Arnot Peak is one of the dozen peaks in Carson-Iceberg Wilderness that is over 10,000 ft. Airola Peak (visible near the junction with the creek) is named for John and Emma Airola who homesteaded in Calaveras County in the 1890's and ran cattle in the area in the early 1900's. The trail option to the left at the junction takes you to Woods Gulch. This gulch (as well as Wood Lake in Emigrant Wilderness) is named for a cattleman, Bill Wood.

Need to Know: Cattle graze this area during the summer. The creeks are substantial even late in the season; be careful crossing them (particularly early in the season when snow melt adds to the volume of water).

Want A Loop? There is a loop option but it involves a substantially greater distance (total of more than 15 miles) and elevation change and requires a shuttle between this trailhead and Disaster Creek Trailhead. To do this loop, take the right trail branch towards Upper Gardner Meadow then pick up the trail down Disaster Creek to the Disaster Creek Trailhead. If you want more but do not wish to do this gargantuan loop, head up either trail for a short ways to explore the area. The trail to Woods Gulch is the left branch at the trail junction; this trail crosses the large feeder creek and then begins to climb via switchbacks up to a ridge that gives you some great views.

Directions to Trailhead: Go east on 108 past Donnell Lake Scenic Vista until Clark Fork Road. Turn left onto Clark Fork Road and go 0.8 miles. After crossing the second bridge, stay on Clark Fork Road which veers to the right. Continue on the road for another 4.8 miles (5.6 miles total). Turn left onto Forest Service Road 7N13 that is marked with a sign indicating the Arnot Creek Trailhead. This road passes turnoffs to the left for private camps; stay on the main road. Continue 0.6 miles down this road. Just before the trailhead, there is a big circle parking area. If you veer to the left of the big circle, you can see the Arnot Creek Trailhead sign. Total distance from 108 is 6.2 miles.

Burgson Lake from Wheats Meadow Trailhead

Highlights: This hike offers scenic views of the Dardanelles (striking volcanic formations) and Double Dome Rock across Highway 108, numerous creek crossings, and the destination of a beautiful lake (color photo page 163) that is inset on a granite bench high above Donnell Reservoir. The trail has it challenges, too; it goes up and down repeatedly and the spur trail to Burgson is a primitive one and easy to miss.

Distance: ~3.4 miles to Burgson Lake (~6.8 miles roundtrip)

Elevation Changes: Cumulative ascent to the lake is ~770 ft but ~680 ft on the return trip; elevation ~6400-6700 ft

Difficulty: Strenuous in terms of elevation change

Seasonality: This trail is best during summer to fall months. There are some areas that are exposed which can make for some hot hiking in the heat of summer. The roads to this area are closed during winter months.

User Groups/Permits: The trail is used by hikers, backpackers and horseback riders. Motorized vehicles are prohibited. Permits are not needed to park or day hike but wilderness permits are required for overnight stays.

Parking/Facilities: There is a parking area on the right of Forest Service Road 6N06 across from the trailhead which is on the left. There are no facilities here or on the trail.

Topographic Map: USGS Donnell Lake, CA Quadrangle (7.5 Minute Series)

Hike Description: The hike begins to the left of the trailhead sign and begins to climb for 0.2 miles (passing the wilderness boundary sign in the process) before dropping to a small pond on the left. You begin dropping to a small creek (or dry bed) located at 0.5 miles. At this point you begin a ~0.8 mile climb on switchbacks to a granite bench with some great views of the Dardanelles. From here, you drop to a trail junction at ~1.6 miles. The right branch takes you along Dardanelles Creek up towards a junction with the Sword Lake Trail. The left branch takes you to Wheats Meadow; head left.

From here, the trail drops down to a crossing of Dardanelles Creek at nearly 1.9 miles. You begin to climb again to ~2.1 miles before dropping to a creek (or dry bed) at 2.3 miles. The trail levels out for a short while and you need to watch carefully for the unmarked, not very distinct trail to the left that takes you to Burgson Lake; it is ~1/4 mile from the previously mentioned creek bed. This trail takes you out onto a granite bench. You head in a generally downward direction veering a bit to the right; if you lose the trail, keep heading in this direction. The trail will bring you to the north side of the lake ~3.4 miles into the hike.

Trail Tidbits: Burgson Lake is most likely named for cattleman Ed Burgson who owned the B & G Cattle Company in Sonora and grazed cattle in the area. Although Carson-Iceberg was designated as a wilderness area in 1984, grazing still continues today. This is because grazing rights were established in the 1880's and have been passed down through generations of family. There are 10 specific grazing allotments in the Carson-Iceberg Wilderness (9 for cattle, 1 for sheep) and the grazing is monitored by the US Forest Service and regulated through a grazing management plan. Cattlemen pay a fee to the US Forest Service annually to graze cattle in the high country.

Need to Know: The trail to Burgson Lake is primitive and disappears at times on the granite shelving; if you follow the general direction it is heading, you can find the trail again. The dust on the trail can become quite thick during the summer due to the stock animals that are brought into the area. Other sections are rocky. This area is grazed during the summer.

Want A Loop? To do a loop, you could go cross-country to Wheats Meadow by heading northwest. [Note: only attempt this if you are familiar with cross-country travel and have skills using a compass and topographic map.] Once you are at Wheats Meadow, you can take the main trail back to the trailhead. If you just want more and don't want to travel cross-country, head back to the main trail, head left and take it into Wheats Meadow. Return on the same trail to the trailhead.

Directions to Trailhead: Go east on 108 past Donnell Lake Scenic Vista until Clark Fork Road. Turn left onto Clark Fork Road and go 0.8 miles. After crossing the second bridge turn left onto Forest Road 6N06. Drive 3.9 miles until you see the Wheats Meadow Trailhead sign on the left. Total distance from 108 is 4.7 miles.

Clark Fork River Trail

Highlights: This hike offers a shady, forested trail along the clear, cool and well-fed Clark Fork River with a moderate amount of elevation gain. There are numerous stopping places along the river to cool your feet or listen to the rushing river while appreciating the scenery.

Distance: ~2.6 miles to junction with Boulder Creek (~5.2 miles roundtrip)

Elevation Changes: Cumulative ascent to the junction with Boulder Creek is ~500 ft and ~100 ft on the return trip; elevation ~6600-7050 ft

Difficulty: Moderate in terms of elevation change

Seasonality: This trail is best during summer and autumn months and can be attempted on warmer days as there is a reasonable amount of cover. The roads to this area are closed during winter months.

User Groups/Permits: The trail is used by hikers, backpackers and horseback riders. Motorized vehicles are prohibited. Permits are not needed to park or day hike but wilderness permits are required for any overnight stays. Fees are charged at the campgrounds along Clark Fork River.

Parking/Facilities: There is a parking area at the end of Clark Fork Road. There are no facilities here or on the trail; however, there are facilities found at the picnic and camping areas along Clark Fork Road.

Topographic Map: USGS Disaster Peak, CA Quadrangle (7.5 Minute Series)

Hike Description: The trailhead sign marks the start of the trail just to the right at the end of Clark Fork Road. The trail then takes you around Iceberg Meadow (enclosed by barbed wire) with views of 'The Iceberg' across the meadow, to the crossing of Disaster Creek at ~0.25 miles. Just past the creek, you pass the wilderness boundary sign and then begin to ascend more than 100 ft over the next 0.2 miles. After the climb, you drop down gradually to the level of the river. For the next ~2 miles, you encounter a few gradual hills with minimal ascents as well as a number of stream (or dry bed) crossings at 1.6, 2.0 and 2.25 miles. At ~2.5 miles, the trail begins to head away from the river and climbs ~85 ft until reaching the trail marker that indicates the junction of the Clark Fork Trail with the trail to Boulder Lake. Boulder Creek is just past the trail marker to the right and is the turnaround point for this hike.

Trail Tidbits: The Clark Fork River is a primary watershed for the Carson-Iceberg Wilderness. It feeds into the Middle Fork of the Stanislaus River (upstream of Donnell Reservoir). The Clark Fork was named for the commissioner of Tuolumne County in 1862. Clark and other commission members from 3 counties were given the task to find and build a wagon road that connected Sonora with the eastern side of the Sierras; they chose a route along today's Clark Fork River up to St. Mary's Pass and then on to Sonora Pass. The road, when built, actually followed the Middle Fork of the Stanislaus River up to Kennedy Meadows then Sonora Pass, thereby avoiding the steep terrain on the approach to St. Mary's Pass.

Need to Know: There are cattle that are grazed in this area during the summer. I have also noted biting flies along the trail. Be aware that afternoon thunderstorms can arrive rapidly so plan accordingly.

Want More? It is not possible to do an easy loop along this trail; however, if you would like to add more mileage to your hike, continue another ~1.2 miles up the Boulder Lake Trail to Boulder Lake or stay on the original trail, cross Boulder Creek and continue upwards. There are some waterfalls <0.5 miles further up the Clark Fork River Trail. The trail does take you all the way to Clark Fork Meadow (~5.4 miles further), but the trail becomes sketchy as you climb a granitic section up to the meadow.

Directions to Trailhead: Go east on 108 past Donnell Lake Scenic Vista until Clark Fork Road. Turn left onto Clark Fork Road and go 0.8 miles. After crossing the second bridge, stay on Clark Fork Road which veers to the right. Continue on the road until it ends (another 8.3 miles). Total distance from 108 is 9.1 miles.

Photo: Bear on the Clark Fork River Trail

Disaster Creek Trail

Highlights: This hike offers a shady, forested trail along the rushing, cool waters of Disaster Creek with significant elevation gain, particularly at the start of the trail. Along the way, you are treated to close-up views of 'The Iceberg' (color photo page 168) as well as more distant views of Red Peak, Bald Peak, Lightning Mountain and Disaster Peak.

Distance: ~3.0 miles to the junction for Paradise Valley and Gardner Meadow at Adams Camp (~6.0 miles roundtrip)

Elevation Changes: Cumulative ascent to Adams Camp is ~1200 ft and ~10 ft on the return trip; elevation ~6600-7850 ft

Difficulty: Difficult in terms of elevation change

Seasonality: This trail is best during summer or autumn months and can be attempted on warmer days as there is a reasonable amount of cover. The roads to this area are closed during winter months.

User Groups/Permits: The trail is used by hikers, backpackers and horseback riders. Motorized vehicles are prohibited. Permits are not needed to park or day hike but wilderness permits are required for any overnight stays. Fees are charged at the campgrounds along Clark Fork River.

Parking/Facilities: There is limited parking near the trailhead sign off of Clark Fork Road. There are no facilities here or on the trail; however, there are facilities found at the picnic and camping areas along Clark Fork Road.

Topographic Map: USGS Disaster Peak and Dardanelles Cone, CA Quadrangles (7.5 Minute Series)

Hike Description: The trailhead sign marks the start of the trail. For the first mile, you climb steadily via switchbacks with Disaster Creek audible on the left. On your way upward, you pass the wilderness boundary sign at <0.25 miles from the trailhead. Unobstructed views of 'The Iceberg' occur on the right just before the first mile ends. Shortly after, there are small waterfalls on Disaster Creek. Just past 1.1 miles into the hike, there is a faint trail that takes you down to some pools on Disaster Creek. This is a nice spot to sit and take in your surroundings. The trail at this point still climbs but not as steeply as before. You cross some small streams at ~1.3 and ~1.6 miles before reaching a plateau. You cross an open meadow that is quite swampy due to springs at ~2.1 miles. Additional climbing is required ~0.2 miles further up the trail. At ~2.7 miles there is a faint, unmarked trail heading off towards the right and Disaster Peak. You cross the main feeder creek for Disaster Creek just before Adams Camp and the junction with Paradise Valley and Gardner Meadow Trails. This trail junction is at 3 miles and is the turnaround point for this hike.

Trail Tidbits: Disaster Peak earned its name when the topographer for the Wheeler Party, in 1878, loosened a boulder causing him to fall 15 ft. In the fall, the boulder rolled over him and broke both of his legs. The creek was soon referred to as Disaster Creek. 'The Iceberg' is a large granitic formation that looks like its namesake, looming over Disaster Creek and surrounding areas. It was most likely named by the US Geologic Survey; however, it appeared on later map editions than Iceberg Peak, located elsewhere in the Carson-Iceberg Wilderness. At first, the Iceberg area was destined to be an administrative site for the US Forest Service but these plans were abandoned.

Need to Know: There are cattle that are grazed in this area during the summer. Parts of the trail can be thick with dust and other areas are rocky.

Want A Loop? There are a couple of loops that you could do but both would entail high mileage and additional amounts of climbing. The shorter loop would require a shuttle car at Arnot Creek Trailhead. For this option, take the left trail at the Adams Camp junction to Upper Gardner Meadow. From there, take the Arnot Creek Trail back to the Arnot Creek Trailhead. For the longer loop, take the right trail at the Adams Camp junction to Paradise Valley. Follow this trail until it reaches the Pacific Crest Trail; head right until you reach the primitive trail down to Boulder Lake. Continue past Boulder Lake on the primitive trail until you reach the Clark Fork River Trail; turn right and take this to the Clark Fork Trailhead which is just down the road from the Disaster Creek Trailhead.

Directions to Trailhead: Go east on 108 past Donnell Lake Scenic Vista until Clark Fork Road. Turn left onto Clark Fork Road and go 0.8 miles. After crossing the second bridge, stay on Clark Fork Road which veers to the right. Continue on the road until just before it ends (another 8.3 miles). Look for the trailhead on the left. Total distance from 108 is 9.1 miles.

Iceberg Meadow from Saint Mary's Pass Trailhead

Highlights: This hike offers great views from Saint Mary's Pass (color photo page 170), an interesting cross-country descent to Clark Fork Meadow, spring and creek crossings, waterfalls with the drop of the Clark Fork River through steep gorges and numerous stopping places to rest along the river. Once you reach the river, the trail is primarily shaded with mixed conifer trees and occasional aspen stands. If you do this hike one-way (with a shuttle), the majority of the uphill is at the start when you climb Saint Mary's Pass; after reaching the pass, you primarily descend along the river until reaching Iceberg Meadow at the Clark Fork Trailhead. This hike does involve some cross-country travel; you need to feel comfortable navigating without a trail.

Distance: ~11.5 miles to Iceberg Meadow at the Clark Fork Trailhead (use a shuttle for the one-way hike)

Elevation Changes: Cumulative ascent to the top of Saint Mary's Pass is ~900 ft and an additional ~380 ft to the Clark Fork Trailhead; elevation ~6600-10400 ft

Difficulty: Difficult in terms of elevation change

Seasonality: This trail is best during mid-late summer and early fall; it should not be attempted at the start of summer as there may be too much water flowing in the river and streams. The roads to this area are closed during winter months.

User Groups/Permits: The trail is used by hikers, backpackers and horseback riders. Motorized vehicles are prohibited. Permits are not needed to park or day hike but wilderness permits are required for any overnight stays. Fees are charged at the campgrounds along Clark Fork River Road.

Parking/Facilities: There is a parking area at the Saint Mary's Pass Trailhead as well as at the end of the Clark Fork Road at Iceberg Meadow. There are no facilities at either of these locations; however, there are facilities found at the picnic and camping areas along Clark Fork Road.

Topographic Map: USGS Disaster Peak and Sonora Pass, CA Quadrangles (7.5 Minute Series)

Hike Description: The trail starts with an uphill jaunt from Saint Mary's Pass Trailhead to the gap that is visible to the left (Saint Mary's Pass). Enjoy the views as you ascend: Sonora Peak off to the northeast (right), Leavitt Peak to the south (across 108), Tower Peak to the southeast and even 'The Three Chimneys' to the southwest. You reach the summit and wilderness boundary sign in ~1.1 miles. The trail splits into 3 branches here. The right branch takes you to Sonora Peak and the faint left branch peters out very soon. You want to take the trail that is straight and heads gently downhill. This trail leads you to Stanislaus Peak (now visible ahead of you); however, you need to peel off of this trail in ~0.2 miles to head downhill towards Clark Fork Meadow visible in the distance. Some maps show this as an actual trail but others show no trail. Regardless, if there is or was a trail, it has not been maintained and is no longer identifiable. Jump off the trail when you see a small drainage off to the left and head down it cross-country. As the draw becomes steeper, skirt to the right to find the easiest way down. Keep working your way to the right and downhill; avoid the dense volcanic rock to the far right. Once you have reached the canyon floor, walk along the left side of the river to drop further down to Clark Fork Meadow. At some point you might see 'ducks' along the way to mark a 'trail' but they do not appear consistently. Once you reach the Clark Fork Meadow, head to the far end of it on the right side of the river. As you leave the meadow, the going is easy as you walk along the river but then the river begins to drop steeply through narrow gorges. At this point, you want to head much further right, finding an easier path down. Again, there are 'ducks' here and there to mark 'a trail' but then they disappear. Once you have reached the bottom of the steep section, head closer to the river. A trail appears and leads you through brushy willows along streams that empty into the Clark Fork River. This trail seems to disappear and reappear regularly for another 0.5 miles or so; the key is to stay near the river and continue to follow it downhill until you reach the well-established trail. At ~7.4 miles into the hike, you can see a faint trail that heads off to the left. This is the trail junction with the Seven Pines Trail which crosses the river and begins to work its way uphill. Continue on the main trail and ~1 mile from the Seven Pines Trail junction (8.4 miles total), there are numerous waterfalls as the river plunges down more steep gorges providing plenty of picture-taking opportunities. After the waterfalls and before Iceberg Meadow, there are ample beaches to sit and cool your feet in the river. You cross Boulder Creek and reach the Boulder Creek Trail junction at ~8.9 miles into the hike. Continue on your mostly downhill trek towards the wilderness boundary sign and Disaster Creek at ~11.3 miles. The Clark Fork Trailhead is ~0.2 miles further.

Trail Tidbits: There are cattle that are grazed in this area during the summer. Ranchers that graze cattle in the mountains tend to drive them out at the end of September or into early October before the onset of winter weather. Be aware that cattle drives can occur on Clark Fork Road. Unfortunately, it is frustrating getting stuck behind slow-moving bovine for several miles! The earliest settlers, the Bartleson-Bidwell Party, crossed the Sierras in 1841 and came through this area, following the Clark Fork River from Disaster Creek to the Middle Fork of the Stanislaus River.

Need to Know: A portion of this hike is done without a trail. You should feel comfortable with cross-country travel and be able to use a compass, map or GPS device to help you navigate. Hiking poles could be useful on this hike as footing can be tricky in places. Be sure to allot extra time for the shuttle. A car needs to be left at Saint Mary's Pass Trailhead as well as the Clark Fork Trailhead. There are numerous stream and creek crossings; the water is cold and flowing swiftly early in the season.

Want a Loop? It would be fairly difficult to do a loop without adding many more miles and a ton more climbing. If you are game though, you can turn right onto the primitive Boulder Lake Trail at its junction with the Clark Fork River Trail and take it all the way to the Pacific Crest Trail. At the PCT, turn right and continue to Sonora Pass Trailhead. From here, head down the road nearly 1 mile to the Saint Mary's Pass Trailhead. If you are unable to do the written hike as a shuttle, you can hike roundtrip from Saint Mary's Pass Trailhead to the end of Clark Fork Meadow. This would be ~3.5 miles one-way (~7.0 miles roundtrip) and would involve a cumulative ascent of ~900 ft to the meadow and another climb of ~1400 ft to return to the trailhead (a strenuous hike in terms of elevation changes).

Directions to Trailhead: Go east on 108 past Donnell Lake Scenic Vista until Clark Fork Road. Turn left onto Clark Fork Road and go 0.8 miles. After crossing the second bridge, stay on Clark Fork Road which veers to the right. Continue on the road until it ends (another 8.3 miles). Total distance from 108 to the first shuttle drop off is 9.1 miles. To get to the other trailhead, go back to 108 and head left towards Kennedy Meadows. Just before you reach Sonora Pass Trailhead, you will see a short dirt road off to the left that immediately puts you into the parking area for Saint Mary's Pass Trailhead. You can see the trailhead sign from the road. Total distance from 108 to this trailhead is 0 miles.

Photo: Clark Fork River below the Clark Fork Meadow

McCormick Creek from County Line Trailhead

Highlights: This hike offers scenic views of the Dardanelles and Spicer Meadow Reservoir (if you do the loop) as well as traipses through tranquil meadows and across gurgling creeks. This trail is less traveled and at times difficult to follow. If you plan on doing the loop be prepared for some off-trail hiking always keeping the westernmost Dardanelles on your left.

Distance: ~2.1 miles (~4.2 miles roundtrip)

Elevation Changes: Cumulative ascent is <360 ft on the way out and <90 ft on the return trip; elevation ~7200-7500 ft

Difficulty: Moderately easy in terms of elevation

Seasonality: This trail is best during summer or autumn months. The roads to this area are closed during winter months.

User Groups/Permits: The trail is used by hikers, backpackers and horseback riders. Motorized vehicles are prohibited. Permits are not needed to park or day hike but wilderness permits are required for overnight stays.

Parking/Facilities: There is a parking area at the end of Forest Service Road 6N06 at the County Line Trailhead for this hike. There are no facilities here or on the trail.

Topographic Map: USGS Spicer Meadow, CA Quadrangle (7.5 Minute Series)

Hike Description: Start on the main trail at the trailhead but veer right in ~10 yards on a fainter trail. Less than 0.2 miles into the hike, the trail is overgrown and you need to zig and zag around a tree and then a dead branch. Once around these obstacles, you should be able to find the trail. Do not head off on the remnants of an old road to the left at ~0.3 miles; stay right to head downhill. You cross a small creek at nearly 0.5 miles and just past this creek is the wilderness boundary sign. For the next 0.8 miles, you head up and down through a forested area with small meadows and numerous seasonal rivulets. At ~1.3 miles into the hike, the trail takes you out in a large open meadow and as you walk further into the meadow, the westernmost and southernmost Dardanelles come into view. Cross the meadow for ~0.3 miles fording a number of small creek beds before reaching a short granitic section. The trail continues to parallel the westernmost Dardanelles as it takes you through additional meadows with aspen stands and across more creek beds. At just past 1.9 miles you cross a slightly bigger creek and <0.1 miles later, there is an easy-to- miss trail junction just before a marsh meadow. Even if you miss this junction, cross the marsh meadow over to an open, sandy area with some large boulders off to the left (trail disappears here). Head left towards the boulders (note the campsite) and then veer right to McCormick Creek at a spot where you can reach the water (less willows here).

Photo: The Dardanelles as seen from Highway 108 (from left to right: western, northern, southern and cone structures)

Trail Tidbits: McCormick Creek was named for an early settler although the spelling on earlier maps shows 'McCormack'. An 1879 map indicates that a house existed at that time. The Dardanelles are unique volcanic structures. Locals have nicknames for the individual formations that include 'Elephant Back', 'Bookcase' and 'The Fortress'. There is also the Dardanelles Cone. Use your imagination to figure out which structure is which.

Need to Know: The trail is not always easy to follow, particularly when crossing through meadows. The loop trail (seen on USGS maps) is very difficult to follow, particularly if there is snow on the north-facing side. To do the loop, you need to be comfortable traveling without a trail while circumnavigating the western Dardanelles.

Want A Loop? To do the loop, cross the marsh meadow and find the easy-to-miss junction; turn right. Follow this trail as it heads away from the creek and then parallels a small creek that feeds into McCormick Creek. The trail becomes hard to follow when it reaches a shelf. Find a way up the shelf and then orient yourself to ascend through the saddle between the western and northern Dardanelles. Once you crest the top of the saddle, head down to the meadow visible ~200 ft below. There is a creek running through the meadow; do not cross over it but follow it downstream a short ways. At this point, you might pick up the trail again but if not, hike cross-country around the western Dardanelles trying not to lose too much in elevation. Continue this way for the next ~3 miles, enjoying the views of Spicer Meadow Reservoir and the wilderness areas around it. You finally reach the main trail in a flat-topped meadow area at ~6 miles into the loop. Veering left on the main trail brings you back to the parking area in another 0.75 mile whereas turning right will take you to Sword Lake. Roundtrip distance is 6.75 miles for a moderately difficult hike.

Directions to Trailhead: Go east on 108 past Donnell Lake Scenic Vista until Clark Fork Road. Turn left onto Clark Fork Road and go 0.8 miles. After crossing the second bridge turn left onto Forest Service Road 6N06. Drive 6.3 miles to the end of the road ignoring the smaller side roads (4 miles down this road you will pass Wheats Meadow Trailhead). Total distance from 108 is 7.1 miles.

Photo: The southern Dardanelles structure as seen from McCormick Creek (photo by Wendy Hesse)

Sonora Peak from Saint Mary's Pass Trailhead

Highlights: After a butt-busting climb, you are rewarded with incredible 360 degree views and a huge sense of accomplishment!

Distance: ~2.0 miles to Sonora Peak (~4.0 miles roundtrip)

Elevation Changes: Cumulative ascent to the top of Saint Mary's Pass is ~900 ft with an additional ~1130 ft to Sonora Peak; elevation ~9430-11460 ft

Difficulty: Strenuous in terms of elevation change   **Photo:** Sonora Peak

Seasonality: This trail is best during mid-late summer and early fall; if snow is on the trail, it may be more difficult to navigate to the peak. The road to this area is closed during winter months.

User Groups/Permits: The trail is used by hikers, backpackers and horseback riders. Motorized vehicles are prohibited. Permits are not needed to park or day hike but wilderness permits are required for overnight stays.

Parking/Facilities: There is a parking area at the Saint Mary's Pass Trailhead. There are no facilities here or on the trail. There is a vault toilet at the Sonora Pass Trailhead ~1 mile further up the road.

Topographic Map: USGS Sonora Pass, CA Quadrangle (7.5 Minute Series)

Hike Description: Follow the trail next to the trailhead sign on an upward jaunt to the pass. Enjoy the views as you ascend: Sonora Peak off to the northeast (right), Leavitt Peak to the south (across 108), Tower Peak to the southeast and Nightcap Peak and 'The Three Chimneys' to the southwest.

You reach Saint Mary's Pass and the wilderness boundary sign in ~1.1 miles. The trail splits into 3 branches here. The right branch takes you towards Sonora Peak. The trail peters out after a short climb up to an open bowl where you can see a couple of wilderness boundary markers (use these markers as landmarks on your return trip). Walk uphill across the bowl heading northeast; shoot for the area just to the left of Sonora Peak but to the right of the lower bump on the left spine of the peak. The trail picks up again once you have crossed the bowl. Follow the trail up to the peak and take some time to savor the views.

Trail Tidbits: Sonora Peak and Pass were named for the town of Sonora. Emigrants traveling over the pass in this area were headed to Sonora which was the hub for the southern gold mining camps. The town of Sonora, established in 1848 by Mexican miners, was named for the state of Sonora in Mexico. Sonora Peak is the highest peak in the Carson-Iceberg Wilderness and stands at 11,462 ft.

Need to Know: The area is above tree-line and very exposed. Be aware that afternoon thunderstorms can arrive rapidly so plan accordingly. In addition, protect yourself against the intensity of the sun and the wind at this elevation. The higher you go up the peak, the steeper and rockier it becomes; it helps to stay on the trail where there is less loose rock. Take extra precautions on the descent, particularly if there is snow on the trail.

Want A Loop? From the peak, you can see the Pacific Crest Trail that heads to Sonora Pass. If you want a loop and you feel comfortable and capable of cross-country travel, hike to the PCT (either at Wolf Creek Lake just below White Mountain or directly down the southeast spine of the peak until you encounter the PCT). Turn right at the PCT to head back to Sonora Pass Trailhead and then walk the road down to Saint Mary's Pass Trailhead. Another option, if you want more, is to hike back to St. Mary's Pass, take the trail to Stanislaus Peak then return back to the trailhead for a total roundtrip distance of 9.2 miles (see Stanislaus Peak hike).

Directions to Trailhead: Go east on 108 past Kennedy Meadows (8.3 miles). The trailhead is 1.7 miles past the 9000 ft elevation sign. Look for a short dirt road off to the left that immediately brings you into the parking area for Saint Mary's Pass Trailhead. You can see the trailhead sign from the road. Sonora Pass Trailhead is less than a mile further. Total distance from 108 to this trailhead is 0 miles.

Stanislaus Peak from Saint Mary's Pass Trailhead

Highlights: This hike offers tremendous views the entire trip (color photos page 161 and 170)! After the hefty ascent to Saint Mary's Pass, the trail traverses a wide bowl overlooking the Clark Fork River Canyon with only some additional elevation changes. There are numerous springs throughout the bowl even late in the season; wildflowers abound in the summer.

Distance: ~3.5 miles to the southeast flank of Stanislaus Peak on the granitic section (~7.0 miles roundtrip)

Elevation Changes: Cumulative ascent to the top of Saint Mary's Pass is ~900 ft with an additional ~300 ft to southeast flank of Stanislaus Peak and ~290 ft on the return trip; elevation ~9430-10500 ft

Difficulty: Strenuous in terms of elevation change

Seasonality: This trail is best during mid-late summer and early fall. If snow is on the trail, it may be difficult to navigate to the peak. The road to this area is closed during winter months.

User Groups/Permits: The trail is used by hikers, backpackers and horseback riders. Motorized vehicles are prohibited. Permits are not needed to park or day hike but wilderness permits are required for overnight stays.

Parking/Facilities: There is a parking area at the Saint Mary's Pass Trailhead. There are no facilities here or on the trail.

Topographic Map: USGS Sonora Pass, CA Quadrangle (7.5 Minute Series)

Hike Description: Follow the trail on an upward jaunt to the pass. Enjoy the views as you ascend: Sonora Peak off to the northeast (right), Leavitt Peak to the south (across 108), Tower Peak to the southeast and Nightcap Peak and 'The Three Chimneys' to the southwest. You reach the summit and wilderness boundary sign in ~1.1 miles. The trail splits into 3 branches here. The right branch takes you to Sonora Peak and the faint trail to the left peters out very soon. You want to take the trail that is straight and heads gently downhill. This trail leads you to Stanislaus Peak (now visible ahead of you) by traversing the wide bowl that you are now entering. As you walk along the edge of the bowl, you cross numerous springs which keep the area wet and lush. At ~1.8 miles, you cross a spring and then climb a short distance. The trail then traverses another bowl until you are opposite Stanislaus Peak. Continue to follow the trail as it brings you around to the granitic section on the SE flank of Stanislaus Peak which overlooks a meadow and a primitive trail that heads to Clark Fork Meadow. This is the turnaround point; you can try scrambling up the peak further but the slope is covered with scrub brush and loose volcanic rock making the ascent difficult.

Trail Tidbits: Stanislaus Peak is one of a dozen peaks greater than 10,000 ft in the Carson-Iceberg Wilderness. The moniker 'Stanislaus' has its origins with a Me-Wuk Indian, who was baptized at the San Jose Mission and given the name Estanislao after the Polish saint, Saint Stanislas. Estanislao left the Mission with other converted Native Americans to fight the Mexican Government in California. After he was defeated in 1829, a river was named Rio Estanislao in his honor. Fremont anglicized the name in 1844 to the Stanislaus River. The peak was named Stanislaus Peak, after the river, in the 1870's.

Need to Know: The area is above tree-line and is very exposed. Be aware that afternoon thunderstorms can arrive rapidly so plan accordingly. In addition, protect yourself against the intensity of the sun at this elevation and realize that conditions can also be quite windy. There are numerous stream and creek crossings; the water is cold and flowing swiftly early in the season.

Want A Loop? A very challenging loop would be to take the primitive trail down to Clark Fork Meadow and then follow the head waters of the river upstream until you reach the granitic wall that is just below the bowl you traversed to get to Stanislaus Peak. You would then need to find an easy way (stay on the side closest to Stanislaus Peak) up the wall and into the bowl before ascending back to Saint Mary's Pass. If this sounds like it might be a little too much but you want to do more, then head back to Saint Mary's Pass and then up the trail to Sonora Peak before returning to the trailhead for a total roundtrip distance of 9.2 miles (see Sonora Peak hike).

Directions to Trailhead: Go east on 108 past Kennedy Meadows (8.3 miles). The trailhead is 1.7 miles past the 9000 ft elevation sign. Look for a short dirt road off to the left that immediately brings you into the parking area for Saint Mary's Pass Trailhead. You can see the trailhead sign from the road. Total distance from 108 to this trailhead is 0 miles.

Sword & Lost Lakes from County Line Trailhead

Highlights: This hike offers scenic views of the Dardanelles and Spicer Meadow Reservoir as well as the opportunity to visit 2 lovely lakes. Lost Lake is less visited but Sword Lake has a reputation for being a premier swimming lake.

Distance: ~2.7 miles to Sword Lake (~5.4 miles roundtrip) and ~3.0 miles to Lost Lake (~6 miles roundtrip)

Elevation Changes: Cumulative ascent to the lakes is ~400 ft but ~600 ft on the return trip; elevation ~6850-7400 ft

Difficulty: Moderately difficult in terms of elevation change

Seasonality: This trail is best during summer or autumn months; there are areas with little to no cover so it can be a hot hike particularly on the uphill return. The roads to this area are closed during winter months.

User Groups/Permits: The trail is used by hikers, backpackers (including many large groups) and horseback riders. Motorized vehicles are prohibited. Permits are not needed to park or day hike but wilderness permits are required for any overnight stays.

Parking/Facilities: There is a parking area at the end of Forest Service Road 6N06 at the County Line Trailhead for this hike. There are no facilities here or on the trail.

Topographic Map: USGS Spicer Meadow, CA Quadrangle (7.5 Minute Series)

Hike Description: Follow the main trail that veers left behind the trailhead sign. The trail climbs significantly in the first 0.4 miles. Just before you reach the crest of this ascent, you should see the wilderness boundary sign. When you reach this point, be sure to step off the trail to the left about 10 yards for a scenic view of the Middle Fork of the Stanislaus River Canyon and Double Dome Rock across Highway 108. The trail now skirts the edge of the western Dardanelles with some up and down. At ~0.7 miles you reach a meadow and a view of the granite peaks around Spicer Meadow Reservoir. When you reach the end of the meadow, you begin a ~1.2 mile descent dropping ~500 ft. During this descent, you cross a stream or dry bed (~1.2 miles), squish your way through spring runoff (1.6 miles), see interesting rock formations (~1.75 miles), cross another stream or dry bed (~2 miles) and have some excellent views of the Dardanelles and Spicer Meadow Reservoir. Once you are 2 miles into the hike, the trail gentle meanders through a forest. You pass the first stagnant pond and a sign post (stay straight) at ~2.25 miles then a second stagnant pond at ~2.45 and another trail junction at ~2.6 miles (veer left). At 2.7 miles you can see Sword Lake. A trail to the right takes you around the near side of the lake but to continue on the trail that heads to Lost Lake, head left and up and over a saddle. There are many small trails leading to different parts of Sword Lake; however, follow the one that heads away from the lake for a short while. At ~2.8 miles you reach a 'Y'. Either direction will take you to Lost Lake. The trail that goes left heads through a small campground and then becomes more difficult to follow. It is easier to follow the trail to the right but then you must veer left just before reaching the edge of a marshy part of the lake. From here, head uphill past a large group camping area and just above this camping area, you should see a stagnant pond. Head to the right of this and follow the trail to the lake.

Trail Tidbits: The Carson-Iceberg Wilderness offers a spectrum of elevations that differ by as much as 6000 ft and includes volcanic rock (as seen in the area of the Dardanelles) as well as granitic rock such as the rock that surrounds Sword and Lost Lakes. The Dardanelles, remnants of an ancient volcanic lava flow, are easily visible and recognized throughout various vantage points in the county. They most likely are named for similar rock formations found on 'The Dardanelles', a straight between the Sea of Marmara and the Aegean Sea that connects European Turkey with Asian Turkey.

Need to Know: The trail is quite popular, particularly on weekends and it is not uncommon to find large groups of backpackers using it throughout the week. The dust on the trail can become quite thick, especially by the end of summer, due to the stock animals that are brought into the area. I have also noted biting flies near the trailhead. Be aware that afternoon thunderstorms can arrive rapidly so plan accordingly.

Want A Loop? To do a loop, you could head to the Wheats Meadow Trailhead via the Dardanelles Creek Trail (4.5 miles from Sword Lake); however, you will need to arrange a shuttle to return to your vehicle at

County Line Trailhead or plan to walk up the forest service road for another 2.3 miles to reach County Line Trailhead. Another option, if you want more, would be to loop around Sword and Lost Lakes or head down to Spicer Meadow Reservoir. To get to Spicer, take the trail that skirts to the left side of the stagnant pond just before Lost Lake and head uphill. At the top you reach a granitic area that has ducks or cairns that mark a trail. From here you can see Spicer Meadow Reservoir and you can work your way towards it.

Directions to Trailhead: Go east on 108 past Donnell Lake Scenic Vista until Clark Fork Road. Turn left onto Clark Fork Road and go 0.8 miles. After crossing the second bridge turn left onto Forest Service Road 6N06. Drive 6.3 miles to the end of the road ignoring the smaller side roads (4 miles down this road you will pass Wheats Meadow Trailhead). Total distance from 108 is 7.1 miles.

Photo: Lost Lake

Wheats Meadow from Wheats Meadow Trailhead

Highlights: This hike offers scenic views on top of granite benches, thick forest cover down in creek canyons, views of the Dardanelles (color photo page 162), numerous creek crossings, and the destination of a large, wide-open, beautiful meadow in the midst of the wilderness.

Distance: ~3.2 miles to Wheats Meadow (~6.4 miles roundtrip)

Elevation Changes: Cumulative ascent to the meadow is ~770 ft but ~560 ft on the return trip; elevation ~6400-6700 ft

Difficulty: Difficult in terms of elevation

Seasonality: This trail is best during summer to fall months. There are some areas that are exposed which can make for some hot hiking in the heat of summer. The roads to this area are closed during winter months.

User Groups/Permits: The trail is used by hikers, backpackers and horseback riders. Motorized vehicles are prohibited. Permits are not needed to park or day hike but wilderness permits are required for overnight stays.

Parking/Facilities: There is a parking area on the right of Forest Service Road 6N06 across from the trailhead (on the left). There are no facilities here or on the trail.

Topographic Map: USGS Donnell Lake, CA Quadrangle (7.5 Minute Series)

Hike Description: The hike begins to the left of the trailhead sign and begins to climb for 0.2 miles (passing the wilderness boundary sign in the process) before dropping to a small pond on the left. You continue dropping to a small creek (or dry bed) until you reach 0.5 miles. At this point you begin a ~0.8 mile climb on switchbacks to a granite bench with some great views of the Dardanelles. From here, drop to a trail junction at ~1.6 miles. The right branch takes you along Dardanelles Creek up towards a junction with the Sword Lake Trail. The left branch takes you to Wheats Meadow; head left. From here, the trail drops down to a crossing of Dardanelles Creek at nearly 1.9 miles. You begin to climb again to ~2.1 miles before dropping to a creek (dry bed) at 2.3 miles. The trail levels out for a short while, passes the unmarked primitive trail to Burgson Lake on the left at ~2.55 miles and then climbs to a pond on the right at ~2.8 miles. From here, you drop down to a creek bed which you follow into Wheats Meadow. It is ~3.2 miles to the trail junction at Wheats Meadow Creek where you can see an old, collapsed structure across the creek. This is the turnaround point.

Trail Tidbits: Wheats Meadow and Creek were named for an early settler, named Wheat. Despite the fact that there was no land patent for anyone named Wheat, his house appeared on an 1879 General Land Office plat as well as in surveyor notes. Apparently, the absence of a patent did not prevent Wheat from using the area to live and graze cattle. This area was used by the US Forest Service as an administrative site beginning in 1907.

Need to Know: This area is grazed during the summer. The dust on the trail can become quite thick as the summer progresses due to the stock animals that are brought into the area. Other sections are rocky. Be aware that afternoon thunderstorms can arrive rapidly so plan accordingly.

Want A Loop? To do a loop, you would need to travel on some primitive trails with trail junctions that are not marked. You should only attempt this if you have decent skills reading a topographic map and using a compass since the primitive trails in this area often disappear for short sections. This is particularly true in cow meadows as the cows create numerous 'false' trails. To do this loop, head right at the trail junction at the creek in Wheats Meadow. Follow the creek for a short while and look for a primitive trail that heads to the east near the place where the other trail crosses the creek (and heads to Spicer Reservoir). Take this primitive trail until you reach the Dardanelles Creek Trail junction. Head south (right) on the Dardanelles Creek Trail; it brings you to the trail junction with the Wheats Meadow Trail. Return to the trailhead the way you came.

Directions to Trailhead: Go east on 108 past Donnell Lake Scenic Vista until Clark Fork Road. Turn left onto Clark Fork Road and go 0.8 miles. After crossing the second bridge turn left onto Forest Service Road 6N06. Drive 3.9 miles until you see the Wheats Meadow Trailhead sign on the left. Total distance from 108 is 4.7 miles.

Photo: Stanislaus Peak in Carson-Iceberg Wilderness

Photo: Bear Lake in Emigrant Wilderness

Photo: Dardanelles structure at dusk returning to Wheats Meadow Trailhead in Carson-Iceberg Wilderness

Photo Left: Lahar structure along the Trail of the Gargoyles

Photo Below: Burgson Lake in Carson-Iceberg Wilderness

Photo: Leavitt Peak and Deadman Lake in Emigrant Wilderness

Photo:

Volcanic structures as viewed from Cooper Meadow in Emigrant Wilderness

Photo: Granitic splendor of Emigrant Wilderness near Waterhouse Lake

Photo: Wolf Creek Lake in Humboldt-Toiyabe National Forest

Photo: Creek from Blue Canyon Lake in Emigrant Wilderness

Photo: Bridge over Middle Fork Stanislaus River above Kennedy Meadow

Photo: Top of Table Mountain

Photo: Bell Meadow in Emigrant Wilderness

Photo: 'The Iceberg' as seen from Disaster Creek in Carson-Iceberg Wilderness

Photo: View of Leavitt and Koenig Lakes heading south from Sonora Pass

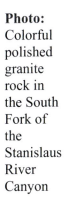
Photo: Colorful polished granite rock in the South Fork of the Stanislaus River Canyon

Photo: View on the way to St. Mary's Pass in Carson-Iceberg Wilderness

Photo: Granitic rock 'ship' on the Middle Fork of the Stanislaus River on the China Flat and Sand Bar Trails

Emigrant Wilderness Trails

The Emigrant Wilderness has been protected since 1931 when it was designated as the Emigrant Basin Primitive Area. In 1975, its status was changed to the Emigrant Wilderness. It consists of 112,277 acres that spread into the shape of a parallelogram, 25 miles wide and 15 miles long. It is located along the Sierra Nevada crest and its western slope, sandwiched between Humboldt-Toiyabe National Forest (east), Yosemite National Park (south), Carson-Iceberg Wilderness and Highway 108 (north) and more of the Stanislaus National Forest (west). The entire wilderness area is part of the Stanislaus National Forest. The Pacific Crest Trail skirts in and out of the northeast edge of the wilderness area.

The Emigrant Wilderness was named after the historic Emigrant Pass (originally referred to as Sonora Pass but located 9 miles south of current Sonora Pass). The West Walker route crossed the Sierra Nevada Mountains through Emigrant Pass and a few emigrant parties successfully managed to reach Sonora using this arduous route. Since the route was deemed too difficult, it never became popular.

Known primarily for its granitic landscapes and alpine lakes, the Emigrant Wilderness is stunning. Although the northeast corner is dominated by volcanic ridges, peaks and rock formations, the remaining part of the wilderness area is predominantly exposed granite ridges, peaks, cones and cliffs. Glacial polishing is evident in a large number of areas. Despite the small size in area, Emigrant Wilderness has more than its fair share of pristine, high elevation lakes and beautiful mountain meadows. Its elevation ranges from 5000 ft around Cherry Lake to 11,570 ft at Leavitt Peak.

There are a number of trailheads for Emigrant Wilderness along the 108 corridor. They include Leavitt Lake, Sonora Pass, Kennedy Meadow, Eagle Meadow, Coyote Meadow, Waterhouse, Gianelli Cabin, Crabtree Camp, Bell Meadow, Box Spring and Bourland Meadow. There is at least 1 hike leaving from each of these trailheads in this book. A few of the hikes are short enough that they never make it into the Emigrant Wilderness (especially considering that the parking areas for most of these trailheads are quite a distance from the wilderness boundaries). There are more visitors to Emigrant Wilderness than its neighbor, the Carson-Iceberg Wilderness, most likely because it has more lakes and scenic overlooks. However, if you want to leave the people behind in the Emigrant Wilderness, you can choose to hike from one of the less popular trailheads or hike further from them. The signage in Emigrant Wilderness is significantly better than that in Carson-Iceberg Wilderness but there are still areas in the less traveled regions that have unmarked trails.

Photo: Emigrant Wilderness as viewed from Burst Rock area

Blue Canyon Lake from Blue Canyon Trailhead

Highlights: Despite the barren appearance from the highway, this trail offers a huge variety of wildflower displays throughout the summer, several stream crossings (color photo page 166) and a beautiful blue mountain tarn set in a bowl surrounded by volcanic peaks that are a purplish-red in color.

Distance: 1.8 miles one way (3.6 miles roundtrip)

Elevation Changes: Cumulative ascent is ~1050 ft on the way out and <100 ft on the return; elevation ~8950-10,050 ft

Difficulty: Difficult in terms of elevation and elevation change

Seasonality: This trail is best during summer months to early fall. The road to this area is closed during winter months.

User Groups/Permits: The trail is used by hikers and backpackers. Permits are not needed to park or day hike but wilderness permits are required for any overnight stays.

Parking/Facilities: There is a small widened shoulder directly off of 108 on the right side just before the 9000 ft elevation sign (heading towards Sonora Pass). There are no facilities here or on the trail.

Topographic Map: USGS Sonora Pass, CA Quadrangle (7.5 Minute Series)

Hike Description: Descend to cross Deadman Creek which parallels the highway. Head up the scree trail to the right (facing SE). At ~0.1 miles you pass a sign that says 'Entering Fire Zone'. At this point you should already note the seeps and abundance of wildflowers. Just past 0.3 miles, you enter the Emigrant Wilderness (note National Forest Wilderness sign). Look upwards and you should see an unnamed volcanic structure (the 'Matterhorn') that you pass on its right. Cross a creek just past the wilderness sign and make a little side trip off to the right of the trail to see a waterfall at ~0.4 miles. You begin climbing at 0.8 miles, ascending nearly 200 ft within 0.1 miles on a trail that is slippery with scree (loose rock). From here, you descend a short bit then gradually climb before crossing another creek at ~1 mile. Climb another steep ascent before reaching a stunning plateau. At 1.3

miles, there is a tricky downhill section on scree bringing you down to the outlet from Blue Canyon Lake. Cross this creek and head up its right side for a short distance before crossing back over to its left side. At 1.6 miles, you begin to head away from the creek and then come back to it at 1.7 miles. Go 0.1 miles further to reach Blue Canyon Lake.

Trail Tidbits: The blue of the lake is created by the amount of powdered rock found in it and the cold temperatures which inhibit alga growth. The northeastern third of Emigrant Wilderness consists primarily of volcanic peaks and ridges as evidenced by the rhyolite found at Blue Canyon Lake. This is in contrast to the rest of Emigrant Wilderness which is primarily granitic. Snow fields can be found at this lake into summer months. For those interested in birding, the gray-crowned rosy-finch can be found in abundance at the snow line at this lake.

Need to Know: There is scree in a number of areas on the trail that makes secure footing challenging. Choose your steps carefully. Stream crossings can be difficult early in the season. It is often windy at high elevation lakes so it might be a good idea to pack additional layers. Also, afternoon thunderstorms are a serious consideration at high elevations; start early.

Want A Loop? You can do a loop to this hike by heading cross-country to Deadman Lake. If you are not comfortable with cross-country travel using a map and compass, then this loop is not for you. Look for the notch that is to the left of the needle-like rock structure on the ridge on the right side of the trail as you leave the lake (just where the trail returns to the lake outlet). Climb the scree slope to the notch. Follow the faint trail on the ridge that takes you past the far side of the 'needle', heading southeast. At the end of the ridge, the trail veers left and climbs a saddle. Deadman Lake is at the base of Leavitt Peak on the other side of the saddle. From Deadman Lake, head northeast to a large meadow bowl on a steep descent and to the right of the 'Matterhorn'. Continue back to the trailhead by following the drainage leaving the bowl. As this drainage is one of the creeks that you originally crossed at the mile mark, it will bring you back to the main trail. Elevation gain is now closer to 1900 ft and roundtrip distance for the loop is ~5 miles.

Directions to Trailhead: Go east on 108 past Kennedy Meadows. The Blue Canyon Lake 'Trailhead' is a widened shoulder on the right just before the 9000 ft elevation sign west of Sonora Pass; park off the road on the widened shoulder. Distance from 108 is 0 miles.

'Bourland' Lake from Bourland Meadow Trailhead

Highlights: This hike is to a lake that is unnamed on some maps but referred to as Bourland Lake in other resources. The lake is near but not in Emigrant Wilderness. Most people use Bourland Trailhead as an access point to Emigrant Wilderness and are unaware of the primitive trail on the other side of the creek that eventually brings you to this 'lost' lake set in a wooded bowl. You have to work to get here though. The drive to the trailhead is long and the trail disappears in places as it is not maintained. Once you reach this lake though, you most likely will have it to yourself.

Distance: ~2.0 miles to the lake (~4.0 miles roundtrip)

Elevation Changes: Cumulative ascent to the lake is ~230 ft and another ~80 ft on the return; elevation ~7200-7440 ft

Difficulty: Moderately easy in terms of elevation changes

Seasonality: This trail is best during early-mid summer months when there is more water in Bourland Creek. The lake is still substantial even towards mid-fall. The roads to this area are closed during the winter season.

User Groups/Permits: The trail is used by hikers, backpackers, hunters and horseback riders. No permits are needed to day hike in this area.

Parking/Facilities: There is some parking at the Bourland Meadow Trailhead. There are no facilities here or on the trail.

Topographic Map: USGS Cherry Lake North Quadrangle (7.5 Minute Series)

Hike Description: The trail starts to the right of the trailhead sign. However, you split left off the main tract in <0.1 miles at a spot that looks like a drainage channel to Bourland Creek. The trail drops then follows the creek upstream before crossing near a large boulder (~0.2 miles into the hike). If you lose this trail, find a way down to the creek and cross it. Once you are on the other side of Bourland Creek, the trail is much more evident (the trail is not always next to the creek so walk uphill from the creek until you intersect it). Turn right onto the trail and head in the upstream direction. At ~0.5 miles, you pass through an opening (gate) in a barbed wire fence. Continue on the trail through the forest. At nearly 0.75 miles into the hike, you can see a marshy pond through the trees on the right and ~0.1 miles further you come out of the trees into a very large, expansive meadow which is Bourland Meadow. The trail heads down the left length of the meadow but then disappears; continue on this line along the left edge of this meadow section. You reach the end of the larger portion of the meadow at ~1.25 miles and from here you want to stay just to the left of the creek drainage where the trail reappears for a short bit. Just as the trail becomes faint again (at close to 1.4 miles), you can just make out a 'Y' intersection. Head left (northeast) from this point towards the end of this smaller meadow section and a pair of tall, dead co-joined pines atop a small rocky hill. You pick up the trail to the left of the pines and begin to climb upwards fairly gradually in a northeast direction (to the right from the meadow). The trail takes you above the thicker part of the forest and the majority of the boulders. Once above the worst of this, it drops you down to the wooded bowl that contains the lake. If you lose the trail, traverse the ridge until you can see where the trees open up for the lake then drop down to it. Another option is to follow the overgrown creek drainage upstream.

Trail Tidbits: Bourland Creek, Meadow and Lake were named for John Bourland who ran cattle in this area in the summer. John Bourland crossed Sonora Pass in 1864 and settled in Sonora. He served as sheriff for Tuolumne County in the 1860's. Bourland Creek is one of 3 main feeder creeks that serve as the headwaters for the Clavey River. You cross both the Clavey River and Bourland Creek on your way to the trailhead.

Need to Know: The trail is primitive and not well-maintained; as a result, it is easy to lose. If you prefer hiking with a distinct and obvious trail, then this hike is not for you. Cattle are grazed in this area during the summer months. There is lots of loose barbed wire alongside the outside of the barbed wire fence; watch your step. Note your surroundings when you cross the creek at the start of your hike as it will not be obvious to you when to get off the trail and cross back on your return trip (the trail paralleling the creek continues on for a distance before running into the road that heads to Box Springs).

Want More? There is another unnamed lake that feeds into 'Bourland' Lake. There is no marked trail to get to this other lake but if you want more, you could explore this area (follow the inlet upstream). The other lake is on the USGS Pinecrest Quadrangle (7.5 Minute Series) and is ~ 340 ft higher.

Directions to Trailhead: Go east on 108 past Sierra Village. Turn right at the 2nd Long Barn exit (shortly after the divided highway begins). Take the 2nd left onto Forest Service Road 3N01 (0.1 miles) and drive on this road for 20.6 miles (crossing the Clavey River at 16.2 miles and Bourland Creek at 20.2 miles). The road becomes a dirt road 18.2 miles from its start. Turn left on Forest Service Road 3N16 (you will see a sign for Box Springs Trailhead) and go 6.1 miles until it dead ends at the trailhead (the turnoff for the Forest Service Road to Box Springs is on the left before the Bourland Trailhead). Total distance from 108 is 26.8 miles.

Photo: 'Bourland' Lake

Camp and Bear Lakes from Crabtree Camp Trailhead

Highlights: The hike to these 2 lakes is very popular for a reason; they are beautiful mountain lakes set in granite basins with scattered stands of pines surrounding them (color photo page 162). On the way, you encounter numerous meadows rampant with wildflowers.

Distance: ~2.5 miles to Camp Lake (5.0 miles roundtrip); ~3.8 miles to Bear Lake (7.6 miles roundtrip)

Elevation Changes: Cumulative ascent to Camp Lake is ~500 ft and another 120 ft to Bear Lake and ~150 ft on the return; elevation ~7160-7710 ft

Difficulty: Moderate in terms of elevation changes

Seasonality: This trail is best during summer months and early fall. The roads to this area are closed during the winter months.

User Groups/Permits: The trail is very popular and sees lots of use by hikers, backpackers and horseback riders with pack animals. No permit is needed for day hikes but a wilderness permit is needed for overnight stays.

Parking/Facilities: There is a large parking area at the Crabtree Trailhead (it does fill on weekends and holidays). There are also several vault toilets but no water. One night of camping is allowed at the trailhead.

Topographic Map: USGS Pinecrest & Cooper Peak Quadrangles (7.5 Minute Series)

Hike Description: Look for the trailhead sign and start the hike there. You cross a bridge over Bell Creek 100 yards from the sign. Shortly after, you reach a trail junction; head right to go towards Camp Lake. Over 0.1 miles into the hike, you cross a creek bed and then begin the first ascent of ~150 ft over the next 0.3 miles. You then reach a segment of the hike where you go up and down some. At 0.9 miles, you begin your second 0.3 mile climb but this one is ~350 ft. At 1.4 miles, you reach a trail marker; continue straight for Camp Lake (the right takes you to Pine Valley). At this point, you begin to walk along a ridge and within 0.2 miles you begin to get some spectacular but typical views of the granitic wonder that is Emigrant Wilderness. Take some time to enjoy the panoramic display. Nearly 1.9 miles into the hike, you reach an area that is heavily vegetated and a short distance later, you pass a pond that is in succession (turning into a meadow). Almost 2.3 miles into the hike, you reach the wilderness boundary sign. From here, you have a short climb up to the lip of the basin that holds Camp Lake. The trail continues along the right side of the lake. At 2.8 miles into the hike, you reach another trail marker; head left to Bear Lake (right takes you to Piute Meadow). You know you are on the right path if you see a stagnant pond off to the right shortly after taking the trail. From here, it is a fairly easy hike with some gradual ascents to Bear Lake. On the way, you pass through some meadows that can be vibrant with wildflowers in early summer. A little more than 0.1 miles before Bear Lake, you encounter its outlet (Lily Creek) and at 3.8 miles you reach the granite lip around Bear Lake.

Trail Tidbits: Since both Camp and Bear Lakes see many visitors, they have been prone to overuse issues particularly when campers set up base close to the waterline. Much effort has gone into restoring the shorelines of both lakes over the past decades. Although there are many lakes in the Emigrant Wilderness, it is the lakes closest to trailheads that are subject to overuse and as a result, camping is limited to one night at these lakes. Crabtree Camp earned its name from O. S. Crabtree, a resident of Knight's Ferry who took out a patent for land in this area under the Swamp & Overflow Act. The patent was later rescinded as the land in this area did not meet the criteria for the Swamp & Overflow Act (i.e. it was not swampy).

Need to Know: Crabtree Trailhead is one of the more popular trailheads for Emigrant Wilderness with the majority of users heading out on the Camp Lake/ Pine Valley Trail. Due to the number of pack animals and foot traffic on the trail, it becomes thick with dust by August. Mosquitoes can be horrific in meadow areas when they are wet and boggy; biting flies can be lurking in the trailhead area as well.

Want More? There is no easy way to do a loop unless you want to work out a cross-country route (using a topo map and compass) that heads up the steep incline to Chewing Gum Lake and then return to the trailhead using the Chewing Gum Lake Trail. If you want more, you could take the time to explore around Bear Lake and follow its inlet (Lily Creek) upstream all the way up towards Y Meadow Lake or, after a short hike up the inlet, head off on a cross-country trek to the northeast to Granite Lake.

Directions to Trailhead: Go east on 108 past Cold Springs. Turn right onto Crabtree Road (4N26) and drive 6.6 miles to Aspen Pack Station. Stay straight on Forest Service Road 4N26 at the pack station and continue another 2.8 miles before turning right at the sign for Crabtree TH. You will reach the parking area 0.7 miles down this road. Total distance from 108 is 10.1 miles.

Photo: Camp Lake is visible through the trees

Chain Lakes from Box Springs Trailhead

Highlights: The hike to this lovely group of lakes is definitely on the trail less traveled. The hike is fairly short and not difficult, passes through some meadow areas rampant with growth and ends at a picturesque lake set amongst a granite backdrop with other lakes scattered around the area. So what is the catch? Getting to the trailhead requires driving a decent distance on forest service roads (some unpaved).

Distance: ~2.2 miles to the first of the Chain Lakes (4.4 miles roundtrip)

Elevation Changes: Cumulative ascent to Chain Lakes is ~350 ft and about ~250 ft on the return trip; elevation ~7300-7600 ft

Difficulty: Moderate in terms of elevation changes

Seasonality: This trail is best during summer months and early fall. The roads to this area are closed during the winter season.

User Groups/Permits: The trail is used by hikers, backpackers and horseback riders. No permit is needed for day hikes but you will need a wilderness permit for overnight stays in the Chain Lakes area.

Parking/Facilities: There is some parking at the Box Springs Trailhead. The trailhead is primitive so there are no facilities here or on the trail.

Topographic Map: USGS Pinecrest & Cooper Peak Quadrangles (7.5 Minute Series)

Hike Description: The trail drops behind the trailhead sign. Initially, the trail is narrow and thick with dust as it passes through a lush, forested area. At just past 0.1 miles, you pass Box Springs. The trail then meanders through an area full of dead trees, both standing and down, before climbing a small saddle. The dead trees are remnants of a 2007 forest fire. At nearly 0.7 miles, you cross a swampy area on a fallen tree trunk and then pass a small pond shortly after. From here, you drop gradually down to Lily Pad Lake (a pond really) at nearly 1 mile. Near the lake there is the start of a primitive trail on the left that takes you to Pine Valley (currently obscured by fallen trees). To continue to the Chain Lakes, head right to travel on the right side of the lake.

You cross a stream bed at nearly 1.4 miles. You then climb another small saddle on a rocky section of the trail entering an area that starts to look more like Emigrant Wilderness with it characteristic granite. After traversing this short section (at ~1.7 miles), you begin to climb 170 ft over the next 0.4 miles. You reach the wilderness boundary sign at ~2.1 miles and then head down to the lake that you can see between the trees. This is the first of the Chain Lakes; the others are smaller with some succeeding into meadows.

Trail Tidbits: The 2 main watersheds of Emigrant Wilderness are the Stanislaus and Tuolumne Rivers. The Clavey River, one of the few undammed rivers in California, has its origins in the Emigrant Wilderness and flows into the Tuolumne River. The Clavey River is one of the most pristine rivers in California and has a reputation for wonderful swimming holes. Plan to stop at the Clavey River when you cross it on your way home from the Box Springs Trailhead. The Clavey River was named for William Clavey, a rancher who grazed his sheep in the area during the late 1800's.

Need to Know: The trail is primitive and not well-maintained. This means that it is often a narrow tract with bushes growing over it making it difficult to see rocks or tree limbs that could be hidden along the path. There are also a number of downed tree trunks that you need to step up and over. Due to the number of dead trees, the trail in these sections is exposed with little shade.

Want a Loop? There is a 7-8 mile loop you could do but it would require some cross-country travel and skills with a compass and topographic map. To do this loop, head northeast off-trail from the Chain Lakes to Grouse Lake then pick up the Pine Valley Trail towards Bell Meadow. Turn left on the trail that heads towards Mud Lake. Turn left again before reaching Mud Lake on a 'hard to follow' and minimally maintained trail that will bring you back to Lily Pad Lake. Return to Box Springs Trailhead the way you came. Otherwise, if you want more, spend time exploring the Chain Lakes and see if you can locate them all or head to the dome that overlooks the West Fork of the Cherry River for some great views.

Directions to Trailhead: Go east on 108 past Sierra Village. Turn right at the 2nd Long Barn exit (shortly after the divided highway begins). Take the 2nd left onto Forest Service Road 3N01 (0.1 miles) and drive on this road for 20.6 miles (crossing the Clavey River at 16.2 miles and Bourland Creek at 20.2 miles). The road becomes a dirt road 18.2 miles from its start. Turn left on Forest Service Road 3N16 (you will see a sign for Box Springs Trailhead) and go 5.6 miles on a road that was paved at one time but is no longer maintained. Turn left onto Forest Service Road 3N20Y and go 2.3 miles to the trailhead (stay right 0.3 miles down this road). Total distance from 108 is 28.6 miles.

Photo: One of the Chain Lakes

Chewing Gum Lake from Crabtree Camp Trailhead

Highlights: This is a challenging hike but it is quiet, well-shaded and leads you up through changing conifer forests. Often it travels along or over seasonal streams. There are numerous opportunities for grand views of the granitic splendor of Emigrant Wilderness including Bear Lake.

Distance: ~4.3 miles to Chewing Gum Lake (8.6 miles roundtrip)

Elevation Changes: Cumulative ascent to Chewing Gum Lake is ~1740 ft and ~340 ft on the return; elevation ~7160-8960 ft

Difficulty: Strenuous in terms of elevation changes

Seasonality: This trail is best during summer months and early fall. The roads to Crabtree Trailhead are closed during the winter season.

User Groups/Permits: The trail is used by hikers, backpackers and horseback riders with pack animals. No permit is needed for day hikes but you need a wilderness permit for overnight stays.

Parking/Facilities: There is a large parking area at the Crabtree Trailhead (which does fill on weekends and holidays). There are also several vault toilets but no water. One night of camping is allowed at the trailhead.

Topographic Map: USGS Pinecrest & Cooper Peak Quadrangles (7.5 Minute Series)

Hike Description: Look for the trailhead sign and start the hike there. You cross a bridge over Bell Creek 100 yards from the sign. Shortly after, you reach a trail junction; head left to go to Chewing Gum Lake. From here you begin a long climb. Over the next 2 miles, you cross stream beds and encounter a stream running alongside the trail before finally reaching the wilderness boundary sign. Keep climbing for just over another mile before reaching a plateau. If you are interested, you can take a quick side trip to the right to see Bear Lake down below. Otherwise, the trail begins to head downhill encountering more streams or streambeds. Once you reach a granitic plateau, you skirt around the mountain that you are hiking. You then climb a saddle before dropping down to the plateau that contains Chewing

Gum Lake and its tarns. You see the first tarn off to the right at ~3.8 miles into the hike and then the trail travels right past the next one <0.2 miles later. The trail continues to the left side of Chewing Gum Lake and the large group campsite <0.3 miles from the last tarn; this is your first view of the lake.

Trail Tidbits: The tarns around Chewing Gum Lake are home to the rare Sierra Nevada yellow-legged frog. These frogs are endemic to the Sierra Nevada Mountains but their population has declined by over 95% due to the introduction of non-native fish in the high elevation lakes, habitat loss due to grazing, disease and air contaminants. These frogs are up to 3.5 inches long and have variable patterns and colors on their back; however the underside of their back legs is always yellow. They have recently been listed as a Federally Endangered Species. They can be found in a few other high elevation lakes in Emigrant Wilderness.

Need to Know: Crabtree Trailhead is one of the more popular trailheads for Emigrant Wilderness; however the majority of users head out via the Camp Lake/ Pine Valley Trail. This trail does not become thick with dust like the Pine Valley Trail but, after the first mile, it is rocky and requires special attention for footing. Mosquitoes can be horrific in meadow areas when they are wet and boggy; biting flies can be lurking in the trailhead area as well.

Want A Loop? A loop would be difficult without significant cross-country travel. However, if you are willing to do a shuttle to make a loop, you could park one car at Gianelli Cabin Trailhead and the other at Crabtree Camp. The trail at Chewing Gum continues up through the Lakes Valley, up to Burst Rock and then down to Gianelli Cabin Trailhead; however, it would involve far less climbing to do this one-way trip from Gianelli Cabin Trailhead down to Crabtree Camp. Otherwise, if you want more, spend some time exploring Chewing Gum Lake and the tarns around it.

Directions to Trailhead: Go east on 108 past Cold Springs. Turn right onto Crabtree Road (4N26) and drive 6.6 miles to Aspen Pack Station. Stay straight on Forest Service Road 4N26 at the pack station and continue another 2.8 miles before turning right at the sign for Crabtree Camp TH. You will reach the parking area 0.7 miles down this road. Total distance from 108 is 10.1 miles.

Chewing Gum Lake from Gianelli Cabin Trailhead

Highlights: This hike offers incredible views of granitic landscapes from Burst Rock and a trek through the beautiful Lakes Valley which can be an ocean of blue in the summer when the lupine bloom. Your destination is a lovely lake with a multitude of fingers and beach areas that you can call your own for a picnic (particularly on the east side).

Distance: ~4.5 miles to Chewing Gum Lake (9.0 miles roundtrip)

Elevation Changes: Cumulative ascent to Chewing Gum Lake is ~690 ft and ~680 ft on the return; elevation ~8600-9060 ft

Difficulty: Difficult in terms of elevation changes

Seasonality: This trail is best during summer months and early fall. The road to Gianelli Cabin Trailhead is closed during the winter season.

User Groups/Permits: The trail is used by hikers, backpackers and horseback riders with pack animals. No permit is needed for day hikes but you need a wilderness permit for overnight stays.

Parking/Facilities: There is ample parking at the Gianelli Cabin Trailhead. There are no facilities here or on the trail.

Topographic Map: USGS Pinecrest & Cooper Peak Quadrangles (7.5 Minute Series)

Hike Description: Look for the trailhead sign just uphill from the parking area and start the hike there. At this point, you begin a slow climb up through a mixed conifer forest with an increasing amount of granite appearing on your left. About 0.5 miles into the climb, the trail brings you to some granite steps and comes close to the edge of the ridge. Take a side trip off to the left to revel in the views of Emigrant Wilderness to the north and the canyon of the South Fork of the Stanislaus River heading west. Once you are back on the trail, you begin some long switchbacks until you reach the summit of Burst Rock at ~1.2 miles into the hike (~390 ft of elevation gain). There is a sign off to the left that provides some history of the early Sonora Pass crossings. As you head across the plateau, you continue to have views off to the left but now you also have views to the right of southeast portions of Emigrant Wilderness. You encounter the wilderness boundary sign at ~1.4 miles. The trail continues mostly downhill from here and passes a pond on the left at ~1.8 miles. The Powell Lake Trail junction (see Powell Lake hike) occurs at ~2.2 miles; stay straight to continue to Chewing Gum Lake. The trail again begins to climb another ~200 ft and, at this point, you can see the Lake Valley down the ridge off to your right. The trail continues onward with switchbacks down the ridge. The junction with the Lakes Valley Trail is in a deeply forested area at the bottom of the ridge at ~3.7 miles into the hike; be sure to head to the right towards the Lakes Valley. The trail meanders gradually downhill through a valley that is gorgeous when flowers are in bloom. After traversing the valley for ~0.5 miles, the trail veers off to the right to head to the west side of Chewing Gum Lake which is hugged by a granite wall. You reach the lake at ~4.5 miles. Another option is to stay in the meadow and find your way (via cross-country travel) to the east side of the lake.

Trail Tidbits: Gianelli built a cabin in 1905 near the current day location of the trailhead. A 1926 General Land Office Plat lists the structure as 'Diamond's Cabin'. On more recent maps, the area is marked only with the word 'site' indicating the location of the former structure.

Need to Know: The trail can be thick with dust in areas (particularly heading down to the Lakes Valley) by the end of the season. There are also several rocky sections where you will need to watch your footing. As Gianelli Cabin is one of the higher trailheads in Emigrant Wilderness, there is less uphill walking on the way in but it also means the return trip has more uphill walking than usual. There is a creek at the trailhead but there is no water along the trail (other than the pond or a side trip to Powell Lake) until you reach the area around Chewing Gum Lake.

Want A Loop? A shuttle loop is the only real option for a loop in this area. Park one car at Gianelli Cabin Trailhead and the other at Crabtree Camp Trailhead; start the hike at Gianelli Cabin Trailhead. Once you reach Chewing Gum Lake, continue on the trail that heads mostly downhill to Crabtree Camp Trailhead (see Chewing Gum Lake from Crabtree Camp hike). If you don't wish to do a shuttle loop but would like to hike more, spend some time exploring Chewing Gum Lake and the tarns around it. See if you can spot a rare Sierra Nevada yellow-legged frog; some make their home in these tarns.

Directions to Trailhead: Go east on 108 past Cold Springs. Turn right onto Crabtree Road (4N26) and drive 6.6 miles to Aspen Pack Station. Stay straight on Forest Service Road 4N26 at the pack station and continue another 6.9 miles before reaching Gianelli Cabin TH. Total distance from 108 is 13.5 miles.

Photo: View of a granitic section of Emigrant Wilderness from the shelf surrounding Chewing Gum Lake

Cooper Meadow from Coyote Meadow Trailhead

Highlights: This trail offers a fairly easy walk that skirts Coyote Meadow and Horse and Cow Meadow before descending to Cooper Meadow. On the way you are treated to great views of Burst Rock, Cooper Peak, Castle Rock and The Three Chimneys (color photo page 164) and the merging landscapes of the volcanic north with the granitic south. The cabin and barn located in Cooper Meadow were built in the late 1800's and are still in use today.

Distance: ~3.6 miles (7.2 miles roundtrip) to Cooper Meadow cabin area

Elevation Changes: Cumulative ascent is ~300 ft on the way there and ~400 ft on the return; elevation ~8500-8800 ft

Difficulty: Moderate in terms of elevation changes

Seasonality: This trail is best during the summer and early fall. The roads to this area are closed during the winter season. The section of road above the campgrounds becomes incredibly icy if there is any snow on it. The wildflowers in the meadow are rampant during late spring to early summer. The aspen change color in the fall but there is less water at this time.

User Groups/Permits: The trail is used by hikers, backpackers and horseback riders. No motorized vehicles are allowed. No permits are needed to park or use the trail for day hikes; however, a wilderness permit is required for overnight stays.

Parking/Facilities: There is a small parking area at the trailhead. There are no facilities here or on the trail.

Topographic Map: USGS Pinecrest and Cooper Peak Quadrangles (7.5 Minute Series)

Hike Description: Follow the path to the left of the trailhead sign. The trail takes you across the end of Coyote Meadow and then up into a mixed conifer forest. At ~0.2 miles, stay right on what looks to be the most used trail. You encounter the wilderness boundary sign at 0.5 miles. You now traverse the ridge that Cooper Peak sits atop and at ~1.3 miles you reach an open area with many lahar (volcanic mixture of mud and lava) outcroppings on the ridge to your left. You cross a number of seasonal creek beds over the next 0.5 miles and have great vistas of the ridge across the South Fork of the Stanislaus River including Burst Rock about ~1.5 miles into the hike. The traverse takes you around the end of the ridge and then you skirt Horse and Cow Meadow with a granitic bench visible on the right. At nearly 2.1 miles, you can see the sudden switch from volcanic rock to granitic rock on the left. At the end of the meadow is a cow pond (~2.5 miles) and, just after this pond, you begin your descent to Cooper Meadow. Nearly 0.8 miles from the pond (3.3 miles into the hike) there is a 'Y' in the trail; stay left and then when you reach the next 'Y' veer right off the main trail to head towards the cabin area (left is the official trail that takes you to the junction with the trails for Eagle Pass and Hay Meadow). Since cows graze this area, there are numerous cow tracks heading off in different directions making it difficult to stick to the 'real trail'. If you lose the trail, don't worry; just head downhill towards the meadow then head right to reach the cabin area at ~3.6 miles.

Trail Tidbits: W. F. Cooper was the original cattle grazer in Cooper Meadow from 1861 to 1900. The barn, which was the original cabin, was built in 1865 and the cabin that you see today, was built in 1875. The peak and the meadow were named after Cooper on maps as early as 1898. Look for the tree with the name 'Cooper' and year '1861' carved into it. The grazing rights have been passed down through generations and this area is currently grazed today by members of the Sanguinetti family. The small creeks running through Cooper Meadow are part of the headwaters for the South Fork of the Stanislaus River which flows down into Pinecrest Lake.

Need to Know: The area is grazed by cattle during the summer to early fall. The trail can be thick with dust particularly later in the season and the section down to Cooper Meadow is slippery with loose rock. Also many of the streams dry up late in the season so be sure to pack plenty of water. The cabin and barn area are still in use today; please be respectful of the people that lease this area from the forest service for grazing.

Want A Loop? A loop is possible but it would involve good cross-country skills. For this option, hike past the Cooper Cabin and head towards the granite area at the end of the meadow to pick up the South Fork of the Stanislaus River. Head downstream and, after passing by Burst Rock on your left, head to the right to Waterhouse Lake. From Waterhouse Lake, head up the granitic wall until you find the trail at the top (see Waterhouse hike). Hike to the Waterhouse Trailhead and then turn right on 5N67. It is one mile back to Coyote Meadow Trailhead (or plan a shuttle). A long shuttle option would be to leave a car at the Eagle Meadow Trailhead as well as the trailhead at Coyote Meadow. Then, from the official junction at Cooper Meadow, hike the trail up to Eagle Pass and then down to Eagle Meadow. If the loops are too much and you still want more, hike towards the southwest end of the meadow and explore the South Fork of the Stanislaus River.

Directions to Trailhead: Go east on 108 past Strawberry. Turn right on Herring Creek Road. Continue on this road for ~6.8 miles until it 'T's' (it becomes Forest Service Road 4N12 at ~4.5 miles and is no longer paved at ~5.5 miles). At the 'T', turn right to remain on 4N12. When the road becomes a 'Y' (0.1 miles further), take the right branch to stay on 4N12. Cross a bridge ~0.4 miles further (7.3 miles total) and go past a campground. Continue another ~2.2 miles up 4N12 (9.5 miles total) and then veer left to stay on 4N12 (right puts you on 5N31). Go 1.8 miles (11.3 miles total) further then turn right onto 5N67. Drive 1 mile on 5N67 and then turn left into the parking area for Coyote Meadow at the location where you see the sign for Coyote Meadow Horse Camp. Total distance from 108 is 12.3 miles.

Photo: The original house (now a barn) at Cooper Meadow

Deadman Lake from Blue Canyon Trailhead

Highlights: Despite the barren volcanic appearance from the highway, this rugged hike offers a splendid display of a huge variety of wildflowers throughout the summer, particularly along the drainage below the huge meadow tucked in a bowl. The meadow bowl is a wonderful destination in itself as several waterfalls feed the streams and streamlets heading into it. The leg to Deadman Lake is challenging but the sight of Leavitt and other peaks standing over the small tarn, set amongst scree boulders, is impressive (color photo on page 164).

Distance: 2.4 miles one way (4.8 miles roundtrip)

Elevation Changes: Cumulative ascent is ~1700 ft and ~250 ft on the return trip, elevation ~8950-10,500 ft

Difficulty: Strenuous in terms of elevation and elevation change

Seasonality: This trail is best during summer months to early fall. The road to this area is closed during winter months.

User Groups/Permits: The trail is used by hikers and backpackers. Permits are not needed to park or day hike but wilderness permits are required for any overnight stays.

Parking/Facilities: There is a small widened shoulder area directly off of 108 on the right side of the road just before the 9000 ft elevation sign (heading towards Sonora Pass). There are no facilities here or on the trail.

Topographic Map: USGS Sonora Pass, CA Quadrangle (7.5 Minute Series)

Hike Description: From the road, descend to cross Deadman Creek which parallels the highway. Head up the trail to other side. At ~0.1 miles you pass a sign that says 'Entering Fire Zone'. At this point you should already note the seeps and abundance of wildflowers. Just past 0.3 miles you enter Emigrant Wilderness (note National Forest Wilderness sign). Look upwards and you should see an unnamed volcanic structure (the 'Matterhorn') that you will pass on its left. You begin climbing at 0.8 miles, ascending nearly 200 ft within 0.1 miles on a trail that is slippery with scree (loose rock). From here, you descend a short bit before climbing again (~0.9 miles). At this point, you have a choice to make. Option one is to leave the trail and head up the gentle ascending ridge to the left until you reach the large meadow in the bowl. Option two is to continue to the stream crossing at ~1 mile then leave the trail and work your way along the stream edge until you arrive at the meadow (occasionally you can see a faint trail). Once you reach this large, high elevation meadow, enjoy its beauty (~1.3 miles into the hike). To continue to Deadman Lake, cross the meadow on the right side of the stream and head towards the low rise at the southern end of the bowl. On your way, you pass a number of seeps and streamlets that feed into the larger stream. Hike up the low rise where you soon realize that you have yet more to climb (>600 ft). As you climb, work your way to the right of the large, lumpy projection along the high ridge. As you reach the saddle just before this rock projection, head right and you should see Deadman Lake below you. As the lake is surrounded by scree boulders and steep terrain, travel along the ridge overlooking the lake to the right, until you reach the far end where the ridge has dropped enough to make it easier to reach the lake.

Trail Tidbits: Deadman Lake shares its name with Deadman Creek which parallels Highway 108. The creek used to be known as Rattlesnake Creek up until the 1860's. The creek was renamed Deadman Creek after the frozen body of a foot traveler, Tim Whitaker, was found alongside the creek (further downstream from the trailhead crossing) following a severe blizzard in 1865. The gentlemen that found the body buried him near the creek and marked a tree near the grave.

Need to Know: This hike is significantly off-trail; you need to feel comfortable with cross-country travel using a topographic map and compass (or GPS device). There is scree in a number of areas on the trail that makes secure footing challenging; choose your steps carefully. Stream crossings can be difficult early in the season. It is often windy at high elevation lakes so it might be a good idea to pack additional layers. Also, afternoon thunderstorms are a serious consideration at high elevations; come prepared.

Want A Loop? You can create a loop to this hike by heading cross-country to Blue Canyon Lake. Climb back up the low saddle that overlooks Deadman Lake and, as you head down the other side, veer to the left (west). You should see a needle-like outcropping of rock to the left; you want to keep it on your left as you head down the ridge where it sits. You might note a faint trail to help you navigate past the structure. Once the ridge drops down to a plateau (after passing the needle-like structure), choose a spot to drop down off its left side that would give you the least steep path down to Blue Canyon Lake (should be visible from the top of the ridge). To reach the trailhead, take the established trail back from Blue Canyon Lake. Elevation gain for this loop is now closer to 1900 ft and roundtrip distance is closer to 5 miles.

Directions to Trailhead: Go east on 108 past Kennedy Meadows. The Blue Canyon Lake 'Trailhead' is a widened shoulder on the right just before the 9000 ft elevation sign west of Sonora Pass; park off the road on the widened shoulder. Distance from 108 is 0 miles.

Photo: Creek flowing from large meadow bowl below Deadman Lake

Eagle Meadow Loop

Highlights: This is an easy jaunt around the edges of Eagle Meadow (near but not in Emigrant Wilderness) with views of Eagle Peak to the southwest. This hike is particularly pretty in the fall when the aspen are changing color but would also be gorgeous in the early summer when wildflowers are blooming. You could do this hike and then travel down Eagle Meadow Road another 5 miles to see the oldest, living tree, the Bennett Juniper.

Distance: ~2.3 miles for the loop

Elevation Changes: Cumulative ascent on loop is ~120 ft; elevation ~7550-7650 ft

Difficulty: Easy in terms of elevation change

Seasonality: This trail is best during summer to fall months; the aspen change color in fall but there is less water available at that time. The roads to this area are closed during winter months.

Photo: Eagle Meadow

User Groups/Permits: The trail is used by hikers, backpackers and horseback riders. Motorized vehicles are prohibited. Permits are not needed to park or day hike; fees are charged at the campgrounds along Eagle Meadow Road for overnight stays.

Parking/Facilities: There is a parking area at the back of the Eagle Meadow Horse Camp. There are vault toilets located in the horse camp.

Topographic Map: USGS Dardanelle, CA Quadrangle (7.5 Minute Series)

Hike Description: The trailhead sign marks the start of the trail which is just to its right. Initially you walk near a barbed wire fence but then you go through a gate into the fenced-off area. You climb a short ways and then reach an area where you have excellent views of the meadow. At the far end of Eagle Meadow (nearly 1 mile into the hike), you head into an aspen forest. At ~1.2 miles, you reach a junction with another trail; head left to return along the other side of the meadow (right takes you to Eagle Pass). The trail heads back through the meadow keeping Eagle Creek on your right-hand side. At ~2.2 miles, there is a trail that crosses the creek and heads to the corral that is part of Martin's Cow Camp; you want to stay on the left side of the creek where a trail takes you to a 'gate' in the barbed wire fence just in front of the entrance to the horse camp. Be sure to close the fence after exiting the meadow and head back through the horse camp to the trailhead.

Trail Tidbits: Martin's Cow Camp is named for Joe Martin who had a permit to graze cattle in Eagle Meadow in the 1950's. Joe Martin also once owned the land where the Bennett Juniper is located but donated the land to the Nature Conservancy in 1978. They passed it on to its current owners, Save the Redwoods League. The Bennett Juniper, first discovered by Basque sheep ranchers, is considered the largest and oldest specimen of Western Juniper. It is 3000-6000 years old, 86 ft high and 40 ft around and is downright noble. The Juniper was named for Clarence Bennett, a naturalist who first visited the tree in 1932. To protect the Bennett Juniper from vandals, a caretaker lives nearby during the months that the roads are open.

Need to Know: There are cattle that are grazed in Eagle Meadow during the summer. As there is not much water available towards the end of the season, be sure to pack what you need for the hike.

Want More? The hike is written as a loop. If you want more, head right at the trail junction and go uphill for some distance towards Eagle Pass before returning back to the meadow.

Directions to Trailhead: Go east on 108 past Strawberry ~13 miles. Turn right onto Eagle Meadow Road (Forest Service Road 5N01). At ~0.3 miles, turn right to stay on 5N01 (left goes to Niagra Creek Campground). Stay right at 0.9 miles to stay on 5N01. At ~2.9 miles, you cross Niagra Creek and pass Niagra Creek ORV Campground. Continue following the signs for 5N01. At 5.1 miles from 108, stay left when you see a sign for Barn Meadow with an arrow pointing right (onto 5N15X). At 5.3 miles, stay right to stay on

5N01. At 6 miles, stay straight and head downhill for 1 mile on an unpaved part of 5N01 before turning right into Eagle Meadow Horse Camp. Veer left near the entrance to the camp and left again further up until you can see the Eagle Meadow Trailhead sign. Total distance from 108 is 7.2 miles.

To reach the Bennett Juniper, travel 5 more miles on 5N01. Look for a sign on the right that says Bennett Juniper; turn left onto the tract after noting the sign. You can see the caretaker's encampment as you head down the hill.

Photo: The Bennett Juniper

Eagle Pass from Eagle Meadow Trailhead

Highlights: This is a challenging hike that starts off on a meandering shady, forested trail along the edge of Eagle Meadow before ascending on a long, slow climb to Eagle Pass. Once you reach Eagle Pass, you are rewarded with spectacular views of volcanic rock formations such as the Dardanelles, Castle Rock, Cooper Peak, and with a quick jaunt to the east, 'The Three Chimneys'. Down below you can see Cooper Meadow and Cooper Pocket.

Distance: ~4.5 miles to junction Eagle Pass (~9.0 miles roundtrip); ~4.9 miles to the overlook of 'The Three Chimneys' (~9.8 miles roundtrip)

Elevation Changes: Cumulative ascent to Eagle Pass is ~1700 ft and ~80 ft on the return trip; cumulative ascent to 'The Three Chimneys' overlook area is ~230 ft more there and 10 ft on the return trip; elevation ~7550-9250 ft

Difficulty: Strenuous in terms of elevation change

Seasonality: This trail is best during summer to fall months; the aspen change color in fall but there is less water available at that time. The roads to this area are closed during winter months.

User Groups/Permits: The trail is used by hikers, backpackers and horseback riders. Motorized vehicles are prohibited. Permits are not needed to park or day hike but wilderness permits are required for any overnight stays once you reach Eagle Pass and the wilderness boundary. Fees are charged at the campgrounds along Eagle Meadow Road.

Parking/Facilities: There is a parking area at the back of the Eagle Meadow Horse Camp. There are vault toilets located in the horse camp.

Topographic Map: USGS Dardanelle and Cooper Peak, CA Quadrangles (7.5 Minute Series)

Hike Description: The trailhead sign marks the start of the trail which is just to its right. Initially you walk near a barbed wire fence but then you go through a gate into the fenced-off area. Towards the far end of Eagle Meadow (nearly 1 mile into the hike), you head into an aspen forest. At ~1.2 miles you reach a junction with another trail; head right passing the barbed wire fence again. Even though this area is predominantly volcanic rock, you see occasional slabs of granite such as rocks on the right just past the trail junction (there is much more granite once you reach the Emigrant Wilderness). Another 0.25 miles further, you cross Eagle Creek which is the last substantial source of water on this hike (higher up you pass small seasonal creeks). From Eagle Creek, climb for the next 3+ miles before reaching the wilderness boundary sign and Eagle Pass. Spend some time enjoying the view. Behind you, you can see the Dardanelles and Eagle Peak. To the right, note Castle Rock, Cooper Peak and even Burst Rock. In front is Cooper Meadow. The established trail continues down to Cooper Meadow. To get a close-up view of 'The Three Chimneys' though, head cross-country up to the left climbing the rock-strewn rise until the next ridge with 'The Three Chimneys' comes into view. Continue hiking east along the ridge until you are looking directly across at 'The Three Chimneys'.

Trail Tidbits: The origin of the names for Eagle Peak, Eagle Creek and Eagle Meadow is unknown but it is thought that Eagle Peak and Eagle Creek were named by the Wheeler Survey party in 1878-1879. The name for Eagle Meadow appeared on a map in 1898. Castle Rock, which is visible from Eagle Pass, was also named by the Wheeler Survey party in 1878-1879.

Photo: 'The Three Chimneys'

Need to Know: There are cattle that are grazed in the meadow during the summer. Be aware that afternoon thunderstorms can arrive rapidly so plan accordingly. As there is not much water available, particularly towards the end of the season, be sure to pack what you need for the hike.

Want A Loop? A loop is possible if you are willing to do a long-distance shuttle with 2 cars; park one car at Coyote Meadow Trailhead and the other at Eagle Meadow Trailhead. Take the trail from Eagle Pass down into Cooper Meadow (~1 mile). Once you reach the trail junction in Cooper Meadow, head right to climb up and out of the meadow (see Cooper Meadow hike). Follow this trail to Coyote Meadow Trailhead.

Directions to Trailhead: Go east on 108 past Strawberry ~13 miles. Turn right onto Eagle Meadow Road (Forest Service Road 5N01). At ~0.3 miles, turn right to stay on 5N01 (left goes to Niagra Creek Campground). At 2.8 miles, you cross Niagra Creek and pass Niagra Creek ORV Campground. Continue following the signs for 5N01. At 5.2 miles from 108, stay left to stay on 5N01 when you see a sign for Barn Meadow with an arrow pointing right (onto 5N15X). At 6 miles, stay straight to stay on 5N01 and head downhill for 1 mile before turning right into Eagle Meadow Horse Camp. Stay left at the camp and left again further up until you can see the Eagle Meadow Trailhead sign. Total distance from 108 is 7.2 miles.

Photo: Aspen changing color on the trail to Eagle Pass

Grouse Lake from Bell Meadow Trailhead

Highlights: This hike takes you along the edge of gorgeous Bell Meadow (color photo page 168), across Bell Creek and up through a mixed conifer forest with a final climb through volcanic rock. You then drop down into Pine Valley on a fairly level trail until you reach Grouse Lake. The lake is shallow, decorated with lily pads, and is set within a meadow up against granite peaks. Although you can get to Grouse Lake from Crabtree Trailhead, the route from Bell Meadow involves less climbing.

Distance: ~4.9 miles to Grouse Lake (9.8 miles roundtrip)

Elevation Changes: Cumulative ascent to Grouse Lake is ~740 ft and ~260 ft on the return; elevation ~6560-7260 ft

Difficulty: Moderately difficult in terms of elevation changes

Photo: Me-Wuk Indian grinding stone called a 'chasay'

Seasonality: This trail is best during summer months and early fall. The aspen trees change color in Bell Meadow in the fall. The roads to this area are closed during the winter season.

User Groups/Permits: The trail is used by hikers, backpackers and horseback riders with pack animals. No permit is needed for day hikes but you will need a wilderness permit for overnight stays.

Parking/Facilities: There is some parking at the Bell Meadow Trailhead. There are no facilities here or on the trail.

Topographic Map: USGS Pinecrest & Cooper Peak Quadrangles (7.5 Minute Series)

Hike Description: Look for the trailhead sign and start the hike there. Begin walking along the northern edge of Bell Meadow. At ~0.25 miles into the hike, there are some granite shelves off to the left that contain Indian grinding stones. As you travel along the edge of the upper portion of Bell Meadow, you encounter a junction with a trail to Crabtree Camp Trailhead at ~1.25 miles (stay right) and a crossing over Bell Creek a short distance later. You cross another creek ~2.2 miles into the hike then begin climbing through a forested area. Less than 0.1 miles further, there is a trail junction with Mud Lake; stay to the left. The climb continues through a volcanic rock section and provides views across to a ridge on the left where the Crabtree Camp Trail is located. Just before reaching the plateau at ~2.9 miles, you encounter another Crabtree Camp Trail junction (marked as Pine Valley) and as you descend on the other side of the saddle, you find a third Crabtree Camp Trail junction at ~3.2 miles. The trail heads through Pine Valley which contains numerous dead trees left behind from a 2007 forest fire. There is another trail junction with Mud Lake < 0.2 miles further. At ~4 miles into the hike, you cross Lily Creek and then enter the Emigrant Wilderness at 4.2 miles (note boundary sign). Grouse Lake is ~0.7 miles further up the trail. You will need to look for it through the trees off to the right as the trail skirts past it.

Trail Tidbits: Bell and Lily Creeks join a few miles downstream and become the Clavey River. Bell Meadow was named for William Bell, who claimed 320 acres of land in this area with William Tarbox for the purpose of summer grazing. Grazing still occurs today since the practice substantially predates the 1964 Wilderness Act. There are 4 grazing allotments within Emigrant Wilderness and these are monitored by the US Forest Service.

Need to Know: Cattle are grazed in Bell Meadow as well as in the area around Grouse Lake. The trail along the edge of lower Bell Meadow is sandy which makes for some hard walking. The trail through Pine Valley to Grouse Lake can be thick with dust particularly later in the season.

Want A Loop? You could do a loop that involves a car shuttle with one car parked at Crabtree Camp Trailhead and one parked at Bell Meadow Trailhead. On your return, take any one of the 3 different trails that bring you to Crabtree Camp Trailhead.

Directions to Trailhead: Go east on 108 past Cold Springs. Turn right onto Crabtree Road (4N26). Drive 6.6 miles to the intersection just before Aspen Pack Station. Turn right onto Forest Service Road 4N25 and continue ~0.4 miles before turning left onto 4N02Y. You reach the parking area ~1.8 miles down this road. Total distance from 108 is 8.8 miles.

Kennedy Lake from Kennedy Meadow Trailhead

Highlights: This hike involves a decent amount of climbing, some of which is steep, but the viewpoints of a myriad of peaks along the way are well worth the effort. On this hike, you can revel in the beauty of cascading rivers and expansive mountain meadows, experience numerous bridge crossings and stare in awe at trail sections cut out from the edges of granite cliffs.

Distance: 8.2 miles one-way (16.4 miles roundtrip) from the designated trailhead parking; 7.6 miles one-way (15.2 miles roundtrip) from the day parking area past the store

Elevation Changes: Cumulative ascent roundtrip is ~1430 ft to the lake and another ~150 ft on the return trip; elevation ~6320-7820 ft

Difficulty: Strenuous in terms of elevation change

Seasonality: Although this trail can be used during summer and fall months, it can be a zoo in the Kennedy Meadows area during peak resort operational months (summer). If you prefer to travel when there are fewer hikers and pack animals, then do this hike when the pack station and resort area have closed for the season. Water seems to be plentiful even late in the season. The roads to this area are closed during winter months.

User Groups/Permits: The trail is used by hikers, backpackers, horseback riders and pack animals. Motorized vehicles are prohibited. Permits are not needed to park or day hike. For overnight trips, you need a permit and you should be sure to park in the designated trailhead for overnight hikers.

Parking/Facilities: There is a large, designated trailhead parking area before you reach the actual Kennedy Meadows resort area complete with vault toilets and a water spigot. There is a two-night camping limit in designated spots. If you are day hiking, it is sometimes possible to find parking just past the store. Although the hike is written as if traveling from the trailhead parking area, total mileage is included for both parking areas.

Topographic Map: USGS Sonora Pass, CA Quadrangle (7.5 Minute Series)

Hike Description: If you parked at the trailhead, go back to Kennedy

Meadows Road; turn left and follow the road into the resort area and past the day use parking area. Follow the signs for 'the trail'. At ~0.6 miles, the pavement ends and the trail continues as a dirt road that is gated a short distance further. From here you head away from the Middle Fork of the Stanislaus River and climb a small saddle, then just over 0.2 miles later, you head back to the river and Kennedy Meadow comes into view. Skirt the edge of the meadow on the dirt road and then head into a forested area. You encounter first, the Kennedy Meadow Trailhead sign at ~1.6 miles and then the Emigrant Wilderness boundary sign at 1.7 miles into the hike. You do some easy climbing until you cross the Middle Fork of the Stanislaus River on a bridge at ~1.9 miles. After crossing the bridge, the trail becomes fairly steep for the next ~0.6 miles. At ~2.2 miles, you come to the confluence of Kennedy Creek (on the left) with the Middle Fork of the Stanislaus River (on the right). Just past this area, you cross the Middle Fork on a bridge and then find yourself with 2 trail options. The trail on the left is steeper and 0.05 miles shorter; the trail on the right is less steep, longer and travels along the river. Both converge again at a point where you can see waterfalls on the river. At ~2.8 miles, you reach the junction with the Kennedy Lake Trail; head left. Continue climbing and at ~3.2 miles, you pass a 'pond' on the left and, just more than 0.1 miles later, an obvious vista point to the left. Take some time to look at the grandeur around you and catch your breath; you can see Bald Mt and Red Peak in the distance to the north, Night Cap Peak above you, Leavitt Peak to the northeast, East Flange Rock to the southwest and towering behind you, a massive unnamed peak. As you continue upward, the roar of Kennedy Creek can be heard on your left; you cross the creek on a bridge at ~3.6 miles. For the next 3.1 miles you hike through a shady, mixed conifer forest still climbing but with a much gentler slope. During these 3 miles, you encounter the trail junction with the Night Cap Trail (~4.2 miles), cross many seasonal streams, and for a good part of the time, walk in step with Kennedy Creek. At ~6.7 miles, you emerge into a large meadow and skirt its left side while crossing many rivulets until you pass a barbed wire fence (and gate) at ~7.0 miles. From here, you reach a very large meadow that you cut through, while crossing many streams. You should see a small cabin at ~7.4 miles and shortly after this (~7.6 miles), the meadow becomes a huge marsh and it becomes easy to lose the trail. Continue in the same direction, following the creek upstream until it widens into the 'tail' of Kennedy Lake (at ~8 miles) and eventually, you reach the 'body' of the lake at ~8.2 miles.

Trail Tidbits: Kennedy Meadow, Creek, Peak and Lake were all named for

Photo: Large meadow near Kennedy Lake

brothers, Andrew and J. F. Kennedy. Andrew claimed land around Kennedy Lake in 1886 whereas J. F. Kennedy claimed 2000-3000 acres in the vicinity of the creek, meadow and lake in 1896. The 1883 General Land Office Plat made note of a Kennedy Lower Camp, Kennedy Lake and Kennedy Brothers Upper Camp near the lake. One of the four grazing allotments in this wilderness is along Kennedy Creek just downstream of Kennedy Lake.

Need to Know: You will be walking next to the road and into the resort area for the first 0.5 miles; please be careful of motorized vehicle traffic. The trail conditions vary from sandy in some sections, thick dust in others and granite steps and rocks in yet others. The trail is quite busy in the summer particularly with horse traffic. Once you near the lake, the area becomes quite swampy. If you wish to keep your feet dry, cross Kennedy Creek near the cabin and approach the lake from the other side.

Want More? A loop is possible with this hike but it requires travel on a primitive trail (used for driving cattle), adds substantially more climbing and involves some descents on very steep sections. However, the views in certain places are spectacular, including those of Relief Reservoir, Granite Dome and Kennedy Meadow. To take this loop, return the way you came until you reach the trail junction with Night Cap; take the right branch and head uphill. The cattle create many trails on their treks through this area but all the trails finally merge to one. Once you reach the plateau, you traverse for a short distance (with several viewing opportunities), then you begin a steep descent. You repeat this pattern a number of times before making the final descent to the water tower on the trail leading back to the resort (you can see cars traveling on 108). This loop shortens the roundtrip hike by ~0.3-0.4 miles.

Directions to Trailhead: Go east on 108 past Dardanelles Resort. Turn right onto Kennedy Meadows Road. Go 0.6 miles and turn left into the trailhead parking area. Go 0.1 miles to park. Day hikers can try to find parking in the day use area past the resort. Total distance from 108 is 0.7 miles.

Note: the meadow and trailhead are called Kennedy Meadow since there is one meadow, while the resort and its road are named Kennedy Meadows.

Photo: Numerous peaks preside over Kennedy Lake

Koenig Lake from Leavitt Lake Trailhead

Highlights: This is an easy hike from one gorgeous lake to another. Leavitt Lake quietly sits beneath a volcanic peak on its south side with few people around to admire it (most likely because it is difficult to reach). Koenig Lake is a beautiful glacial blue lake with a neighboring unnamed lake. Although Leavitt Lake is a trailhead for Emigrant Wilderness, Koenig Lake is not in Emigrant Wilderness but is part of the Bridgeport Winter Recreation Area.

Distance: 0.75 miles one-way from the north side of Leavitt Lake (1.5 miles roundtrip); 1.25 miles one-way from the Leavitt Lake Trailhead located on the east shore of the lake (2.5 miles roundtrip)

Elevation Changes: Cumulative ascent to the lake is ~130 ft and ~130 ft on the return trip from the north shore of the lake but cumulative ascent to the lake is ~170 ft to and ~310 ft from the trailhead; elevation ~9650-9700 ft

Difficulty: Easy in terms of elevation change from the north shore; moderately easy from the trailhead

Seasonality: This trail is best during summer months to early fall. The roads to this area are closed during winter months.

User Groups/Permits: The trail is used by hikers, campers and fishermen. There are also dirt roads that are open to motorized vehicles. Permits are not needed to park, day hike or camp as the lake is currently not part of any wilderness area.

Parking/Facilities: There is parking off the dirt road near the north shore of the lake as well as on the east side of the lake at the Leavitt Lake Trailhead. There are no facilities here or on the trail.

Topographic Map: USGS Pickel Meadow and Sonora Pass, CA Quadrangles (7.5 Minute Series)

Hike Description: From the trailhead, follow the road back down towards Leavitt Lake. Cross the lake's outlet and follow the trail up and over the hill on its northwest corner. Once you crest the hill, you should be able to see the unnamed neighbor lake. Further in the distance, is Koenig Lake.

Trail Tidbits: Koenig and Latopie Lakes are in an area managed by the Humboldt-Toiyabe National Forest. In 1984, 47,000 acres including Koenig and Latopie Lakes became part of the Proposed Hoover Wilderness Addition. The Humboldt-Toiyabe National Forest released 7000 acres from the proposed addition for use by snowmobiles during winter months. This area is now known as the Bridgeport Winter Recreation Area and includes Koenig and Latopie Lakes (but not Leavitt Lake and its access road). The loss of the 7000 acres from the proposed wilderness addition is not without controversy; conservation groups are battling with winter recreation enthusiasts regarding the status of this area.

Need to Know: This area is difficult to get to from Highway 108. The road requires a 4-wheel drive vehicle with high clearance as the road is very rough with stream crossings. Do not attempt to drive this road with a regular car. Since the lake is above tree line, it can get quite windy; be prepared with extra layers of clothing. Also, afternoon thunderstorms are a serious consideration at high elevations; be prepared.

Want A Loop? You can return to Leavitt Lake on a different trail that follows alongside the drainage from Koenig Lake on the left side. The trail will eventually cross the drainage and bring you back to Leavitt Lake. Roundtrip mileage will be an additional 0.3 miles. If you want more, you can make the attempt to climb up the scree slope and head to Latopie Lake from Koenig Lake; however, this requires sure-footedness as the slope can be quite slippery. Latopie Lake is an additional 0.4 miles from Koenig Lake.

Directions to Trailhead: Go east on 108 past Sonora Pass. The dirt road to Leavitt Lake is on the right, 3.8 miles from Sonora Pass (< 1 mile once you cross Sardine Creek on 108). The road is not marked other than with a sign saying 'Rd 32077' and it is located on a hairpin turn. If you reach the Mono County 4.0 mile marker, you have gone too far. From here, the fun begins! Leavitt Lake is located 2.7 miles down a deeply rutted road with strategically placed boulders to make the journey even more difficult. On top of this, you make 3 stream crossings which should not be attempted if the water is running fast and deep. Once you reach the lake, follow the dirt road to the left and up another 0.4 miles before reaching the trailhead parking on the left. Distance from 108 is 3.1 'hairy' miles.

Latopie Lake from Sonora Pass Trailhead

Highlights: This is the hike to do if you want your fill of spectacular views! Despite the high elevation and early ascent, the uphill is a steady rise and not too steep and the views begin within a few miles from the start. At some point you will be able to survey Sonora and Stanislaus Peak in the Carson-Iceberg Wilderness, Leavitt Peak and Blue Canyon in the Emigrant Wilderness, Sardine Creek & McCay Creek drainages in Humboldt-Toiyabe National Forest as well as the distant peaks of the Hoover Wilderness (within the Humboldt-Toiyabe National Forest). Once you reach the 'notch', a number of high alpine lakes decorate the scenery (color photo page 169), including Latopie Lake. Although you pass through Emigrant Wilderness, this lake is not in the wilderness area.

Distance: 4.8 miles one way (9.6 miles roundtrip)

Elevation Changes: Cumulative ascent to the lake is ~1340 ft and ~700 ft on the return trip; elevation ~9600-10,850 ft

Difficulty: Strenuous in terms of elevation and elevation change

Seasonality: This trail is best during summer months to early fall. The road to this area is closed during winter months. The trail can be treacherous if there is still snow on it in the late spring/ early summer weeks.

User Groups/Permits: The trail is used by hikers, backpackers and horseback riders. Permits are not needed to park or day hike but wilderness permits are required for any overnight stays.

Parking/Facilities: There is moderately large parking area at the trailhead with picnic tables and a vault toilet.

Topographic Map: USGS Sonora Pass, CA Quadrangle (7.5 Minute Series)

Hike Description: As you are heading into the one-way section of the parking area, you should note a trail that heads off to the right; follow this trail over a small hill and down to highway 108. Cross the road and head up to the trailhead sign on the other side. From here the trail climbs for the next 0.3 miles and then drops down on a short section where you cross a stream bed at ~0.6 miles and various streamlets of Sardine Creek (above its falls) 0.8-0.9 miles. At this point, you begin some long switchbacks over the next 1.6 miles, reaching the top and the Emigrant Wilderness boundary at 2.5 miles. Be sure to take in the views along the way! From here, you traverse the ridge that overlooks Blue Canyon for 1.2 miles (on the right). There is a short trail to an overlook off to the left at ~3 miles. About 3.7 miles into the hike, you once again descend, this time for ~260 ft over the next 0.4 miles before climbing for another 0.3 miles (4.4 miles) to the 'notch' on the ridge that overlooks the Leavitt Lake area and more spectacular views. Continue another 0.1 miles down the trail and take the primitive trail heading off to the left and down to Latopie Lake (a drop of ~350 ft). The trail is visible most of the way down but it is also slippery due to loose rock; watch your footing. Latopie Lake is a beautiful high elevation gem and a worthy destination.

Trail Tidbits: The trail crosses Highway 108 at Sonora Pass, the second highest vehicular pass in California at 9624 ft. Members of the Clark-Skidmore came west through the Sonora Pass area in 1852 (they actually passed through today's Emigrant Pass); however, this route never became popular as it was too arduous for wagon trains. With the advent of mining areas on the east side of the Sierras, the Sonora and Mono Wagon Road, was established in 1864 to transport ores to the west side of the Sierra Nevada Range. The steepness of the road (20% grade in some places) is still notorious and is not advised for large vehicles.

Need to Know: The steep sections of the trail can be slippery on descents due to some loose rubble. The trail is often cut into the sides of steep mountains; be sure to stay on the trail in these sections and do not attempt to hike if the trail is covered with snow unless you have proper gear. This area is fairly exposed and there is no water except at lakes; be sure to pack enough for your hike. It is often windy at high elevations so it might be a good idea to pack additional layers. Also, afternoon thunderstorms are a serious consideration at high elevations; be prepared.

Want A Loop? There is a very long loop (~16.5 miles) that could be done but you also need the USGS Pickel Meadow CA Quadrangle (7.5 minute series). This should only be attempted if you are sure-footed, can handle walking down steep sections of scree (loose rock) and can travel comfortably on sketchy trails. Follow the faint trail to the left of the drainage at Latopie Lake down to Koenig Lake (5.7 miles). Once at Koenig Lake, pick up the trail on the far side and head to Leavitt Lake (6.6 miles). At Leavitt Lake, follow the dirt road across its outlet and up to the trailhead marker (left at the 'Y' at 7.5 miles). Follow the trail along switchbacks up the shoulder of the peak overlooking Leavitt Lake until you reach the crest at 8.3 miles. At the junction with the PCT (8.4 miles), head north (right) and continue on this trail and eventually, you reach the junction with the Latopie Lake trail (12.0 miles) and shortly after, the 'notch'. Head back to the trailhead the way you originally came.

Directions to Trailhead: Go east on 108 past Kennedy Meadows. The Sonora Pass Trailhead is just before the pass on the left. Distance from 108 is 0 miles.

Photo: Latopie Lake as seen from the Pacific Crest Trail

Leavitt Peak from Leavitt Lake Trailhead

Highlights: This is a challenging hike that provides more than its fair share of incredible scenery of mountain peaks and occasional high alpine lakes. The views spread out in all directions from a multitude of perspectives and give the impression that you are at the top of the world (after the ascent)!

Distance: 3.6 miles one way (7.2 miles roundtrip)

Elevation Changes: Cumulative ascent to the peak is ~1350 ft and ~50 ft on the return trip; elevation ~9650-11,000 ft

Difficulty: Strenuous in terms of elevation and elevation change

Seasonality: This trail is best during summer months to early fall. The roads to this area are closed during winter months.

User Groups/Permits: The trail is used by hikers, backpackers and horseback riders. Permits are not needed to park or day hike but wilderness permits are required for any overnight stays when you are within wilderness boundaries (Leavitt Lake is not within a wilderness boundary).

Parking/Facilities: There is moderately large parking area at the trailhead but no facilities here or on the trail.

Topographic Map: USGS Pickel Meadow and Sonora Pass, CA Quadrangles (7.5 Minute Series)

Hike Description: From the trailhead, follow the trail past the gated area. Continue on the trail which switchbacks up the shoulder of the volcanic peak overlooking Leavitt Lake. You reach a gate at 1.1 miles and the Hoover Wilderness boundary sign just beyond. At ~1.2 miles, you are at the crest (~10,650 ft) of this ridge. Another 0.1 miles further, you encounter the junction with the Pacific Crest Trail (1.3 miles). Head north (right) and continue on this trail as it heads around the ridge through scrub areas and loose volcanic rock. Along the way you can see Lost Lake in the far distance (in Emigrant Wilderness) and the drainage that heads down to Kennedy Lake. Once you reach the shoulder of Leavitt Peak at ~3.6 miles, Kennedy Lake is visible down below. This is the turnaround point.

Trail Tidbits: The trail that heads up the shoulder of the volcanic peak overlooking Leavitt Lake used to be an old mining road. You can see it continue into the distance beyond the crest. Leavitt Peak, Creek, Meadow and Falls were named for Hiram Leavitt. Hiram Leavitt joined the hostelry business in 1863, when he opened a stage stop establishment on the east side of Sonora Pass near Leavitt Meadow. He served travelers heading over the mountains via the Sonora Mono Road (opened officially in 1864). Mr. Leavitt later became a Mono County judge.

Need to Know: This area is difficult to get to from Highway 108. The road requires a 4-wheel drive vehicle with high clearance as the road is very rough with stream crossings. This should not be attempted by a regular car. Since the lake is above tree line, it can get quite windy so be prepared with layers of clothing. Also, afternoon thunderstorms are a serious consideration at high elevations. The steep sections of the trail can be slippery on descents due to some loose rubble. This area is fairly exposed and there is no water except at lakes; be sure to pack enough for your hike.

Want A Loop? There is an 8.3 mile loop that includes downhill travel on steep sections and primitive trails. For this loop, continue on the PCT past Leavitt Peak, then take the turn right 4.9 miles into the hike to Latopie Lake. Once at Latopie Lake, follow the faint trail to the left of the drainage down to Koenig Lake (the trail fades here and there but find the easiest way down). Once at Koenig Lake, pick up the trail on the far side of the lake and head to Leavitt Lake. At Leavitt Lake, follow the dirt road across its outlet and up to the trailhead parking area. If you arrange a shuttle with someone ahead of time, you could do a shuttle loop to Sonora Pass. For this, continue along the trail until you reach Sonora Pass by following the PCT. It is an additional 5.8 miles to Highway 108 from the shoulder of Leavitt Peak.

Directions to Trailhead: Go east on 108 past Sonora Pass. The dirt road to Leavitt Lake is on the right, 3.8 miles from Sonora Pass. The road is not marked other than with a sign saying 'Rd 32077'; it is located on a hairpin turn. If you reach the Mono County 4.0 mile marker, you have gone too far. From here, the fun begins! Leavitt Lake is located 2.7 miles down a deeply rutted road with strategically placed boulders to make the journey even more difficult. On top of this, you make 3 stream crossings which should not be attempted if the water is running fast and deep. Once you reach the lake, follow the dirt road to the left 0.4 miles to reach the trailhead parking on the left. Distance from 108 is 3.1 'hairy' miles.

Leavitt Peak from Sonora Pass Trailhead

Highlights: This is a challenging hike with incredible scenery of both granitic and volcanic mountain peaks, gorgeous lakes, delicate wildflowers and lush drainages. You climb the first 2.5 miles but most of it is along extended and gradual switchbacks. The entire hike provides visual stimulation and the climb gives you a great sense of accomplishment.

Distance: 5.8 miles one way (11.6 miles roundtrip)

Elevation Changes: Cumulative ascent to the peak is ~1520 ft and ~570 ft on the return trip; elevation ~9600-11,000 ft

Difficulty: Strenuous in terms of elevation change

Photo: Leavitt Peak

Seasonality: This trail is best from summer to early fall. The road to this area is closed during winter months.

User Groups/Permits: The trail is used by hikers, backpackers and horseback riders. Permits are not needed to park or day hike but wilderness permits are required for any overnight stays.

Parking/Facilities: There is moderately large parking area at the trailhead with picnic tables and a vault toilet.

Topographic Map: USGS Sonora Pass, CA Quadrangle (7.5 Minute Series)

Hike Description: As you are heading into the one-way section of the parking area, you should note a trail that heads off to the right; follow this trail over a small hill and down to Highway 108. Cross the road and head up to the trailhead sign on the other side. From here the trail climbs for the next 0.3 miles. You then drop for a bit and cross a stream bed at 0.6 miles and various streamlets of Sardine Creek (above its falls) between 0.8-0.9 miles. At this point, you begin some long switchbacks over the next 1.6 miles, reaching the top at 2.5 miles where you enter Emigrant Wilderness. Be sure to take in the views along the way! From here, you traverse the ridge that overlooks Blue Canyon (for 1.2 miles) which gives you a view of Leavitt Peak. There is a short trail to an overlook off to the left at ~3 miles. At 3.8 miles into the hike, you descend for the next 0.4 miles and then you climb for 0.3 miles to the 'notch' on the ridge that overlooks the Leavitt Lake area and more spectacular views. Continue another 1.3 miles along the ridge until you have reached the shoulder of Leavitt Peak which is on the right. You should be able to see Kennedy Lake and Kennedy Creek drainage over the edge.

Trail Tidbits: Leavitt Peak is the highest point in the Emigrant Wilderness and stands at an elevation of 11,570 ft. The peak was named for Hiram Leavitt who was well known on both sides of Sonora Pass. In addition to his judgeship and hostelry business on the east side, he made claim to lands on the west side for agriculture and grazing. His lands were located on the 'Ice Trail', a ridge between the Stanislaus (South Fork) and Tuolumne (North Fork) Rivers which was part of the difficult Walker River Trail used by some emigrants to cross the Sierra Nevada Mountains.

Need to Know: The steep sections of the trail can be slippery on the descent due to some loose rubble. The trail is often cut into the sides of steep mountains; be sure to stay on the trail in these sections and do not hike if the trail is covered with snow unless you have proper gear. This area is fairly exposed and there is no water except at lakes; be sure to pack enough water for your hike. It is often windy at high elevations so pack additional layers. Also, afternoon thunderstorms are a serious consideration at high elevations.

Want A Loop? If you arrange a shuttle with someone ahead of time, you can continue along the trail until you reach Leavitt Lake. Follow the PCT until you reach the junction with the Leavitt Lake Trail. Take this trail (left) down to Leavitt Lake. Add 4.1 miles to your total if you reach the outlet for the lake; add another 2.7 if you hike to the highway. Otherwise, if you want more without doing a shuttle, look for the primitive trail that heads up Leavitt Peak and explore the area. It is back the way you came on the uphill side of the trail; usually it is marked with a rock arrow.

Directions to Trailhead: Go east on 108 past Kennedy Meadows. The trailhead is just before the pass on the left. Distance from 108 is 0 miles.

Powell Lake from Gianelli Cabin Trailhead

Highlights: This is an excellent hike for everyone including kids. There is a short climb at the start but once you reach the plateau at Burst Rock, it is downhill a short ways to Powell Lake. The views are incredible along both sides of the plateau giving you a glimpse of the granitic splendor of the Emigrant Wilderness. The lake is perfect for a quick dip on a hot day.

Distance: ~2.4 miles to Powell Lake (4.8 miles roundtrip)

Elevation Changes: Cumulative ascent to Powell Lake is ~460 ft and ~320 ft on the return; elevation ~8600-9060 ft

Difficulty: Moderate in terms of elevation changes

Seasonality: This trail is best during summer and early fall. The roads to this area are closed during the winter season.

User Groups/Permits: The trail is used by hikers, backpackers and horseback riders with pack animals. No permit is needed for day hikes but you will need a wilderness permit for overnight stays.

Parking/Facilities: There is ample parking at the Gianelli Cabin Trailhead. There are no facilities here or on the trail.

Topographic Map: USGS Pinecrest & Cooper Peak Quadrangles (7.5 Minute Series)

Hike Description: Begin the hike with a slow climb through a mixed conifer forest. About 0.5 miles into the climb, the trail brings you to some granite steps and comes close to the edge of the ridge on the left. Take a short side trip off towards the edge to savor the views of Emigrant Wilderness to the north and the canyon of the South Fork of the Stanislaus River heading west. Once back on the trail, you begin some long switchbacks until finally you reach the summit of Burst Rock at ~1.2 miles into the hike (~390 ft of elevation gain). There is a sign off to the left that provides some history of the early Sonora Pass crossings. As you head across the plateau you again have the views off to the left but now you also have views of southeast portions of Emigrant Wilderness to the right. The wilderness boundary sign appears at ~1.4 miles. The trail continues mostly downhill from here and passes a pond on the left at ~1.8 miles. The Powell Lake Trail junction occurs at ~2.2 miles; head left towards the lake for ~0.2 miles. There are many trails that cut off in various directions down to the lake but the main trail appears to be the easiest way to reach the lake at a nice wide grassy area.

Trail Tidbits: The Sonora Pass emigrant trail traveled directly over Burst Rock and then along Dodge Ridge heading towards Sonora. The name Burst Rock is derived from the moniker 'Birth Rock', so named when at least 2 babies from emigrant mothers were born on this granitic formation in 1853.

Need to Know: The trail can be thick with dust in areas by the end of the season. There are a few rocky sections where you will need to watch your footing carefully. Although less visited than Camp and Bear Lakes, Powell Lake is a popular destination since it is fairly accessible to a wide range of people. As a result, it has a one night camping policy. Please protect this high use area by minimizing your impact.

Want More? There is not an easy loop to do that would include Powell Lake due to the steep granitic walls on Burst Rock. If you would like to do more, consider heading down to Chewing Gum Lake (see Chewing Gum Lake from Gianelli Cabin Trailhead hike) or you could explore the far edges of Powell Lake and the tarns that are below the granitic shelf on its north side.

Directions to Trailhead: Go east on 108 past Cold Springs. Turn right onto Crabtree Road (4N26) and drive 6.6 miles to Aspen Pack Station. Stay

straight on Forest Service Road 4N26 at the pack station and continue another 6.9 miles before reaching Gianelli Cabin TH. Total distance from 108 is 13.5 miles.

Photo: Powell Lake

Relief Reservoir Dam from Kennedy Meadow Trailhead

Highlights: Although this hike involves some climbing, some of which is steep, it is a hike of great beauty and variety. You visit a scenic mountain meadow, see cascading rivers, cross numerous bridges (color photo page 167), hike trail sections cut out from the edges of granite cliffs, feel inspired beneath the towering mountain peaks and find historic remnants left from the construction of Relief Reservoir Dam. The only downside to this hike is the immense number of people who mob the area during the summer months.

Distance: 3.5 miles one-way (7.0 miles roundtrip) from the designated trailhead parking to the dam

Elevation Changes: Cumulative ascent roundtrip is ~990 ft to the reservoir dam and another 200 ft on the return trip; elevation ~6300-7160 ft

Difficulty: Difficult in terms of elevation change

Seasonality: Although this trail can be used during summer and fall months, it can be a zoo in the Kennedy Meadows area during the summer. If you prefer to travel when there are fewer hikers and pack animals, then do this hike when the pack station and resort area are closed. The roads to this area are closed during winter months.

User Groups/Permits: The trail is used by hikers, backpackers, horseback riders and pack animals. Motorized vehicles are prohibited. Permits are not needed to park or day hike. If you plan to stay overnight, you need a permit and you should park in the designated trailhead for overnight hikers.

Parking/Facilities: There is a large, designated trailhead parking area before you reach the Kennedy Meadows resort area that has vault toilets and a water spigot. There is a two-night camping limit in designated spots around the parking area. Day hikers can sometimes find parking just past the store; take 1 mile off the roundtrip total if you park near the store.

Topographic Map: USGS Sonora Pass, CA Quadrangle (7.5 Minute Series)

Hike Description: The trail begins on the dirt trail near the vault toilet. This trail takes you back to Kennedy Meadows Road; turn left and follow the road into the resort area (there are signs for 'the trail'). At ~0.6 mile, the pavement ends and the trail continues as a dirt road that is gated a short distance further. From here, you head away from the Middle Fork of the Stanislaus River and climb a small saddle then, just over 0.2 miles later, you drop back to the river and Kennedy Meadow comes into view. Skirt the edge of the meadow on the dirt road and then into a forested area. You encounter the Kennedy Meadow Trailhead sign at ~1.6 miles and the wilderness boundary sign at 1.7 miles into the hike. You do some easy climbing until you cross the Middle Fork of the Stanislaus River on a bridge at ~1.9 miles. Once across the bridge, the trail becomes fairly steep for the next ~0.6 miles. At ~2.2 miles, you come to the confluence of Kennedy Creek (on the left) with the Middle Fork of the Stanislaus River (on the right). Just past this area, you cross the Middle Fork on a bridge and find yourself with 2 trail options. The trail on the left is steeper and 0.05 miles shorter; the trail on the right is less steep, longer and travels along the river. Both converge again at a point where you can see waterfalls on the river. Less than 0.1 miles from this point (~2.45 miles into the hike), you should see some equipment left behind from the dam construction in the early 1900's. The trail climbs less steeply the next 0.1 miles. At ~2.8 miles, you reach the junction with the Kennedy Lake Trail; stay straight. Continue climbing and at ~3.2 miles, you reach an obvious vista area. Take some time to view your surroundings and catch your breath. As you get back on the trail, you should note some more equipment left on the side of the trail. Look carefully and note the faint trail heading off to the right. Take this trail to Relief Reservoir (the main trail heads uphill and passes high above the lake). As you climb up, you can see the old powder room on the right where dynamite was stored during dam construction. Once you crest the small ridge, Relief Reservoir should be visible below. There are many trails that head down towards the water's edge; take a more obvious trail down to what looks like the remnants of an old road littered with many more relics left from the construction period. Head to the right on this 'road' and it will take you to the dam for Relief Reservoir.

Trail Tidbits: In 1852, the Clark-Skidmore party was the first group of emigrants to take the Walker River Trail over Sonora Pass. With their supplies running low on this difficult trail, it was decided that a small group would ride ahead to Sonora and return with relief supplies. Meanwhile, the remaining group continued the struggle towards the crest with the wagons and their meager stores; eventually, they abandoned the wagons and traveled on foot to the western slope. The relief party met them (9 days after they had set out) at a spot now referred to as Relief Camp. Relief Camp was at the site of present day Relief Reservoir. Construction on Relief Reservoir Dam was begun in the early 1900's by Union Construction for the purpose of generating electricity and conserving water.

Note: the meadow and trailhead are called Kennedy Meadow since there is one meadow, while the resort and its road are named Kennedy Meadows.

Need to Know: Be careful of motorized vehicle traffic the first 0.5 miles when you are walking along the road. The trail conditions vary from sandy in some sections, thick dust in others and granite steps and rocks in yet others. The trail is quite busy in the summer particularly with horse traffic.

Want More? A loop is not possible with this hike. If you want more, cross the dam and spend some time exploring the area around the reservoir.

Directions to Trailhead: Go east on 108 past the Dardanelles Resort. Turn right onto Kennedy Meadows Road. Go 0.6 miles and turn left into the designated trailhead parking area. Go 0.1 miles up to park. Total distance from 108 is 0.7 miles.

Photo:
Relief
Reservoir

Waterhouse Lake Trail

Highlights: This trail offers an initial downhill meander through beautiful meadows, stunning views of the granitic South Fork of the Stanislaus River Canyon when the trail crests, adventurous scrambling across rock slabs before finally reaching a small pristine mountain lake nestled among mountain ridges in the Emigrant Wilderness. Unfortunately, it is mostly uphill on the return trip (color photo page 165).

Distance: ~1.6 miles (3.2 miles roundtrip) but can vary on path taken

Elevation Changes: Cumulative ascent is ~65 ft on the way out and ~760 ft on the return; elevation ~7420-8180 ft

Difficulty: Moderately difficult in terms of elevation changes

Seasonality: This trail is best during the summer and early fall. The roads to this area are closed during winter months. The wildflowers in the meadow are rampant during late spring to early summer.

User Groups/Permits: The trail is used by hikers and backpackers. No motorized vehicles are allowed. No permits are needed to park or use the trail for day hikes; however, a wilderness permit is required for overnight stays.

Parking/Facilities: There is a parking area at the trailhead. There are no facilities here or on the trail.

Topographic Map: USGS Pinecrest Quadrangle (7.5 Minute Series)

Hike Description: There is a sign that indicates that you are at the Waterhouse Trailhead. The trail heads down a gentle slope through a gorgeous meadow. At 0.25 miles into the hike, you begin descending at a greater rate following small creeks and walking through additional lush meadows. At times you cross seasonal creeks. You reach an Emigrant Wilderness boundary sign ~0.8 miles into the hike. The trail takes you another 0.1 miles to the lip of the river canyon; spend some time relishing the view. Also, you should take note of your surroundings so that you can find this part of the trail again on your return. The trail heads off to the left and then basically disappears as it continues down granite ridges and slabs.

People have placed cairns (or 'ducks') to mark various trails; some bring you to Waterhouse Lake but others bring you down to the drainage coming out of Waterhouse Lake (note the brown stains) or perhaps further to the South Fork of the Stanislaus River. Your goal is to head down part way and then work your way left. It is OK if you find yourself heading straight down towards the drainage area as you can then climb up to Waterhouse Lake following the water stains. At ~ 1.6 miles, you crest a granite bowl and reach the lake tucked inside. On your return, follow the cairns that leave the lake on the uphill side of the outlet. They lead you across and up. If you lose the cairns, shoot for the area that you took note of before your descent.

Trail Tidbits: One of the watersheds in the Emigrant Wilderness is the Stanislaus River; one of its forks, the South Fork, is visible in this carved canyon. The headwaters of the South Fork of the Stanislaus River begin upstream in Horse and Cow, Cooper, Hay and Whitesides Meadows. In the 1920's, Fred Leighton began building 18 check dams throughout Emigrant Wilderness so that water could be released at a slower rate resulting in a larger store of water in the rivers and lakes during the California dry season. Two of these check dams were located at Cooper Meadow and Whitesides Meadow and directly impacted the flow of the South Fork prior to its arrival in Pinecrest Lake. Since 1975, the fate of these man-made check dams had been part of a political controversy with one side stating that man-made structures are not in keeping with the intent of the 1964 Wilderness Act and the other side contending that the dams are legal since their origins predate the Wilderness Act and any dismantling of them would result in decreased trout habitat and low water levels in the summer. The Stanislaus National Forest attempted to find some middle ground by allowing some of the dams to deteriorate (including Whitesides and Cooper) while maintaining others. In 2006, the US Court System determined that none of the check dams in Emigrant Wilderness should be maintained and all should be allowed to reach their own natural demise over time.

Need to Know: Once you reach the crest of the river canyon, you need to carefully pick a trail down the granite slabs and ridges as some sections are steep and rocks can be loose. If you are the type of person that needs to follow a specific and well-marked trail, then this is not the hike for you.

Want More? There really isn't a loop that you can do for this hike; however, if you want more, spend time exploring the river canyon. Head over to the drainage area for the South Fork of the Stanislaus River and follow it down a ways. If you arrange a shuttle, you could follow the river the entire way to Pinecrest Lake.

Directions to Trailhead: Go east on 108 past Strawberry. Turn right on Herring Creek Road. Continue on this road for ~6.8 miles (it becomes 4N12 at ~4.5 miles and is no longer paved at ~5.5 miles) until it reaches a 'T'. At the 'T', turn right to remain on 4N12. When the road reaches a 'Y' (0.1 miles further), take the right branch to stay on 4N12 (the left takes you to the Herring Reservoir Campground). Cross a bridge ~0.4 miles further (7.3 miles total) and pass another campground. Continue another ~2.2 miles up 4N12 (9.5 miles total) and then turn right onto 5N31. Go 0.6 miles up this road then head left on 5N67. The Waterhouse Lake Trailhead is off to the right just as you turn onto 5N67. Total distance from 108 is 10.1 miles.

Photo: Waterhouse Lake

Humboldt-Toiyabe National Forest Trails

Scattered in various locations in eastern California and Nevada from Idaho to Utah, the Humboldt-Toiyabe National Forest consists of 6.3 million acres, which makes it the largest National Forest in the continental United States. The forest is split into two parts: the Humboldt National Forest (primarily the northern and eastern sections) and the Toiyabe National Forest (primarily the southwest sections). The forest is divided into 10 Ranger Districts but only 2 include acreage in California: the Carson and Bridgeport Ranger Districts. The area east of Sonora Pass along 108 is part of the Toiyabe National Forest, Bridgeport Ranger District (one of the largest).

Due to the fact that the Humboldt-Toiyabe National Forest is non-contiguous and is spread over such large areas, it boasts a diverse group of habitats. These range from near-desert to riparian areas, and include the Great Basin as well as subalpine and alpine meadows and peaks. The elevation ranges from 4100 ft to 12,374 ft. The highest peak is Dunderberg Peak located in eastern California in the Bridgeport Ranger District.

The name 'Humboldt-Toiyabe' has some interesting origins. The Humboldt portion came from the East Humboldt Mountain Range and Humboldt River which were named by Fremont in honor of a German naturalist. Toiyabe comes from a Shoshone word that means 'mountain'.

The Humboldt-Toiyabe National Forest website states that there are '80,000-100,000 prehistoric and historic archeological sites within the forest boundaries which include emigrant trails, mining towns, Native American camps, logging sites and rock art'. The Native Americans that occupied this vast area include the Northern and Southern Piute, Washoe and Western Shoshone. Today, the Humboldt-Toiyabe National Forest is a destination for recreation including hunting, fishing, camping, swimming, hiking, backpacking, horseback riding, bird watching and picnicking, off-highway vehicle activities, photography, cross-country skiing, snowshoeing, snowmobiling, rock climbing and gold panning.

Since only ~11% of the Humboldt-Toiyabe National Forest is located in California and even less of this is located along the Highway 108 corridor, there are only 4 hikes in this book that travel into this area. Two of them leave from the Leavitt Meadow Trailhead, one from Sardine Meadow and the other from Sonora Pass heading north. All of these trailheads are fairly high in elevation and take you into fairly dry subalpine and alpine areas.

Roosevelt and Lane Lakes from Leavitt Meadow Trailhead

Highlights: This is a hike of variety. It starts off by crossing and following the West Walker River through desert scrub brush, typical of the eastern Sierra Nevada Mountains, then climbs into coniferous forest cover before heading down to beautiful Roosevelt and Lane Lakes (neighbor lakes).

Distance: 3.15 miles one way (6.3 miles roundtrip) to Roosevelt Lake; 3.7 miles one way (7.4 miles roundtrip) to far side of Lane Lake

Elevation Changes: Cumulative ascent to the Roosevelt Lake is ~350 ft and ~240 ft on the return trip; cumulative ascent to Lane Lake is an additional ~40 ft to the lake and an additional ~40 ft on the return trip; elevation is ~7150-7500 ft

Difficulty: Moderate in terms of elevation change

Seasonality: This trail is best during summer months to early fall; the numerous aspen along the trail will be changing color in the fall. The road to this area is closed during winter months.

User Groups/Permits: The trail is used by hikers, backpackers, fishermen and horseback riders. Permits are not needed to day hike but wilderness permits are required for any overnight stays at the two lakes. There is a fee for camping in Leavitt Meadow campground.

Parking/Facilities: There is no fee for the large parking area at the trailhead that has a vault toilet. There are additional vault toilets at the campground. There is a fee for parking at the Leavitt Meadow Campground for the day.

Topographic Map: USGS Pickel Meadow, CA Quadrangle (7.5 Minute Series)

Hike Description: From the trailhead parking area, take the path near its entrance that heads east towards the Leavitt Meadow Campground. Follow the dirt trail, then cross the creek on the log bridge and walk along the campground road that overlooks the river. Head east until you reach the bridge that crosses the West Walker River (~0.2 miles from the trailhead parking area). Cross the bridge and head up to the right on a short hill then continue 0.2 miles further until you reach a trail junction. The trail to the left takes you to Secret and Poore Lakes. The trail to the right heads up the West Walker River; head right. Just past this trail junction, you reach a 'Y'. Take the left to continue on the trail (the right branch heads down to the river). You then walk through an area of scrub brush with huge mounds of volcanic rock rubble to the left. There is another trail that goes off to the left 0.2 miles from the 'Y' (~0.6 miles from start); this trail also takes you to the Secret & Poore Lakes trail. Stay on the main trail heading up the drainage. Eventually you walk along a ridge above the West Walker River where you should see numerous groves of aspen and other river-loving vegetation that thrive along the river plain. Occasionally there are trails that head off to the right to go down to the river; stay on the main trail. You begin to climb at ~1.8 miles leaving the river plain and heading up into granitic areas with coniferous forest and more cover from the sun. In general, you climb for the next 0.8 miles. There is a trail that heads off to the right at ~2.3 miles; stay straight. Nearly 2.6 miles into the hike, you reach another junction with Secret and Poore Lakes; continue on the main trail. Less than 0.1 miles from this junction, you encounter the Hoover Wilderness boundary sign. Head downhill to Roosevelt Lake which is <0.5 miles from the boundary sign (3.1 miles from the trailhead). To continue to Lane Lake, circle to the right of Roosevelt Lake. Hike over a saddle and down the other side. As you are coming down, you can see Lane Lake off to the left; however, the easiest access to the lake is to continue down the saddle until it reaches the far side. This is ~0.5 miles from Roosevelt Lake.

Trail Tidbits: The trail takes you into the Hoover Wilderness. This wilderness area is shared between Toiyabe National Forest and Inyo National Forest. The Hoover Wilderness borders Yosemite National Park to the south, Emigrant Wilderness to the west and the Great Basin to the east and consists of over 48,000 acres. It originally was designated as a primitive area by the US Forest Service in 1931 until it became a Wilderness Area following the 1964 Wilderness Act. It was named in honor of President Herbert Hoover.

Need to Know: This area is fairly exposed at the start so it would be best to get an early start on warm days. Even though you are following the West Walker River, water is not very accessible (until you reach the lakes) since you are on a ridge above the river. The trail is sandy much of the way which can make walking a bit more difficult. Since there is a pack station just west of Leavitt Meadow, you may encounter pack animals on the trail.

Want A Loop? Head back from Lane and Roosevelt as you came until you reach the boundary sign for the wilderness area. Keep your eye out for the trail junction for Secret and Poore Lakes (<0.1 miles further). Turn right onto this trail. Very quickly you come to a trail that heads off to the left that takes you to Secret Lake or you could continue another 0.2 miles until you reach another trail on the left that takes you to Secret Lake. Regardless of which trail you take, Secret Lake is just over 0.5 miles from the junction with the Roosevelt and Lane Lakes Trail. Once at Secret Lake, follow the trail on the west side of the lake that heads north and up and away from the lake. Go ~2.2 miles before reaching one of the junctions with the West Walker Trail (close to the bridge at the campground). Head back to the trailhead parking the way you came. Total distance for this loop is just under 8 miles (if you have traveled to both Roosevelt and Lane Lakes). If you don't wish to do a loop but you want more, head down to the river and explore level trails that head upstream or downstream.

Directions to Trailhead: Go east on 108 past Sonora Pass. The Leavitt Lake Trailhead is ~7.7 miles from Sonora Pass on the right. It is located past the Leavitt Meadow Pack Station but before the Leavitt Meadow Campground. Distance from 108 is 0 miles.

Photo: Roosevelt Lake with Mt. Emma in the background

Sardine Falls Trail

Highlights: Despite the high elevation of the trailhead, this hike is a great hike for the entire family. The highlights include a creek crossing, a pleasant meander through a meadow and numerous waterfalls within a short distance from Highway 108.

Distance: ~1.05 mile one way (2.1 miles roundtrip)

Elevation Changes: Cumulative ascent is just over 200 ft on the way there and ~5 ft on the return trip; elevation ~8800-9050 ft

Difficulty: Moderately easy in terms of elevation change

Seasonality: This trail is best during summer months to early fall. More impressive waterfalls can be seen earlier in the season; however, Sardine Creek may be difficult to cross too early in the season. The road to this area is closed during winter months.

User Groups/Permits: The trail is used by hikers, picnickers and cattlemen. Permits are not needed to park or hike.

Parking/Facilities: There is pull-out parking area just to the right of 108 that can accommodate a few vehicles. There are no facilities here or on the trail.

Topographic Map: USGS Pickel Meadow, CA Quadrangle (7.5 Minute Series)

Hike Description: From the parking area, cross Sardine Meadow along a faint trail (or not). Cross Sardine Creek about 400 ft from the parking area then follow the very obvious grassy tract up the hill. At ~0.5 miles the tract narrows to more of a trail then heads up to the right and around a hill. Just over 0.1 miles further, you come to a 'Y'. The right will take you directly up to Upper Sardine Falls on McKay Creek. The left will take you to an area where you can see 4 other falls (if there is enough water flowing), also on McKay Creek, before leading you back to the main trail that takes you to Upper Sardine Falls. If you decide to take the left route, you encounter 'The Wall' waterfall <0.1 miles further. Just past this waterfall, you can see Lower Sardine Falls and hear 2 other waterfalls that are below. You might want to spend some time exploring this area before following the faint trail to the right of Lower Sardine Falls back to the main trail. Continue up the trail, which will head away from the water for a bit. Then at ~0.9 miles, the trail returns to water and you cross a small stream. Head up and to the right and, very shortly, Upper Sardine Falls will be visible. Return to the parking area by staying on the main trail the entire way back.

Trail Tidbits: Although these falls are on McKay Creek, they are called Sardine Falls. This generates some confusion as there is also a waterfall on Sardine Creek just to the southeast of Sonora Pass (visible from the highway). To keep things straight, the waterfall on Sardine Creek is referred to as Sardine Creek Falls.

Need to Know: Cattle graze in this area. There is some scree around Upper Sardine Falls; watch your footing. Sardine Creek may be difficult to cross early in the season and other parts of the trail may be boggy if there is lots of running water.

Photo: Lower Sardine Falls on McKay Creek

Want More? A small loop for this hike was already suggested by taking the left branch to Lower Sardine Falls and 'The Wall'. However, if you want more, spend time exploring the lower waterfalls or hike further up McKay Creek to the basin above Sardine Falls. There is a trail that takes you to the basin that starts to the right of the falls (in the woods).

Directions to Trailhead: Go east on 108 past Sonora Pass. On your descent from Sonora Pass, look for the 9000 ft elevation sign where you can see Upper Sardine Falls off to the right in the distance. The road will descend a bit further before leveling out at Sardine Meadow. Pull off the road to the right where the shoulder expands to accommodate parked vehicles. This 'parking area' is 2.6 miles from Sonora Pass. Distance from 108 is 0 miles.

Secret and Poore Lakes from Leavitt Meadow Trailhead

Highlights: This hike is very typical of an eastern Sierra hike. It travels mainly through scrub brush areas with occasional passes through stands of conifers. You climb a significant ascent up to a high plateau that gives you stupendous views of Mt. Emma to the southeast, Tower Peak to the south and Leavitt Meadow to the west. As you come off the plateau, Secret Lake surprises you with it aqua-colored waters beneath the gray mountain ridge that Mt. Emma presides over. Poore Lake is a large, shallow lake reminiscent of salt-flat lakes; if you arrive late in the season, particularly during a drought year, there won't be much water left in this lake.

Distance: 2.6 miles one way (5.2 miles roundtrip) to Secret Lake; 3.4 miles one way (6.8 miles roundtrip) to the tip of Poore Lake

Elevation Changes: Cumulative ascent to Secret Lake is ~750 ft and ~420 ft on the return trip; cumulative ascent to Poore Lake is an additional ~70 ft to the lake and an additional ~300 ft on the return; elevation is ~7150-7800 ft

Difficulty: Difficult in terms of elevation change

Seasonality: This trail is best during summer months to early fall. The numerous aspen along the trail change color in the fall but Poore Lake may have evaporated considerably by then. The road to this area is closed during winter months.

User Groups/Permits: The trail is used by hikers, backpackers, fishermen and horseback riders. Permits are not needed to day hike nor are they required for any overnight stays at the lakes. There is a fee for camping in Leavitt Meadow Campground.

Parking/Facilities: There is no fee for the large parking area at the trailhead that has a vault toilet. There are additional vault toilets at the campground. There is a fee for parking at the Leavitt Meadow Campground for the day.

Topographic Map: USGS Pickel Meadow, CA Quadrangle (7.5 Minute Series)

Hike Description: From the trailhead parking area, take the path near its entrance that heads east towards the Leavitt Meadow Campground. Follow the dirt trail, then cross the creek on a log bridge and walk along the campground road that overlooks the river. Head east until you reach the bridge that crosses the West Walker River (~0.2 miles from the trailhead parking area). Cross the bridge and head up to the right. Continue 0.2 miles further until you reach a trail junction. The left branch takes you to Secret Lake. Less than 0.1 miles further, you reach another trail junction; stay left for Secret Lake. Climb a small saddle (and head down again) before beginning a longer, more substantial climb of over 600 ft in phases over the next 1.2 miles. With the climbs, you hit plateaus on occasion that offer great views of Tower Peak and other mountains to the south and Leavitt Meadow to the west. Once you reach the high plateau at ~1.9 miles into the hike, you have great views of the gray mountain ridge to the east with Mt. Emma sitting on its southeast edge. You might also catch a glimpse of Poore Lake down to the left. At ~2.3 miles, you begin heading down and Secret Lake soon becomes visible between the trees. The trail takes you down to the west side of the lake, a distance of 2.6 miles. To continue to Poore Lake, follow the trail along the lake heading south (ignore the other trail that leaves the lake on the west shore). After a short distance, this trail leaves the lake to climb a saddle on its southwest corner before bringing you back down to the lake on the southeast side. From here, you head up a short rocky draw. You pass a pond on the left ~0.25 miles from the western shore of Secret Lake (2.85 miles total). Just past the pond, you reach a trail junction. The faint trail to the left takes you down to the tip of Poore Lake in just under 0.5 miles. The trail to the right heads to the junction with the Roosevelt and Lane Lakes Trail (see Want a Loop?).

Trail Tidbits: The West Walker Emigrant Trail passed through Pickel Meadow, crossed the West Walker River and followed Poore Creek up to Poore Lake. From here the trail climbed the ridge between Poore Lake and Leavitt Meadow and continued past Roosevelt and Lane Lakes. In 1852, the Clark-Skidmore party became the first group of emigrants to take this grueling trail over Sonora Pass. It was at Poore Lake that the group decided to send a relief party ahead on horseback to gather desperately needed supplies. Those that were left behind continued the struggle of moving wagons up the steep, difficult trail. Although a few other emigrant parties traveled this trail the next year, it was quickly abandoned as a reasonable route to Sonora.

Need to Know: This area is fairly exposed at the start so it would be best to get an early start on warm days. Water is not accessible until you reach Secret Lake (except at the bridge crossing); be sure to pack enough water for the hike. Since there is a pack station just west of Leavitt Meadow, you may encounter pack animals on the trail.

Want A Loop? From <u>Secret Lake</u>, take the trail from the **west** shore for ~0.5 miles until it reaches a trail junction; head right. Go <0.1 miles to reach the Roosevelt & Lane Lakes Trail junction. From <u>Poore Lake</u>, head back the way you came but instead of turning right to head to the pond and Secret Lake, continue straight until reaching the Roosevelt and Lane Lakes Trail junction ~0.25 miles further. Regardless of which lake you come from, once you reach the Roosevelt & Lane Lakes Trail junction, turn right to return to Leavitt Meadow along the West Walker River. It is ~2.2 miles before you reach the junction where you first turned to go to Secret Lake; stay left to go back to the campground. Total distance for a loop that involves just Secret Lake is ~5.75 miles; total distance for a loop that includes both Secret and Poore Lakes is ~6.7 miles.

Directions to Trailhead: Go east on 108 past Sonora Pass. The Leavitt Lake Trailhead is ~7.7 miles from Sonora Pass on the right. It is located past the Leavitt Meadow Pack Station but before the Leavitt Meadow Campground. Distance from 108 is 0 miles.

Photo:
Poore
Lake
greatly
diminished

Wolf Creek Lake from Sonora Pass Trailhead

Highlights: This trail offers a multitude of wildflower displays due to a number of small streams and seeps, interesting geologic rock formations and spectacular views of Carson-Iceberg, Emigrant, Toiyabe and Yosemite peaks and ranges (color photo page 165).

Distance: 3.8 miles one way (7.6 miles roundtrip)

Elevation Changes: Cumulative ascent to the lake is ~1200 ft and ~750 ft on the return trip; elevationn ~9600-10,550 ft

Difficulty:
Strenuous in terms of elevation change

Seasonality:
This trail is best during summer months to early fall. The road to this area is closed during winter months.

Photo: View from Sonora Pass Trail

User Groups/Permits: The trail is used by hikers, backpackers and horseback riders. Permits are not needed to park or day hike but wilderness permits are required for any overnight stays.

Parking/Facilities: There is a moderately large parking area at the trailhead with picnic tables and a vault toilet.

Topographic Map: USGS Sonora Pass & Pickel Meadow, CA Quadrangles (7.5 Minute Series)

Hike Description: From the parking area head towards the vault toilet and trailhead sign. The trail heads off to the left and within 100 yards, meets up with the Pacific Crest Trail (PCT) and the Carson-Iceberg Wilderness boundary sign. Continue up to the right and around a small ridge. You then begin a long switchback to the left, crossing numerous streams (or dry beds), gradually climbing most of the way but hitting a few steeper areas as well. At just over 1.5 miles, the trail switchbacks to the right and you continue to climb, gradually in some areas but more steeply in others, crossing many of the same streams that you crossed below. Finally, at ~2.6 miles, you reach the top of the ridge and begin a traverse along it. At ~3.2 miles, Wolf Creek Lake becomes visible down below on the right. The trail begins a fairly steep descent on granitic rocks. Watch for a faint trail off to the right at~3.6 miles that takes you down to Wolf Creek Lake; otherwise, you can continue on the PCT until you reach its junction with the Wolf Creek Trail. Turn right and backtrack to the lake.

Trail Tidbits: White Mountain looks down upon Wolf Creek Lake. This name was most likely given to the mountain by the USGS in the 1890's due to its distinct white coloring. This section of trail is part of the Pacific Crest National Scenic Trail (PCT) which stretches 2650 miles through California, Oregon and Washington along the Sierra Nevada and Cascade Mountains. It is very popular with hardcore backpackers.

Need to Know: The steep sections of the trail can be slippery on the descent due to some loose rubble. It is often windy at high elevations so it might be a good idea to pack additional layers. Also, afternoon thunderstorms are a serious consideration at high elevations; be prepared.

Want More? There is a loop that you can do but it requires some cross-country travel when trails disappear. To do this loop, continue along the PCT heading north. Turn left on a primitive trail that takes you to Sonora Peak (the highest point across the East Fork of Carson River from White Mountain). If you can't find the trail, travel cross-country along the easiest line to Sonora Peak. Once there, head down its north flank then west across the open bowl until you pick up the trail to Saint Mary's Pass Trailhead (see Sonora Peak hike). Once you reach this trailhead, you need to hike along 108 back to Sonora Pass Trailhead. Instead, if you want more, you could hike down the Wolf Creek Trail a short distance.

Directions to Trailhead: Go east on 108 past Kennedy Meadows. The Sonora Pass Trailhead is just before the pass on the left. Distance from 108 is 0 miles.

Photo: Tree 'face' along the trail from St. Mary's Pass to Iceberg Meadow

Sources

Atkins, Thomas. "Journey to the Center of Table Mountain." *Twain Harte News.* N.p., 4 Mar. 2014. Web. 31 Mar. 2014.

Bridgeport Ranger District." *Humboldt-Toiyabe National Forest - Recreation Passes & Permits.* United States National Forest Service, n.d. Web. 29 Mar. 2014.

Browning, Peter. *Place Names of the Sierra Nevada: From Abbot to Zumwalt.* Berkeley: Wilderness, 1991. Print.

Carson-Iceberg Wilderness, Stanislaus and Toiyabe National Forests, California: 1987. N.p.: n.p., 1987. Print.

"Carson-Iceberg Wilderness." *Stanislaus National Forest -.* N.p., n.d. Web. 12 Mar. 2014.

Condor Earth. "Century-Old Canal Still Going Strong: Oakdale Irrigation District - Condor Earth Technologies, Inc. News." *Century-Old Canal Still Going Strong: Oakdale Irrigation District - Condor Earth Technologies, Inc. News.* Condor Earth Technologies, Inc., n.d. Web. 31 Mar. 2014.

"Emigrant Wilderness." *Emigrant Wilderness.* N.p., n.d. Web. 12 Mar. 2014.

Emigrant Wilderness, Stanislaus National Forest, California: Mt. Diablo Meridian, 2001. San Francisco: Regional Office, USDA Forest Service, Pacific Southwest Region, 2002. Print.

"Evaluate Channel Restoration and Aggregate Source Potential for Two-mile Bar on the Stanislaus River." *AFRP Managed Projects.* U.S. Fish & Wildlife Service, 27 July 2010. Web. 31 Mar. 2014.

Farquhar, Francis Peloubet. *History of the Sierra Nevada.* Berkeley: University of California, 1965. Print.

Foothill Resources, Ltd., and Francis Heritage, LLC. *11) Tuolumne Utilities District Ditch Sustainability Project Historic Resource Evaluation Report.* N.p.: n.p., 2012. Web. 12 Mar. 2014.

"Geology - Rocks and Minerals." *Geology - Rocks and Minerals.* University of Aukland, New Zealand, n.d. Web. 25 Mar. 2014.

"The History of Knights Ferry." *Sunshine Rafting*. N.p., 2014. Web. 31 Mar. 2014.

"Humboldt-Toiyabe National Forest - Home." *Humboldt-Toiyabe National Forest - Home*. N.p., n.d. Web. 29 Mar. 2014.

Johnson, Dave H. "The Battle Over Fish Check Dams in the Emigrant Wilderness." *Ezine Articles*. N.p., n.d. Web. 23 Mar. 2014.

Johnson, David H. *Sonora Pass Pioneers: California Bound Emigrants and Explorers 1841-1864*. Sonora, CA: Tuolumne County Historical Society, 2006. Print.

Kellogg, Rachelle. "Visit Sonora Dragoon Gulch." *Visit Sonora*. City of Sonora, n.d. Web. 31 Mar. 2014.

Lang, H. O. *A History of Tuolumne County, California: Compiled from the Most Authentic Records*. Sonora, CA: Tuolumne County Historical Society, 1973. Print.

"OID Board Hears Tunnel Plan." *OID Board Hears Tunnel Plan*. OakdaleLeader.com, 18 Dec. 2012. Web. 31 Mar. 2014.

"Red Hills Area of Critical Environmental Concern, Mother Lode Field Office, Bureau of Land Management California." *Red Hills Area of Critical Environmental Concern, Mother Lode Field Office, Bureau of Land Management California*. N.p., n.d. Web. 12 Mar. 2014.

"Red Hills, Chinese Camp, CA." *Red Hills*. RM and Bonanza: Scenery of the Ponderosa, n.d. Web. 31 Mar. 2014.

"Rocks of the Sierra Nevada." *Geology of the Sierra Nevada*. Geologic Trips, n.d. Web. 25 Mar. 2014.

"Sierra Railroad 1955." *» Pickering Lumber Corp*. N.p., n.d. Web. 12 Mar. 2014.

"Snowmobiles Threaten Proposed Hoover Wilderness Additions." , *Teton, November/October 2004 Yodeler*. Sierra Club, Nov. 2004. Web. 23 Mar. 2014.

Stoddart, Thomas Robertson, and De Ferrari Carlo M. *Annals of Tuolumne County*. Sonora, CA: Mother Lode, 1963. Print.

Tuolumne County, California ... Issued by the Union Democrat under The Auspices and Direction of the Supervisors of Tuolumne County. Sonora, Cal.: J. A. Van Halingen &, 1909. Print.

United States. National Park Service. "Devils Postpile National Monument (U.S. National Park Service)." *National Parks Service*. U.S. Department of the Interior, 12 Mar. 2014. Web. 25 Mar. 2014.

United States. National Park Service. Historic American Engineering Record. *Spring Gap-Stanislaus Hydroelectric System, Sand Bar Dam*. By Cindy L. Baker. N.p., Feb. 2013. Web. 12 Mar. 2014. <lcweb2.loc.gov/pnp/habshaer/ca/ca4000/ca4054/data/ca4054data.pdf>.

United States. National Park Service. "Sierra Nevada Yellow-Legged Frog." *National Parks Service*. U.S. Department of the Interior, 19 Mar. 2014. Web. 23 Mar. 2014.

"WELCOME TO THE TUOLUMNE COUNTY HISTORICAL SOCIETY." *Tuolumne County Historical Society*. N.p., n.d. Web. 12 Mar. 2014.

"Wildlife, New Melones." *Wildlife, New Melones*. N.p., n.d. Web. 12 Mar. 2014.

Yesavage, Jerry. "UPDATE (11/99)-(8/10) Streamflow Dams in the Emigrant Wilderness Area." Stanford University, n.d. Web. 23 Mar. 2014.

Photo: Bridge across Middle Fork Stanislaus River at Column of the Giants

Photo: Kennedy Creek before its confluence with the Middle Fork of the Stanislaus River (above Kennedy Meadow)

Photo: Kathi on the Sonora Pass Trail with Gloria and Stefano (taken by Sheri Betz)

About the Author

Unlike many outdoor enthusiasts, Kathi was not exposed to hiking, backpacking and camping as a child growing up in a mobile military family. Despite this, she has always been drawn to the outdoors and felt connected to the beauty of rugged rural areas. She began hiking and hosteling (traveling from one hostel to the next) throughout the United Kingdom in high school but did not go on her first true backpacking trip until college. She fell in love with the Sierra Nevada Mountains on a backpacking trip through Yosemite; as is true with others, she finds that the Sierra Nevada resonate with her inner core. While teaching in Davis from the 80's through 2005, she and her husband regularly headed to the Sierra Nevada to backpack, climb, camp and hike (with kids in tow as they made their individual appearances); the Emigrant Wilderness has always been a favorite place for them. After a brief stint in Ohio, the Joye family returned to California to make their home in Tuolumne County literally a stone's throw from a number of different trails. Kathi heads out daily on some type of trail whether for a walk or run or a long trek in the high country.